THE BIG BLOCKADE

ENGAGEMENT BETWEEN H.M.S. "ALCANTARA" AND S.M.S. "GREIF"

From the painting by Charles Dixon, R.I.   In the possession of Vice-Admiral T. E. Wardle, C.B., D.S.O.

THE
BIG BLOCKADE

By

E. KEBLE CHATTERTON

The Naval & Military Press Ltd

WITH COLOURED FRONTISPIECE, 32 ILLUSTRATIONS, AND MAPS

Published by

The Naval & Military Press Ltd

Unit 5 Riverside, Brambleside
Bellbrook Industrial Estate
Uckfield, East Sussex
TN22 1QQ England

Tel: +44 (0)1825 749494

www.naval–military-press.com
www.nmarchive.com

PREFACE

It is far from overstating a plain fact if the claim is made that this account of the Blockade is years overdue. Both the Press and public have wondered how and why no full narrative has ever been presented to show the method by which our late enemies were robbed of all stamina in the great European contest.

"The downfall of the military colossus," remarked Mr. Bonar Law in the House of Commons on the day following Armistice, "was due to the Blockade, which has sapped the whole foundation of Germany." The labours of the 10th Cruiser Squadron (which carried out this Blockade), stated Mr. Balfour, when First Lord of the Admiralty, "were more continuous, more important, and more successful than any other branch of His Majesty's Naval Forces". And, shortly before he died, that veteran Admiral of the Fleet, Lord Fisher, wrote to Admiral de Chair (who was in command of the 10th Cruiser Squadron) : "You should all be publicly praised, but the fact is strict secrecy is so necessary in the important work you are carrying out."

But still the years went by and the complete story remained untold.

More recently, Admiral de Chair himself remarked at a dinner given aboard his old Blockade flagship *Alsatian* (now renamed the *Empress of France*) to his former officers who served so perseveringly during those strenuous years, "The work done by the Squadron has never been accurately recorded. They worked under a cloak of secrecy. . . . The Germans knew more about the Squadron than did our own people."

The following chapters, therefore, represent an attempt to give an authentic account from first-hand information of the greatest and most devastatingly effective blockade since ships first sailed the seas. Without the co-operation of numerous officers who once served in that Squadron it would have been impossible for these pages to be written, and a few years later

PREFACE

it would have been entirely useless to aim at providing any adequate picture. Whilst all sorts of invaluable data have been most courteously placed at my disposal—from private diaries to the log-books of Boarding Officers—these form the backbone rather than the meat. It is from personal conversations and private letters that one obtains so much that alone can give the true version.

Everyone, nowadays, well knows that an official despatch must be looked upon as containing a part, yet not necessarily all, of the truth. It is written too soon after events, and from a restricted viewpoint. Even if it be issued to the public, it does not always contain all that the writer stated, or represent his considered final judgment. But at a convenient period of time—though not long enough to dim memories—when all the various pieces of history have been collected together from survivors ; when these facts have been sifted and arranged in their proper order ; illuminated, too, by lights which have been kept out of cold, departmental reports ; then at last it becomes possible to see events not merely as they happened, but why. Often some totally inexplicable act which might puzzle posterity can be explained in five minutes' personal conversation with the officer responsible.

For their inestimable assistance in affording me information and illustrations, I desire to make acknowledgment to the following in particular : Admiral Sir Dudley de Chair, K.C.B., M.V.O. ; Vice-Admiral T. E. Wardle, C.B., D.S.O. ; Vice-Admiral E. L. Booty, C.B., M.V.O. ; Captain J. Kiddle, O.B.E., R.N. ; Paymaster-Captain V. A. Lawford, C.M.G., D.S.O., R.N. (who for many years was Admiral de Chair's Secretary) ; Captain J. W. Williams, D.S.O., R.N.R. ; Lieutenant J. Barton, R.N.V.R. and finally to Dr. A. C. Roxburgh. These last five officers in their separate capacities served for many long months in the flagship, and their collective experience manifests the various difficulties and trials which Blockaders had to undergo.

I wish to acknowledge, also, the courtesy of Mr. Charles Dixon, R.I., the artist, and of Vice-Admiral Wardle, the owner, of the charming painting which is here reproduced as frontispiece.

E. KEBLE CHATTERTON.

CONTENTS

LIST OF ILLUSTRATIONS

THE BIG BLOCKADE

CHAPTER I

PRINCIPLES AND PRECEDENTS

BEFORE we settle down to watch the detailed story of how an unarmoured, though armed, fleet of liners was directly responsible for Germany's downfall in the Great War, sapping her strength so steadily and persistently that the collapse of our late enemy's national will was inevitable, it is requisite that we should first get quite clearly in our minds certain fundamental principles and important precedents.

For, whilst The Big Blockade was unparalleled not less for its effectiveness than for its unexpected dangers and complicated difficulties, yet it was no mere isolated affair having an historical independence or illegal liberty. On the contrary, it was most closely linked with a bygone period usually characterized by wooden hulls, canvas, and cordage; whilst, on the other hand, it has created new rules and so drastically modified older ones that no blockade in the future can ever be carried out according to conceptions accepted previously. Also, it is to be noted that no section of naval warfare was so closely and consistently under the influence of International Law throughout the entire period of hostilities. The blockaders assuredly have the duty of cutting off the enemy's communication with the outside world by sea, yet this cannot be done in any arbitrary manner. The point will be elaborated in due course, but for the present it is enough to remind ourselves that neutrals have their rights which belligerents must respect, or the Law of Nations will ultimately compel the rivals to suffer for their disrespect.

We shall more readily appreciate the following chapters, with all their drama and bravery, their glorious seamanship, their immensity of effort, if we consider at the outset, quite briefly, the threefold purpose of a navy in the time of war. Nor is any apology for this needed, since the general reader not infrequently believes that the primary duty of the Sea Service is to fight battles.

The navy of a maritime nation exists, and has been brought into being, in order that (1) it may obtain, and preserve, the command of the sea, that is to mean the control of the ocean routes, in order that (a) the army may pass across in safety on its expedition against the enemy, and that (b) seaborne commerce may continue without interruption; (2) it may, conversely, prevent the enemy from bringing his military expeditions against the mother country, or her dominions overseas ; (3) and, lastly, that it may deny the ocean and channels to the enemy not solely in regard of fighting units, but of his merchant vessels that would bring him supplies of food, munitions, and any other stores whatsoever. The aim under this category is to contain the rival belligerent, bring economic pressure to bear heavily, and prohibit his imports and exports, restricting his stores only to such as can be produced in his own country. Such is the nature of a blockade, which may be military or commercial, or both ; again, it may be distant or close.

The classical example in naval history of ignoring the principle in (1) is for ever associated with Napoleon, who provides the plainest lesson that the greatest of generals may know nothing of naval strategy. His expedition to Egypt, magnificent though it seemed, and apparently destined to take the conquest of India in its stride, came to a terrible disaster because Bonaparte had neglected to ensure the command of the Mediterranean. His army had indeed advanced and secured its first objective, but the blow was not fatal, and its sea communications were cut off. Nelson's great victory at the Battle of the Nile settled that point ; there was no French naval force to throw in supplies or reinforcements, and no French ships could come sailing towards the coast. Why ? Because the British Navy was in control of the intervening ocean.

A British Blockade of Alexandria followed during that autumn of 1798, but it was, by reason of the weather, the dangers of the coast, the paucity of small suitable ships, extremely difficult to enforce. Thus Napoleon, after some anxious months, was lucky to escape in a frigate during the temporary absence of the British Blockading Squadron which had sailed to Cyprus to get water. Except for that good fortune, the terror of Europe might have ended his days in Africa and the trend of events have been altered. Bonaparte's scheme collapsed because, in the words of a French writer, he never attained *"le sentiment exact des difficultés maritimes"*.

Let it be noted that the command of the sea may be obtained with little fighting, or even without any engagement at all. Indeed, the strategy has (temporarily at least) broken down when the clash of battle occurs between the rival fleets, and it becomes rather a question of tactics. During the War of 1914–1918 the Grand Fleet, whilst but rarely engaged in all those four years actually firing projectiles, was none the less the power which controlled the maritime paths : even when it was several hundreds of miles away in Scottish waters it still made the English Channel safe for transports to reach France with troops and supplies, and the Atlantic safe for cargo vessels.

It cannot be stressed too firmly that without the existence of the Grand Fleet—effective and intact—no blockading operations, such as we are about to consider, could have been possible. However inactive a main battle fleet may have appeared when riding within Scapa Flow, yet it was just this maritime threat which denied the seas to German surface ships with the exception of an occasional raid, prevented our shores from invasion, and enabled us to place a barrier separating Germany from the overseas world. In the broadest sense, it was the Grand Fleet, then, which carried out the blockade ; though in practice this great task was deputed to a fleet of quite different ships and far more suited for a specialized series of activities. This series was the enforcement of a *commercial* blockade, which endeavoured to stop seaborne goods from leaving or entering Germany and Austria.

One might in truth say that whilst the forces under the immediate command of Admiral Jellicoe made up the Grand

Battle Fleet, it was the squadrons under Admiral de Chair which formed a Grand Examination Fleet. The latter, relying on the former's protection though miles away, was able to be the Battle Fleet's executive : to put into application the massed sea power, to chase, stop, examine, and even arrest, not merely any merchant ship of Germany, but any neutral suspected of carrying cargoes or passengers on Germany's behalf. This meant one long and trying period of patrol, which could never be relaxed in spite of mines and submarines, with always the possibility that an apparently innocent steamer pretending to be Scandinavian might suddenly reveal herself as a raider heavily armed with guns and torpedoes.

We are to address ourselves in our present inquiry to the exacting duties of some two dozen steamers organized into one command, "whose labours", remarked the late Lord (then Mr.) Balfour when First Lord of the Admiralty, "were more continuous, more important, and more successful than any other branch of His Majesty's Naval Forces". Night and day, winter and summer ; through gales of wind, mighty seas, Arctic ice, and the vilest weather which the North Sea and North Atlantic meet to create ; through long months when the sun rarely shone, and it was either mist or inky darkness ; these ex-merchant ships, so recently the crack carriers of the leading passenger lines, were crashing into icy waves, lowering their boats for boarding, and generally doing the one really *decisive* part of the World War.

But it was a protracted business, frequently full of disappointment ; at the best of times a grey monotony, and always nerve-trying for everyone from the commanding officer down to the lowest rating in the stokehold or on deck. Unadvertised, barely noticed, and generally not given a thought by the public, these ships and men kept at it throughout the fateful years, employing the one weapon which was wounding the enemy till he must bleed to death. It seems not a little strange that most of two decades should have elapsed before this first full narrative should be published, but at one time there was a good reason for keeping every item under a veil.

"I've just been looking into the splendid work done by your blockading squadron," wrote that veteran Admiral of the Fleet, Lord Fisher, early in 1915 to Admiral de Chair, "and I cannot refrain from expressing my admiration of the way your Captains, Officers and men must have all worked to attain such results in the face of such terrible bad weather and appalling dangers, and none too splendid ships for such very arduous work. I have told the First Lord, and the Commander-in-Chief, I think you should all be publicly praised, but the fact is strict secrecy is so necessary in the important work you are carrying out."

This was just a private letter sent by a First Sea Lord, who was never known to distribute compliments where they had not been exceptionally well earned. Still, if this blockade was the most efficient since ships first used the seas, yet to this day it is the least known : any student of history knows far more of how we blockaded Brest during the Napoleonic wars. Even as recently as April 12, 1931, when Admiral de Chair once again met his old officers aboard his former flagship of the blockade, he felt it necessary to say to them : "The work done by the Squadron has never been accurately recorded. We worked under a cloak of secrecy. . . . The Germans knew more about the Squadron than our own people know."

How, then, was this very modern blockade connected with past attempts of previous generations ? And in what respects was it limited by the Laws of Nations, so that under no circumstances could force degenerate into piracy ?

Let us begin by clarifying and defining the word which must be used in almost every sentence. We are apt to think of a blockade exclusively as some act corresponding to a siege, though a much wider sense is connoted nowadays ; for, whilst it is a development of that purely military land operation whereby the investing army shuts off the enemy from external succour, yet a blockading fleet cannot act so arbitrarily as an army. The sea is a highway that belongs to all the nations of the world, and ships of neutral States may probably cause considerable embarrassment to the blockaders by breaking through the barrier frequently. This, in turn, may result in a further crisis. Why ? Because there is such a demand, by the blockaded, for the neutrals' commodities at the highest prices, that those very traders who have lost their former markets through the outbreak of hostilities will now be willing to run great risks. This, in turn, will create delicate situations and the inevitable seizing of ships caught running the blockade. Finally, there comes a diplomatic climax with the grave probability of the neutrals entering the war, but in opposition to the blockaders.

Thus by sea, at least, the besiegers cannot operate wholly as they might wish : they are not entirely free agents, and the fear of throwing other States into the arms of the enemy will in itself be a deterrent against overbearing interference with non-belligerents. Nor does history fail to emphasize such conclusion by painful logic.

In its most elementary and ancient form a sea blockade was a close investment, such as may be seen in the illustration facing page 16, which represents the English Fleet under Prince Rupert and the Duke of Albemarle at anchor off the Vlie in August 1666 during operations against the Dutch. But even in those days of the sailing ship a close blockade still differed from a land siege by an army. The fleet before us could not remain anchored if a gale of wind piped up, but would have to keep under way ; and, whilst in our twentieth century we have mechanically propelled vessels with greater abilities, yet no admiral would be so suicidal as to station his fleet so near to the enemy's coast. The introduction of the explosive mine, the torpedo, and the aeroplane, together with the long range of modern guns, have combined to banish a close in favour of a distant blockade.

In effect, the Grand Fleet, whilst several hundred miles away from the German coast, formed the military blockade : the closed door which prevented our enemy from sending his surface ships out into the Atlantic, or his transports of troops to reinforce his colonial army in East Africa ; although it is true that a very few individual German warships did break through the blockade disguised as merchantmen, and the High Sea Fleet did make an occasional raid, but never beyond the North Sea. Even the enemy destroyers did not venture farther west than the Straits of Dover.

But it was the commercial blockade which in the long run became even more decisive than the military, and was more distant still ; yet that included a conception far greater than a mere cordon of ships always under way. If the motive was economic pressure, the denial to the enemy of all access and egress embraced not merely goods and passengers, but all other communications west of the North Sea. Thus every effort was made to destroy Germany's export and import trade, and for this there must be a large patrolling fleet ; but communications nowadays include such items as telegraphy, postal service, and banking systems. Therefore those who stayed at home had still their part to play in censoring messages, unravelling secret codes, sifting intelligence, discovering clever plots to deceive, tracing back to German sources huge payments by some big bank in a neutral country made through intermediaries ; warning the patrols, in time, of a suspicious steamer due perhaps next week ; flashing a signal that some notorious enemy agent was travelling on board the neutral liner which was so fond of steaming at high speed with all lights out, and usually chose an unaccustomed track. And additional to all these considerations there was the sensitive task of trying, by every legitimate means, to discourage the business men in the United States, Holland, Denmark, Norway, and Sweden from the very tempting trade with a beleaguered nation. It seemed, indeed, an impossible problem ; for the economic relationship between one country and another in this our present condition of complicated existence is one of mutual reliance instead of the old self-supporting independence. If, for example, Holland had been wont to sell much of her livestock to Germany, or the United States to send large cargoes of cotton, or Norway to ship her fish, and Britain continued her best efforts in preventing these from entering the enemy's ports, would not the neutral producers rise in their wrath, protest to their respective Governments, whose ambassadors in turn would protest in London ?

This actually did occur, and, notwithstanding the many errors of judgment which were made by British statesmen and officials, one can still look back with some admiration for their tactful restraint, and with even more gratitude for the unrestrained tactlessness that characterized Germany's conduct in regard to non-belligerent nations. Thus, in short, our own failings and defects were obliterated by those Teutonic acts which stirred the most powerful neutral to indignation, eventually bringing her into the war not (as might have been possible) against us but as our ally.

Now the geographical position of England has always affected her history, and given her a key position. This central situation was to her benefit in the sixteenth century when she was able to prevent the Spanish Armada from forming a junction with the Duke of Parma, who was to arrive from the Low Countries with his army preparatory to invading our shores. England was, in the seventeenth century, not less a barrier between the Netherlands and the outer world, for there are but two exits to the Atlantic from the North Sea : one through the narrow neck of the Dover Straits, and the other round the north of Scotland, though even this route is partially restricted by the location of the Shetland Isles. The former, even in the War of 1914-1918, was regarded by the enemy as too dangerous and too narrow (except for occasional voyages in submarines) to counterbalance a considerable shortening of route into the Atlantic Ocean ; and every one of the surface raiders preferred, and used, the north-about route.

In the old sailing-ship days, during the time of war, many a Dutchman homeward bound chose the Shetlands track in spite of increased mileage and navigational dangers. Nature was thus very kind so to have placed Britain as a bulwark between Europe and the outer world that when the wars waged in the eighteenth and early nineteenth centuries with France there still existed a ready-made advantage for the British Fleet whilst blockading Brest. Not merely were the south-westerly gales of winter fair winds back to the Devonshire harbours, enabling the storm-tossed wooden ships to find temporary shelter in Plymouth Sound and Torbay, but the coast was easier to make. "In easterly or moderate weather", wrote Admiral Mahan,[1] "the blockading fleet kept its position without difficulty ; but in westerly gales, when too severe, they bore up for English ports, knowing the French Fleet could not get out till the wind shifted, which equally served to bring them back to their station."

During the Seven Years War of 1756-1763 the close

---

[1] *The Influence of Sea Power upon History*, p. 30.

A SEVENTEENTH-CENTURY BLOCKADE

The English Fleet anchored off the Vlie in August 1666.
[*From a Contemporary Print.*]

blockade of Brest certainly had a bad influence on the moral of the French Fleet, just as the distant blockade one and a half centuries later had on the personnel of the High Sea Fleet. To use Mahan's words, the eighteenth century French sailorhood were kept in a state of "constant inferiority in the practical handling of their ships". But the latter, through an unavoidable absence of the British in 1759, were able to make an escape. And here is to be noted the difference which has come with the steamship age, for Admiral de Chair's vessels were not allowed to leave their patrol areas except in rotation at the end of six or seven weeks, when they were running short of coal. The matter of weather was never to enter into the consideration. These liners had been originally built for ocean work, and keep the northern seas they certainly did, with a continuity that had never been possible through the era of sail.

None the less it is impossible to deny that, in spite of the seaworthiness and ocean kindliness which a modern 15,000-ton steamer possesses, she did try her personnel not merely through perpetual suspense and the necessity of always being on the alert, but because there was no respite from movement. The fleet was always steaming, and that this was practicable for weeks on end is an indication alike of the strain, the skill, and the devotion of the engineers down below. The Grand Fleet could make its occasional sweeps down the North Sea, and after perhaps forty-eight hours they were back within a safe anchorage, where rest and any minor repairs could be made. Very different was life for this fleet of armed merchantmen.

Was it then surprising that at the end of a twelve-month physical or nervous endurance broke down, and officers were transferred to light cruisers, battleships, and even to Q-ships? History was again repeating itself, as it always does; for whilst Nelson was able to boast that through long months his ships had weathered the heaviest gales without losing mast or yard, yet Collingwood admitted that the blockading was endurable only up to a limit. When he wrote complaining that he had scarcely known such a thing as a night of rest "these two months", and that "this incessant cruising seems to me beyond the powers of human nature", so that officers

B

were breaking down, he was merely employing the same phrases which were applicable to his naval successors of a later century. The long nights of winter, the violence of the weather off France and Spain, were just as bad or even worse off the north of Scotland. If the old wooden ships were less easy to handle, at least they had not to keep mindful of the invisible submarine and the silver torpedo which suddenly dealt death. Nor could it be argued that wintry gales, fogs, or long black nights would (as in the days of oak and canvas) deter the enemy : on the contrary, these were just the conditions which German raiders usually awaited, and contraband-carriers generally hoped for, in attempting the blockade.

Maritime nations have always been the wealthy countries, for the reason that the sea is "the great scene of commerce"[1] (to use Mahan's happy phrase); and the prohibition of seaborne commerce to an enemy always has been a tremendous blow to the latter's fighting power. But this prohibition must needs be backed up by penalties which can only be enforced by naval preponderance acting through the Prize Courts. British maritime superiority denied to Napoleon the freedom of the seas, so that in the time of Pitt the merchants of London found that their commerce actually flourished during the war period : there was no French merchantman able to leave port. Similarly, one of the most remarkable aspects of the 1914-1918 War lay in the vast amount of British cargo steamers pursuing their trade along every route, only temporarily inconvenienced by surface raiders until the submarine peril reached its peak in April 1917. On the other hand, German liners and freight-carriers remained dead and doomed within harbour.

A commercial blockade has been shown by history to be "the most systematic, regularized, and extensive form of commerce-destruction known to war . . . it does not necessarily involve fighting", and by universal consent subjects to capture neutrals who attempt to infringe it, because, by attempting to defeat the efforts of one belligerent, they make themselves parties to the war. "Against commerce-destruction by blockade, the recourse of the weaker maritime belligerent

---

[1] *Sea Power in its Relations to the War of* 1812, I, p. 144.

is commerce-destruction by cruisers on the high sea."[1]
This is exactly what the Germans attempted until the last
cruiser was interned by the spring of 1915, when the destruction
was undertaken by submarines plus an occasional cruiser having
the external appearance of a neutral trader.

We pass next to consider the legality of a blockade as it
affects all parties concerned, and the consideration under this
heading is anything but a mere abstract study, dusty with
ages of dull niceties : rather it is full of vital interest and the
human enterprise of seafaring men. It is because crews afloat
in ships, away from the controlling powers on land, enjoying
the immunity of the ocean's wide spaces, have from the earliest
times exhibited a tendency to obey only the laws of nature
and not of man that some set of restrictions became essential
for the good of commerce by sea. In the days of ancient Rome
the spread of piracy necessitated that the offenders be indict-
able as "enemies of the human race". From the moment that
overseas trade became important, there was born the need
for regulation to protect that commerce, and Rome's corn
trade from Egypt was too valuable for extinction.

Similarly, when Richard I of England went out on his
crusade with his navy he must needs ordain a set of rules and
penalties against the bad behaviour of his sailors ; but from the
Levant he brought home the drastic Laws of Oleron, which
regulated maritime procedure in detail. As time went on and
shipping increased, obviously the sea laws had to be extended,
and the question of prizes captured received careful attention.
Thus his successor, John, used to take half of the prizes
captured in the Dover defile by the Cinque Ports seamen,
and this percentage continued till the time of Henry VIII,
Letters of Marque being mentioned even in the thirteenth
century. The licences issued in Tudor times (e.g. the reign of
Edward VI) permitting privateering were expressive of the control which was exercised by the highest authority over shipping
activities. The important fact to bear in mind—for reasons
presently manifest—is that there grew up in England a law and
custom of the sea essentially different and distinct from land
affairs, and with a separate jurisdiction for their enforcement.

---

[1] *Ibid.*, pp. 286-288.

Sea law used to be administered by the Admirals of the North, South, and West, but in the sixteenth century it was the High Court of Admiralty which gradually began to take this duty. Piracy round the British Isles was a serious menace both before, and especially after, the Armada campaign. It had to be stamped out, yet even privateering was lawful only when a commission was granted by the Government and the privateers acted in accordance with the law.

But not till the seventeenth century and the unveiling of the New World to more extensive sea commerce, thereby opening up new avenues to unheard of wealth, did the ocean become so internationally significant. This ocean commerce demanded from the lawyers an attention hitherto unthought of. But, now that the Dutch and English mariners were gathering up the world's trade by longer and longer voyages, it was high time that the legal mind of Europe should look out beyond the limits of municipal law in order to discover the principles which should regulate the conduct as between nation and nation. North America was being colonized; the East Indies were bartering their rich products; the whale fisheries of Greenland, the herring fisheries of the North Sea, already were creating Anglo-Dutch jealousies and friction. So it was scarcely surprising that the brilliant Dutch jurist, Hugo Grotius, comes on to the scene during the first quarter of this seventeenth century laying down for all time the elementary principles that should determine the intercourse among civilized nations.

All law is order, and seventeenth-century sea-trading had become to maritime nations so invaluable that it must be regularized, controlled, guided. Here was the beginning of a new conception, because ships were being built of bigger size, ocean-worthy, and the pilots had at last learned how to find a vessel's latitude. When men fight, or contend in games, they have the instinctive desire to do so in accordance with some definite rules : it is a subconscious appeal to an authority superior beyond themselves—the acknowledgment of an impartial standard. But there exists also the urge of self-preservation.

By the mid-seventeenth century Britain had passed from the adventurous sense of seafaring that characterized

Elizabethan days : the vague yearnings had developed now into a firm national determination to become predominant at sea, and the Navigation Acts beginning from 1651, in Cromwell's time, were expressive of this resolve. As the family of European nations grew, voyaged, became more rich through commerce overseas, with intervals of naval wars during the eighteenth century, so there must inevitably be new international rules to cope with unsuspected problems. Just as citizens in their private capacity are bound by the laws of their country, so it had become apparent that, whether in peaceful voyaging or in the capture of prizes during war, there must be some universal practice binding on all parties, otherwise piracy would be paramount.

The final appeal must be to the Law of Nations, so that we find, by August 4, 1914, that the rules of war and neutrality were of comparatively modern origin, and derived from the following : precedents drawn from the practice of nations, the decisions of Prize Courts—all of the late eighteenth and early nineteenth centuries—together with the Declaration of Paris (1856) and the Declaration of London (1909). As an instance that a rule could be laid down only resulting from experience, there was raised in 1742 the question as to what constituted an effective blockade. France and Denmark agreed that at least two vessels were necessary ; whilst later on Holland and Sicily agreed that six vessels outside the range of gunshot were requisite.

But forasmuch as Great Britain became the greatest maritime nation, both in regard to naval matters and as an ocean carrier of trade, her Prize Courts have always played the chief part in building up those laws which concern contraband, blockade, and the capture of private property at sea ; laws, incidentally, to which most of the civilized world has now given its adhesion. But, again, it needed positive crises arising out of actual hostilities (rather than abstract theories) to develop such legislation and demonstrate the international problem that cried out for solution. We have seen the natural impulse of neutrals to trade with belligerents, and we can appreciate that unless this business is done strictly within defined rules accepted by all parties, international friction must assuredly follow.

For example, after war had broken out with the British colonies of North America in 1775, British cruisers did not hesitate to stop and search neutral merchantmen at sea, with the result that there was an Anglo-Dutch crisis. So, too, during the war of the French Revolution following the Declaration against Britain in 1793, British cruisers could not capture neutral cargo vessels without annoying the Americans. It was just this anxious period which produced in Sir William Scott the greatest authority on shipping law to which Europe has hitherto been indebted. The soundness and fairness of Prize Law to-day date back to the judgments of this monumental personality. He was appointed Judge of the High Court of Admiralty in 1798, that is to say five years after the most recent war had started, and he so continued through the Napoleonic wars, leaving an impress of his clear and impartial reasoning that time cannot efface. His invaluable guidance was still very powerful in settling some of the Prize Court cases that arose during the War of 1914-1918.

Better known to us as Lord Stowell, having been raised to the peerage in 1821, he will ever be remembered for having stressed the essential view that sea law is not national but international. He considered that the "duty of my station" was to administer that justice "which the Law of Nations holds out, without distinction to independent States, some happening to be neutral and some to be belligerent. The seat of judicial authority is, indeed, locally here, in the belligerent country", he laid down in 1799, "but the law itself has no locality."

These last seven words are of the highest importance to us who are about to witness a struggle on sea much greater than was waged in the days of our forefathers. Thanks to the law erected by Stowell during the Napoleonic wars, extended and strengthened by Britain and the United States during the nineteenth century, the Prize Courts of the twentieth century were already in possession of the guiding principles which enabled judges to deal with the unsuspected difficulties of blockade and the complicated ramifications of modern contraband trading. International Law has been defined as consisting of certain rules of conduct which modern States regard as being equally binding on them in their relations with one another as a conscientious person obeys the laws of his own country. And had European civilization not yet reached this agreement, then the period of 1914-1918 would have been gorgeous chaos.

For we must not lose sight of the truth that the ultimate sanction of a blockade is the Prize Court. Every neutral State recognized in principle its authority, its powers and functions, because it administered that Law of Nations which "has no locality". Here, during the late War, was the real protection against piracy, so that if a Scandinavian tramp steamer gambled against the rules of contraband, was caught by the British Blockade, and subsequently condemned by the Prize Court, she had only herself to blame. So, also, notwithstanding the irregularities with which Germany attempted a submarine blockade, she was still held in check lest utter defiance of the sea laws should do her even greater harm.

It is a matter for thankfulness that the integrity of the English Prize Courts has never been questioned, even during the bitterest times of the last war. And if by any circumstance the British Blockade had wrongfully seized some neutral steamer, the owners well understood that the matter would be settled with every impartiality by the Prize Court sitting in London, who would not hesitate to award damages. On the other hand, the certainty that, if the seized cargoes were proved to be of enemy destination or origin, they would be condemned by the Prize Court and there would be no appeal except to the Judicial Committee of the Privy Council, involving further delay and expense—this actually strengthened the Blockaders' hands and made a cautious shipowner, of even Sweden, think twice before accepting goods intended ultimately for Germany.

We are about to watch the working of a Commercial Blockade, but this was a comparatively new form of warfare— as distinct from the Military Blockade—and Europe had first experienced it in 1806, when the rivers Elbe, Ems, and Trave were blockaded as a reprisal for the closure of these North Sea entrances to British shipping at the instigation of Napoleon. "American policy", says Mahan,[1] "showed a

---

[1] *Sea Power in its Relations to the War of* 1812, I, p. 146.

disposition to go astray by denying the legitimacy of a purely commercial blockade." But the American Civil War taught a new lesson which could be learned only in hostilities.

We must now introduce at this stage another new development which was being born during the late eighteenth century, grew up during the nineteenth, and became overbearing in its strength during the twentieth. It was the power of the Foreign Office, that is to say, a permanent body of clerks, which has increased so mightily to this day that it has arrogated to itself functions for which it has no right,[1] usurping the privileges of both King and Parliament, and during the War of 1914-1918 expressing its strong will by the medium of Orders-in-Council, seeking (not altogether successfully) to override the Law of Nations in regard to sea affairs. Throughout the Big Blockade naval officers (as they have assured me) were severely handicapped by what seemed to be the arbitrary decisions of departmental officials sitting in London and ruining the achievements that had been won by gallant boarding efforts.

Admiral Jellicoe scarcely disguised the Navy's indignation when he wrote : "The fate of the detained ship was decided in London on receipt of the report of examination. As was perhaps natural, the sentences on many ships' cargoes pronounced in London were not accepted without question from the Fleet, and a good deal of correspondence passed. . . . The difficulties with which the Foreign Office was faced in regard to neutral susceptibilities were naturally not so apparent in the Fleet as to the authorities in London."[2]

An Order-in-Council is a sovereign order on administrative matter issued by the Privy Council's advice, and a succession of these with vacillating policy caused endless trouble, incidentally creating almost as big a crisis with America as the same machinery brought about in the previous century. Those Orders-in-Council of November 11, 1807, intended as retaliatory measures against the enemy France, though modelled on the general plan of blockades, were intensely annoying to the Americans because interfering with the

---

[1] The subject is fully argued in *The Strength of England*, by G. F. S. Bowles. London, 1926.
[2] *The Grand Fleet*, p. 76.

latter's neutral trade. It is true that the severity of the struggle with Napoleon made the problem of international relations none too easy; but the British Cabinet formulated and enforced against neutrals a restriction of trade which it admitted was unsanctioned by law and justified only by the unwarrantable course of the French Emperor. But, be it noted, this interference with the American carrying trade in defiance of International Law was one of the two immediate causes which brought about the war of 1812, as indeed the Orders-in-Council between 1914 and 1917 seemed destined to turn the United States into allies of Germany.

The overwhelming influence of the British Foreign Office during the hundred years immediately preceding 1914 included the Declaration of Paris of 1856. "Without a single word having been breathed to Parliament or to the English people, the thing for which Lord Nelson and Mr. Pitt would have died again to prevent had been completely accomplished by Europe through the direct agency of the English Foreign Office."[1] However, this still remained the almost Universal Law, inasmuch as it was signed by every civilized State (with the exception of four small American republics, the United States, and Spain, though during the Spanish-American War of 1898 the two latter observed its provisions). It is therefore expedient here to state the four clauses which the Declaration of Paris contains :

(1). Privateering is and remains abolished.

(2). The neutral flag covers enemy's merchandise with the exception of contraband of war.

(3). Neutral merchandise, with the exception of contraband of war, is not capturable under the enemy's flag.

(4). Blockades, in order to be obligatory, must be effective, that is to say, maintained by a force sufficient to really prevent access to the coast of the enemy.

This Declaration was made just after the Crimean War, and it was clause (2) which was to receive so much criticism

---

[1] Bowles, *ut supra*, p. 147.

in Great Britain on the ground that it took away from the British Fleet the right to search neutral ships for enemy's goods. Now it so happened that we were not to be involved in a maritime war for the next fifty-eight years, so that this Declaration was never put to practical test ; yet the fact that the United States had never been a signatory would have prevented it from enjoying a common consent of nations. Thus clause (2), for instance, could not have been upheld by the Prize Courts.

After the Boer War came the Hague Peace Conference, out of which emanated the Declaration of London, dated 1909, which was indeed signed by the representatives of Britain, Germany, Austria, France, the United States, Russia, Netherlands, Spain, Italy, and Japan. But amongst its 71 clauses there was so much which was open to criticism that an agitation (aroused largely by the late Mr. Gibson Bowles) prevented its ever being ratified, and when the Great War broke out in August 1914 it had no binding authority.

Thus, with the arrival of hostilities, the legal position was curious. The Declaration of London was dead, the Declaration of Paris was not binding on the United States, and therefore did not enjoy the universal consent of nations. But what influence would it exercise on the Prize Courts, which are the High Court of Admiralty ? Actually an Order-in-Council, dated March 11, 1915, did reject the offensive clause (2) in the Declaration of Paris, so that Convention went by the board. Then, with all the successive and contradictory Orders-in-Council accumulating, it was not surprising that the United States became puzzled, irritated, indignant. What they said in effect was : "By what set of rules are you carrying out this war against Germany ? We find it impossible to see the consistency in your pretensions." More Orders-in-Council kept emanating at the demand of the Foreign Office, though luckily the Prize Courts judges declined to be bound by such regulations, preferring firmly to continue in the tradition of Lord Stowell ; so that when the supreme tests were made, it was the Law of Nations which "has no locality" that stood forth as the final standard.

With this preliminary survey of the principles and precedents we are now ready to watch the practical application under the exceptional conditions of modern warfare. The strange paradox, however, has to be presented that *technically* there never was a British Blockade during those four fateful years. At no date throughout the Great War did Great Britain declare that a blockade against Germany was in existence ; yet in fact it was because of the blockade that our enemy finally collapsed. Deeds proved themselves more influential than words : results were far more important than mere statements of intention.

CHAPTER II

It is now common knowledge that in 1912 plans were being completed in London with regard to the approaching war, and early that year the Committee of Imperial Defence carefully considered the best means for bringing economic pressure to bear on Germany.

A formal declaration of blockade was deemed inadvisable for strategical and legal reasons; naval experts realized that we could not operate successfully in the Baltic with any continuity. The torpedo had altered the outlook, minefields would doubtless be laid with facility, and these narrow waters would be untenable for an investing fleet. Therefore it would be only an ineffective blockade so long as there remained to the enemy access and egress from that tideless sea; and this lack of completion would certainly lead to complications with neutrals. They would point to Article 4 in the Declaration of Paris—that "Blockades, in order to be obligatory, must be effective".

Moreover, the Baltic is only one of the commercial gates into Germany, and much of her trade arrives via Rotterdam through Holland's inland waterways, by means of those enormous barges known as *rhineschiffs*, so familiar to all who have used the Dutch canal system. Thus it would be wiser not to announce the word "blockade", but to banish the thought of a "close up" barrier.

It was arranged ahead that at the outbreak of hostilities all commercial and financial dealings between Germany and the British Empire should be immediately prohibited, and thereby embarrass the enemy by at once cutting off further supplies of many important articles from jute to wool, rubber to bunker coal. A patrol system was indicated for intercepting vessels bound to or from Germany, and to examine traffic destined by sea for Holland, the general object being to destroy the enemy's inward trade arriving from the Atlantic. As part of the pre-War scheme the following expedients were arranged for hampering the contraband trade between Germany and neutral countries :

(*a*) Lists of articles to be regarded as Absolute Contraband, and others of Conditional Contraband, were to be in readiness.

(*b*) A Proclamation was to prevent British shipping from carrying contraband to any port of Northern Europe.

(*c*) Trade between Germany and neutrals was to be made unattractive by threatening the latter with the denial of any more bunker coal.

(*d*) A Prize Court was to be established to deal with the seizures of ships and cargoes.

So meticulously was all planning detailed that the machinery at once started working without a hitch. On August 4, 1914, came the Royal Proclamation specifying arms, projectiles, explosives, warships, aeroplanes, etc., among the long list of Absolute Contraband ; foodstuffs, forage, vehicles, etc., on the list of Conditional Contraband. Next day a Proclamation was made in fulfilment of (*b*) ;[1] and on August 20 "the Commissioners for executing the office of Lord High Admiral" were ordered to "require His Majesty's High Court of Justice and the judges thereof to take cognizance of and judicially proceed upon" "all manner of captures, seizures, prizes and reprisals of all ships, vessels, and goods that are or shall be taken, and to hear and determine the same ; and according to the course of Admiralty and the Law of Nations . . . to adjudge and condemn all such".

In short, the Big Blockade system, with all its momentous consequences, had been now set going, and there remained only

---

[1] At the beginning of the War, British coal merchants in all parts of the world were requested by the Admiralty not to supply ships suspected as trading on the enemy's behalf. But coal was definitely placed in the prohibited lists of May and July 1915, the Foreign Office issuing to our representatives abroad a catalogue of foreign firms who were to be refused coal.

to be made known which was the set of rules that should be regarded as binding. Were these to be found in the ratified Declaration of Paris, or the unratified Declaration of London ? All doubt was soon dismissed by the Order-in-Council dated August 20, 1914, which laid down that "the Convention known as the Declaration of London shall, subject to the following additions and modifications, be adopted and put in force". These alterations concerned Article 33 of the London Declaration, which read :

Conditional contraband is liable to capture if it is shown to be destined for the use of the armed forces or of a government department of the enemy State, unless in this latter case the circumstances show that the goods cannot in fact be used for the purposes of the war in progress.

So that the August 20 Order read :

The destination referred to in Article 33 may be inferred from any sufficient evidence. . . . Conditional contraband, if shown to have the destination referred to in Article 33, is liable to capture, to whatever port the vessel is bound.

Forthwith, then, we no sooner behold the Declaration of London held out as the standard of sea conduct than this rule is subjected to qualification, so that under no circumstances can the blockaders act strictly in accord with the convention which has already been accepted by Germany. On the other hand, we find laid down for the blockaders in this conditioning clause of August 20 the valuable rule that the ultimate destination of the ship's cargo is the test of Contraband, whether Absolute or Conditional. Thus a neutral steamer's cargo of, for example, cotton would become liable to be condemned if the Prize Court were convinced that its final destination was the enemy's country.

This is known as the "doctrine of continuous voyage", and it is stressed here because (distinct altogether from this Order-in-Council) it was part of the Law of Nations before August 1914, as we shall notice from a later chapter.[1] Of great assistance would become such a rule to the Blockading Fleet at a time when every kind of subterfuge would be perpetrated to carry contraband to Germany, though

---

[1] See Chapter XVI in reference to the Norwegian S.S. *Kim* case.

nominally shipped for Denmark or Scandinavia. The London Declaration had aimed at a compromise, but here was the curious situation of the British Foreign Office enforcing the unratified provisions except for one highly notable feature, which other nations might refuse to respect.

It was the beginning of the vacillating policy at which we have already hinted. But for officers and men of His Majesty's Navy there was only one duty, and that was to obey such rules as were issued. We were now at war, and squadrons were operating on their respective stations : the time for speculation was past, the great trial of sea strength was at hand.

In order that full information may be available whenever another blockade has to be inaugurated, and original documents have long since perished, it is meet that we should trace our subject from its source. *Imprimis*, whose was the personality which did the creative work and accomplished the vast organization ? For answer we look back to the month of June 1914, when Rear-Admiral Dudley R. S. de Chair, M.V.O., who had been serving at the Admiralty as Naval Secretary to the First Lord (Mr. Winston Churchill), was asked by the Board to reorganize the Training Service. It was a big undertaking, since it embraced not merely all the youth of the Royal Navy—cadets, boy artificers, seamen, stokers, the various training establishments round the coast, both strictly naval and semi-naval (e.g. those moored in the Thames) —but a squadron of eight cruisers. This new appointment of "Admiral of the Training Service" demanded an officer of great sea experience, but of unusual organizing ability. It was because Admiral de Chair possessed these special qualifications that the choice fell on him to begin a task which circumstances, however, prevented him from completing.

His career had already been distinguished ; in passing for Lieutenant he had won the Goodenough medal for gunnery, nevertheless he had specialized in torpedo. In later years he had served at the Admiralty as assistant to Admiral Jellicoe when the latter was Third Sea Lord, and at the end of 1912 it was Captain de Chair who had succeeded the future Admiral Beatty as the First Lord's Secretary. All this departmental and sea contact formed an ideal preliminary to the much bigger task which awaited. But he had barely begun his reorganization than the war clouds gathered. The 10th Cruiser (or Training) Squadron consisted of the following very old ships *Edgar* and *Royal Arthur*, launched as far back as the year 1890; *Endymion* and *Hawke*, dating from 1891; *Grafton*, *Theseus*, *Gibraltar* and *Crescent*, which dated from 1892. The last couple were of 7,700 tons, but the others displaced only 7,350 tons. All were therefore quite small units, with a designed speed of 19¼ knots, the main armament in each ship comprising two 9.2-inch and twelve 6-inch guns. In the latter half of July they had assembled at Spithead for the naval review, next done a little cruising down the English Channel, but had then been dispersed to their respective ports, Admiral de Chair (who had flown his flag in the *Crescent*) coming ashore and going back to his office in the Admiralty. On Saturday, July 25, H.M.S. *Crescent* went up Portsmouth harbour, but on the Monday there evolved some excitement over the prospects of war between Austria and Serbia.

On Tuesday it was "Stand by to re-mobilize the Training Squadron", on Friday the Admiralty warning telegram was sent out, and next day Admiral de Chair was ordered back to Portsmouth, where he was to hoist his flag again in H.M.S. *Crescent*, take this 10th Cruiser Squadron to sea, and carry out the Northern Blockade. Within one week, therefore, these antiquated men-of-war had suddenly taken on a new value to the country, for Germany to-day crossed the French frontier and she might speedily be at enmity with Britain. That being so, it was time to despatch squadrons from the English Channel to deny German egress from the North Sea in any attempt to approach the Orkneys and Shetlands route.

On Wednesday morning the Grand Fleet had set forth from Portland, northward, but east-about. Admiral de Chair, who reached Portsmouth by the last train on Saturday night, was to proceed west-about. All was bustle and energy now in a contest to beat the clock. The boys were sent ashore, their places being filled by reservists and retired officers who, till a few hours ago, had imagined their familiarity with the sea was long since finished. But throughout Sunday they came dribbling on board, some having travelled all night, the order to mobilize having been sent out only on August 1. Extraordinary efforts were being made to get the *Crescent*, *Grafton*,

ADMIRAL SIR DUDLEY DE CHAIR, K.C.B., M.V.O.

and *Edgar* ready to leave harbour;[1] but the coincidence that August 2 was a Sunday and August 3 happened to be a Bank Holiday, with all the British train service different from normal weekdays, did not altogether assist those old pensioners who were living miles away. Still, remarked the Admiral, it was "marvellous how quickly they came in".

During the forenoon of Monday officers and men were still rejoining, but it was impossible at this critical August 3 to wait any longer. "I determined to push on with what ships I could get, although several officers and men had not joined, as I felt war might be declared at any moment, and it was quite on the cards Germany would strike without declaring war. I telegraphed to Devonport, Chatham, and Queenstown to find out how the mobilizing was going on, and found it was slower than at Portsmouth. It was also very difficult to get any stores or provisions from the town, shops all being shut ; but my steward luckily turned up and got enough to go on with."

So at 11 a.m. on the day before war broke out between Germany and Britain the *Crescent* alone, without her two consorts, steamed forth past Nelson's old *Victory*, turned west to go out by the Needles, and by midnight was off Plymouth. The three units of the squadron based on that port were not yet ready, but a hastening signal was wirelessed in from the *Crescent* as she sped on towards Land's End and the Irish Sea, being joined on Tuesday by the *Edgar* and *Grafton* from Portsmouth. Another wireless message was flashed across to Queenstown where the *Hawke* was lying, telling her to follow with all despatch ; and now Holyhead was being left astern when, shortly after midnight, arrived through the ether the Admiralty's telegram to commence hostilities against Germany.

Daylight was awaited with expectant interest, guns ready, men at their stations, and all preparations for possible emergency. Throughout Tuesday the ships had been in war routine, and the newcomers were shaking down to an old life that had been temporarily suspended. The morning light showed an horizon clear of shipping, and now the cruisers

---

[1] The *Endymion, Theseus,* and *Gibraltar* were now lying at Devonport ; the *Royal Arthur* was at Chatham ; and the *Hawke* at Queenstown.

sighted the Mull of Cantyre. But at 8.30 a.m. a German tramp steamer, named the *Wilhelm Behrens*, with a cargo of timber, came into view. To her the Admiral detached the *Grafton*, who captured her, but only after the stranger had tried to escape. A shot across the latter's bows soon made the German heave-to, a prize crew was put aboard, and she was taken into the Clyde. Thus, within a few hours of hostilities commencing, one enemy trader had been captured.

Steaming past the Scottish coast, the *Crescent* spoke the tourist S.S. *Arcadian*, full of passengers who had been holiday-making in the Norwegian fjords, and she was now given news of the war's outbreak. Strange contrasts this August was affording ! A pleasure-steamer, and a light cruiser ready for action, both in the same picture ! As the *Crescent* carried on northwards, the fine weather of summer turned to mist, and by the time she was in the Minch, between the Hebrides and the mainland, down came the rain and wind as a gentle hint of what might be expected during ensuing months. But by 9 a.m. of August 6 Admiral de Chair had brought his three ships to anchor in Scapa Flow, exchanging signals whilst entering with Admiral Beatty, whose Battle Cruiser Squadron was just coming out. That same day arrived *Endymion* and *Theseus*; so more than half the 10th Cruiser Squadron were now present and correct.

It is interesting to note that neither Admiral de Chair, nor many other officers, had hitherto visited this fine harbour, which has since become so famous the world over. At once the Squadron's ships' companies were busily employed coaling and sending ashore boats together with woodwork, so as to minimize the effect of shell fire that would inevitably be the cause of serious conflagration during any engagement. For those old-fashioned vessels were notoriously combustible. But already the beach presented a curious spectacle—"one mass of gigs and galleys" hauled up above high-water mark and left behind by the Battle Fleet.[1] That same night the *Crescent* and *Edgar* went out and thus began their first patrol

---

[1] There were optimists in those days, and it is amusing to note how short-lived some considered this newly begun war must be. The officer who was sent ashore from H.M.S. *Crescent* arranged to rent a shed for storing some of the ship's woodwork at five shillings a week. "We never went there again," the cruiser's captain tells me, "and I have often wondered whether the man got his money !"

within two days of the war's commencement. It will be noticed that from the afternoon of August 1, when Admiral de Chair was instructed to leave London, until this evening of August 6, not one hour had been wasted in hurrying towards that North Sea exit which stretches across from the Orkneys to the coast of Norway : yet the arrival had been none too early. Already the first German raider, the fast North German Lloyd liner *Kaiser Wilhelm der Grosse,* had started out from Germany on August 4, steamed up the North Sea close to the Norwegian coast, gone right round Iceland, and on August 7 was hurrying south between Iceland and Greenland into the Atlantic, where she was destined to harass British liners until H.M.S. *Highflyer* brought about her destruction.

Whilst the *Crescent* was departing for her area off the Shetlands, just before dark, she passed the *Gibraltar* arriving to join the Squadron. On her way up to Scapa this cruiser had captured a German merchantman off the Isle of Man and sent her into Liverpool with a prize crew. It was not many hours before six units of the 10th Cruiser Squadron, coaled, stripped of superfluous gear, guns ready, and the "old hands" smartened up by much drilling, were patrolling in such a direction that they would be likely to intercept whatever traffic might essay the track which lies north-east of the Shetlands between Norway and the Icelandic coast. *Crescent, Edgar, Endymion, Theseus, Grafton,* and *Gibraltar* were exercising the utmost vigilance by day, whilst at night they were prepared for sudden attack and defence.

Lucky it was that no engagement was immediately forthcoming. The cruisers' crews were so strange to their respective ships, and there was much to be done ere complete efficiency could be attained, but any moment the dull grey distance might unveil the approaching smoke of the enemy's fleet, or at least one of his daring raiders. The first night faded uneventfully away as the organized squadron of "Edgars" stood off to the north-east, but daylight of the 8th revealed two sailing trawlers, marked respectively B.V.17 and B.V.25, which indicated that they hailed from the German port of Begesack. Certainly both craft were captured, much to the surprise of 14 fishermen aboard each ; for they were amazed to learn of a war, having been at sea and beyond sight of land for the last three weeks. But a similar experience happened to British trawlers from Grimsby and Boston, who were surprised by German destroyers this month and taken prisoners.

The Begesack trawlers were named *Geeste* and *Delme*; their crews were taken off, sent below and given a good meal, while their ships were sunk by shell fire, being quite convenient targets for the reservist gun crews, who practised their skill at 4,000 yards. The position where the Germans became visible was about 90 miles N.E. of the Shetlands and roughly that distance from the Norwegian coast : in other words, right on the track which must have been traversed by an enemy raider bound for the Atlantic from home round the north of Iceland. At noon Admiral de Chair sent *Edgar*, *Theseus*, and *Gibraltar* to patrol in the vicinity of Norway between lat. 61°30′ and 62°30′, so that there was already one division of the squadron working near the Shetlands and the other just clear of neutral waters. Various steamers were examined, but no contraband was discovered.

Now at that first week of hostilities our information was very slight, and an Admiral had to rely largely on inference. The western Norwegian coast is so dotted with a fringe of outlying islands that for a considerable distance north and south a steamer is able to keep within territorial limits and snap her fingers at her enemy. It seemed but reasonable to suppose that German vessels would take advantage of this geographical protection, and we shall observe in a subsequent chapter that this actually did happen. But both at the northern and southern end there comes a stage when this Inner Lead (as the long passage is called) breaks off, and shipping must emerge into the open sea. It was for this reason that the last mentioned three cruisers had been so stationed in the hope of catching some German as he left or entered the northern end.

The wisdom of this plan was confirmed on the very next day, for when various steamers were boarded by the *Endymion* and *Grafton* it was learned that no fewer than 22 German trawlers, together with the *Prinz Friedrich Wilhelm*, were lying at Bergen. The latter was one of the North German Lloyd liners, 8,865 tons, with twin screws and a speed of at least 17 knots. Moreover, the Norwegian newspapers reported that she was making warlike preparations. The trawlers belonged chiefly to Bremerhaven, Cuxhaven, and Geeste-münde. It may be said at once that such was the efficacy of our Northern Patrols, that not one of these twenty-three enemy vessels ever came forth to give trouble : yet throughout the war our blockading units were always mindful of them, and a prudent Boarding Officer would keep a list of their names and fishing numbers at hand when going about his duties. Had the Blockade been weaker, we can be pretty sure that at least some of those interned vessels would have escaped in much the same manner that German ships got away from American and other neutral harbours.

Looking back on those inadequately informed days one has to remember, also, the scares and rumours which fogged clear thinking. Was it true that Norway, with all her numerous havens and useful anchorages, intended to side with Germany ? Could the yarn be substantiated that Stavanger was already being used as a base for German submarines ? We do know now quite definitely that on August 6—that is to say, the same date when the *Crescent* and *Edgar* reached and left Scapa Flow— ten U-boats (numbered 5, 7, 8, 9, 13, 14, 15, 16, 17, and 18) left Heligoland and swept northwards towards the Shetlands-Bergen line. The German naval authorities were anxious to learn details as to the blockade (which they always expected would be instituted when war should break out), so these invisible ten proceeded in line-abreast, expecting to find a definite cordon stretching across the North Sea. They returned with most indifferent information, and minus U-9, who was sent to the bottom by H.M.S. *Birmingham* on August 9.

Not till August 10 did the last two cruisers join Admiral de Chair's other "Edgars", so that he now had *Crescent* (Flag), *Grafton*, *Endymion*, and *Theseus* in his first division, *Edgar*, *Royal Arthur*, *Gibraltar*, and *Hawke* in his second. But it was a totally insufficient force, seeing that it was responsible for the patrol extending from the Shetlands to Norway, a span of more than 150 miles, and included the protection of the Shetland Isles themselves. Rarely, if ever, could all eight units be patrolling simultaneously : each ship must periodically return to coal. In fact, the routine settled down to one unit from each division being in harbour together, so that at the best only six cruisers could be relied upon for the blockade. This allowed no margin for unforeseen defects, losses by enemy action, or special duties. It was, indeed, fortunate that during this very early period the enemy should show such lack of enterprise, and the number of neutral steamers to be examined for contraband was so limited.

At first the Admirality directed that the 10th Cruiser Squadron should have its coaling base at Scapa Flow, but Admiral de Chair very soon realized that this was too far removed from the patrol area, and there was the lurking submarine to bear in mind. It was therefore decided to send two colliers into Lerwick, on the east side of the Shetlands, and another couple to Busta Voe on the west side. Each of these formed a good harbour, well sheltered from any gale, and it would be a great convenience to choose one or the other if threatened by submarines or bad weather. Arrangements were also made for supplies of beef and vegetables in either anchorage, though Lerwick was the more suitable, having a fair-sized town.

Such, then, was the somewhat modest beginning of what was to become so formidable a barrier; but the excitements, the difficulties and trials, were still to come.

CHAPTER III

It was characteristic of an opportunist policy at this period that from quite an early date the 10th Cruiser Squadron (otherwise known as Cruiser Force "B") was not allowed to concentrate its entire energies on the stopping of contraband. Indeed, it is significant that the guiding consideration was less concerned with thwarting neutrals' trade into Germany than with the more military intention of encountering any sudden and expected onrush by the enemy's men-of-war. For some time to come, such an idea as a stringent commercial blockade did not mature, and the air was so full of electrical suspense that sudden shocks were always being felt.

The result was that Admiral de Chair's squadron, either as a whole or as units, had no continuity of purpose permitted to it ; these little cruisers were required by Admiral Jellicoe for special "stunts" as occasion demanded. For instance, those Danish islands called the Faroes which lie most of 200 miles north-west of the Shetlands became suspected of being a base for German submarines, and on August 12 *Endymion*, with *Gibraltar*, was sent thither. But in a strange region of savage scenery, with its precipitous tall cliffs, its sharp-pointed peaks, its strong tides and complete absence of trees, there was nothing to justify suspicion, and the cruisers returned. It was more than a week before they rejoined their Admiral, and in the meanwhile he had been needed to assist the Grand Fleet, who were making a sweep over the North Sea towards the Skaggerak. This occupied a whole week-end, and from time to time the "Edgars" were again called upon for a similar duty.

When the Canadian contingents were coming across the Atlantic, and it was thought some portion of the High Sea

Fleet might make a dash to attack the troopship convoy, the 10th Cruiser Squadron was brought right down south to patrol, during the first part of October, in an area much nearer to the south-west of Norway. The *Crescent* and her sisters, in respect both of speed and armament, would have had no chance against the German battle-cruisers ; but the squadron was so spread that the enemy would have to pass through this area, and at least Admiral Jellicoe could be warned by wireless. No great incident, however, occurred until shortly after that phase.

True, there were minor events during the final weeks of summer when the patrol had been resumed. It was on August 20 that the Norske-Amerika liner *Bergensfjord* was stopped and visited by the *Crescent* between Shetlands and Norway. She is mentioned now because on other occasions this fast steamship keeps rushing backwards and forwards through these waters in a most suspicious manner. But at this date, so gentle was the British attitude in regard to foreign goods that when her Master stated his cargo largely consisted of flour, the vessel was not detained. He was bound from New York to Bergen, and expected that if he fell in with a German man-of-war she would capture *Bergensfjord* in order to obtain such a valuable food product. Next day another Norwegian steamer, the *Norueca*, was boarded in much the same neighbourhood. She was proceeding from Galveston to Christiania, but a couple of German stokers were found and removed before she was allowed to proceed.

And so the routine went on, many vessels being now examined, most of them being of either Norwegian or Danish nationality, the Dutch at this time normally using the English Channel in preference to the northern route. Often enough wind and sea combined to make the manœuvring of cruisers and lowering of boats no easy business. During the first part of September the *Royal Arthur*, whilst proceeding to inspect the Swedish S.S. *Tua*, unfortunately rammed and sank her. Two of the latter's crew were drowned, but the rest were taken by *Royal Arthur* into Cromarty. Before the month was out it became very evident that there would be plenty of days when boat work could not be attempted except with every risk of disaster.

The enemy's submarines, especially as demonstrated by the sinking of three "Cressys" during the last week of this September, now had to be considered a very real menace to Admiral de Chair's vessels. However much the latter zigzagged, there must come a perilous interlude when engines had to be stopped before lowering away or picking up the boat with its boarding party ; and these moments when the cruiser lay rolling idly to the swell were more than enough for a U-boat's captain to send his torpedo straight for the cruiser's side.

Occasionally, too, the ludicrous would happen and vary the monotony. One Saturday morning, just before breakfast, came an urgent message from the Commander-in-Chief that an enemy cruiser had been sighted. At once the "Edgars" were spread so as to cut her off, but these old ladies had some difficulty working up to even 16 knots. For three painful hours they did their best, until another signal came through that the chase was to be abandoned. It was just as well, for the "enemy cruiser" was the British destroyer *Swift*, 1,825 tons. True to her name, she was the quickest thing afloat, with the record speed of 41 miles an hour !

Attending on the squadron was that ancient torpedo-gunboat *Dryad*, of 1893 vintage, yet the sight of this 1,000-ton vessel was never displeasing. She maintained contact between the shore and the ships, bringing out despatches for the Admiral, welcome mails and fresh provisions for all. Heavy was the disappointment when the seas became so atrocious that it was impossible to communicate and she was ordered to seek shelter in Peterhead. Men who had looked forward to letters from home turned aside to curse the weather, the Kaiser, and the day they forsook the shore. But the worst had not yet arrived, the autumn gales were just tuning up, yet on the last Monday in September they were already pretty bad. Whilst on her way into harbour for refuelling, the *Crescent* encountered such a heavy sea, and her engines raced so seriously, that she was compelled to ease down till she was making only three and a half knots.

Those were the days when some of the more modern customs sacred to the Navy yielded to revision under the influence of hard seafaring ; the difference between the spectacular smartness of last July's Naval Review at Spithead and the figures wrapped up in yellow duffel suits to-day was highly significant. The North Sea, with its short steep waves, and the biting blasts which came tearing down from the Arctic, respected neither crews nor ships. Dawn would break at last, after a long turbulent night, and look down over grey hulls, grey seas, grey sky—everything drab. Officers, from Sub-Lieutenants upwards, readapted themselves to the new conditions and started growing beards, with such strange effects that the duffel hoods gave them exactly that portraiture which is shown in the sixteenth-century paintings of Dutch North Sea fishermen.

The dangers to be expected from the once despised submarine were now becoming very real. The flagship (*Antrim*) of another cruiser squadron had two torpedoes fired at her when steaming near the Norwegian coast, and only just failed to ram the enemy. This was on October 9, a day that was ideal for U-boats, for at times there was a thick fog, which reduced patrolling to an 8-knot speed, yet suddenly there would come bright intervals. But six days passed before the tragedy happened. Admiral de Chair had taken the *Crescent* into Cromarty on Monday, the 12th, for coaling and repairs to engines, and that evening H.M.S. *Hawke* left the same harbour to rejoin the 10th Cruiser Squadron, which was working some distance north-east of Buchan Ness examining and boarding steamers.

The first alarm occurred at 1.15 p.m. on October 15, when *Theseus*, being then about 80 miles from the shore (lat. 57°50', long. 0°33'E.), saw a torpedo approaching. Fortunately it missed the target and passed astern. On the receipt of this news the Captain of the *Edgar*, who in the temporary absence of the Admiral was acting as senior officer, promptly ordered *Theseus*, *Endymion*, and *Hawke* to leave the area and proceed at full speed in a north-westerly direction. This would bring them towards Scapa Flow. The first two units obeyed, but no reply came from the wireless of *Hawke*, who was out of sight. In vain did *Edgar* keep calling her up, and *Theseus* could only report that she had finally sighted the missing cruiser at 11.15 a.m., when the latter was steaming to the south-west for the examination of a steamer.

The last position of *Hawke* was a little to the south-west of the spot where *Theseus* had been attacked, and that was all the information at present possessed ; yet it was indeed too suggestive of what really had occurred. From Scapa Flow were despatched the speedy *Swift* with a division of destroyers, who went tearing along a south-east course to search the missing ship's last known position. But 120 miles had to be covered ; the darkness soon shut down the short October day. Meanwhile the news had reached Admiral de Chair, who at 4.30 p.m. put to sea in the *Crescent.* Nothing was discovered during the night, but two more destroyer divisions sallied forth to search the area, and next morning, at 8.45, the *Swift* sighted a raft on which were huddled Lieut.-Commander R. R. Rosoman, R.N., and a score of men, the sole survivors, as it then seemed.

There can be no question that the submarine was definitely occupying this particular spot because it was likely to be fruitful for two reasons : it was through here that the Grand Fleet, on its sweeps towards Heligoland Bight, would most probably pass, and in any case it was on the track of war vessels bound out of Cromarty east to the coast of Norway. The raft was found not more than ten miles to the west of where the *Hawke* made her final plunge ; and that in turn was less than twenty miles from the location of the attack on *Theseus.* It is quite evident, too, that the U-boat was determined to remain till some other targets arrived : it would be fine to reach Germany again and beat the record bag of the three "Cressys" about which everyone was still talking.

But for her speed and cautious handling, the *Swift* also would certainly have fallen a victim, for scarcely had she approached the raft than torpedoes were fired at her, so that she had to keep steaming about among the *Hawke's* wreckage and snatch the 21 survivors aboard whilst the other destroyers screened her movements. It was learnt that when the *Hawke* was torpedoed (amidships abreast the foremost funnel) she turned over and disappeared with the loss of 525 lives ; the only survivors, apart from the one officer and his men, being 49 others who got away in a boat and were rescued from starvation by a neutral steamer.

This was the first big crisis for Admiral de Chair's squadron, and it made a profound impression. The submarine scare had spread up the North Sea, and what the next development might be no one dared contemplate without anxiety. Two decisions of importance were now made by the Commander-in-Chief. Firstly, the 10th Cruiser Squadron was withdrawn much further north, so that it was now on a base line N.W. of the Shetlands, the ships being spread 10 miles apart, steering athwart that line W. by S., and then the opposite direction E. by N. During the daylight hours they kept zigzagging at 12 knots, and when darkness set in the speed was reduced to 9 knots. But, secondly, Admiral Jellicoe felt compelled to seek a distant base right away from the North Sea until such time as Scapa Flow had been rendered proof against submarines, so part of the Battle Fleet came to anchor in the Irish waters of Lough Swilly just a week after the torpedoing of *Hawke*.

Admiral de Chair's units were thus back on their original duties of blockading, and unquestionably they were now much better placed for intercepting traffic. Relieved of casual cruising, they began the immense task which in time was to turn the whole tide of war. This bleak expanse of ocean between the Shetlands and Faroes, where Atlantic and North Sea unite, was the great ocean channel for all manner of ships from the New World seeking Scandinavia and Denmark—one of the principal highways of the Seven Seas. To have neglected it any longer, even in favour of more military operations against submarines or minelayers, would have been to allow the uninterrupted flow of contraband.

Thus at once the "Edgars" observed that the shipping was far more numerous than they had met further south. Not one German vessel dared to come, but steamers and sailing ships bound from the United States and South America believed that this north-about route was more hopeful, especially as U-boats were operating in the narrow English Channel and might sink some neutral in mistake for a British transport. Muckle Flugga, the gaunt extremity of the Shetlands and the most northerly point of Britain's dominions in Europe, took on an attractiveness which this lonely rock had never possessed. It was to be so much a part of the squadron's life that the wags called themselves the "Muckle Flugga Hussars". After the chasing about between the Skaggerak and the Orkneys this Northern Patrol, for all its watery wilderness, was something of a relief, so that one officer did not hesitate to write in his diary : "Intercepting German supplies is better than dodging submarines."

The force, already weakened by one, was still quite inadequate for so essential a task. The *Endymion*, for example, on a particular day was towing a Norwegian sailing ship into Lerwick for examination ; the *Theseus* was examining a suspected Danish steamer ; whilst the *Crescent* had captured a Norwegian, which was sent into Lerwick with a prize crew on board, and presently another steamer of that nationality was arrested with a cargo of gasolene. It was *Endymion's* job to take her ship down into Scapa Flow. A nasty rising wind and sea had made it too risky to send off a boarding party, but it meant that the patrol line would be weakened till the cruiser could return.

Still, the Blockade would increase its power when its numbers could be multiplied, and not otherwise. Every three hours each "Edgar" would alter course 16 points, that is to say, turn from west to east or vice versa, the innermost vessel not approaching Muckle Flugga nearer than seven miles, but the routine of coaling and repairs meant that the patrol line was reduced to three units on certain occasions. Sometimes, too, this line was altered so that it was farther to the east, though continuing north and south. Always some unexpected event would keep obtruding, such as an urgent hospital case who had to be taken by *Endymion* into Busta Voe ; or the friendly *Dryad* had run ashore in Hoy Sound ; or a wireless would bring warning from the Commander-in-Chief that a German minelayer was expected to pass between the Faroes and Shetlands, so five "Edgars" were all on the alert.

Nothing happened that day ; the minelayer was a myth. Within a very few hours, however, considerable activity developed, and there was glorious excitement to quicken bored spirits. It was October 29, and the *Crescent* happened to be in Busta Voe, whither she had gone to coal and make good defects, when across this Scottish fjord came a signal that a suspicious steamer with two funnels and masts was racing full speed for the Norwegian coast. At 1 p.m. the Admiral hurried out in his flagship and ordered a general chase. The stranger was said to be passing north of the Shetlands, but the cruiser line included the *Edgar, Endymion,* and *Theseus,* so away they went in pursuit and working up to the best speed their tired old engines would allow.

At 4.24 p.m. the *Edgar* wirelessed that she had increased to 14 knots, that the suspicious steamer had been sighted by *Endymion* in lat. 61°20' N., long. 0°53' W. (which is to say, some 25 miles north of Muckle Flugga), and the stranger was rushing off to the south-east. From this it was evident that she was heading for the neighbourhood of Bergen, or perhaps the Skaggerak: so the Admiral, after rounding Muckle Flugga, endeavoured to steer such a course as would cut the steamer off before she could make neutral waters. But it seemed to be an unequal contest from the first. The *Crescent* was whacked up to her utmost capacity, and "at one time" (says an officer aboard her) "was doing nearly 17 knots"!

At 5.10 p.m. the *Endymion* signalled her speed just then as 18 knots, but the strange steamer was both hull and funnels down below the horizon and still getting away. As to *Theseus,* she, poor thing, by 6.25 p.m. had broken down under the strain, so that unless she had eased up considerably it would not have been safe to continue at all. But, luckily, at 7.5 p.m. the *Endymion* reported she was gaining on the chase and could now see the latter's stern light. Nothing more happened till half an hour after midnight, when there came the joyful signal from *Endymion* that she had at last overtaken her chase. Now this long adventure had lasted for 130 miles, and been terminated only by the extraordinary efforts of the naval engineering staff, together with some pretty clever navigation and careful steering, but it was well worth it.

Not until she had reached lat. 60°28' N., long. 3°22' E., which was most of the way towards Norwegian waters from Muckle Flugga, did the two-funnelled steamer yield and stop. The *Endymion* lowered a boat, sent off a boarding party, who discovered this was the liner *Bergensfjord* again, one of the two crack passenger mail ships of the Norske-Amerika Company. Built at Birkenhead only a year before the war, this 11,000-tons vessel was registered at Bergen and was regarded by the Norwegians with much the same respect that was bestowed in Britain on the *Mauretania.* But from the month that war had broken out this new passenger route

direct from New York to Scandinavia had attained an importance out of all proportion in comparison with its size of business ; it was the means whereby Germany was able to keep
in personal touch with her agents in the United States.

Her Master, true to the old Viking traditions, was a very
fine sailor man who took some notable risks month after month
backwards and forwards across the Atlantic during four years
of hostilities ; yet he was no friend to the British Navy, whom
he caused more than a little trouble. If ever there was a fine
exponent of blockade-running by a modern vessel, it was
persistently shown by the *Bergensfjord*, though the time soon
came when the Blockading Squadron had her movements
accurately foreseen. She would be intercepted in the given
area on a particular date and temporarily detained, notwithstanding every display of indignation, until a proper examination had been made. If any of those "funny" mystery men
were on their way between Germany and New York, you could
be fairly certain they were travelling under an assumed name
either in the *Bergensfjord* or at least her sister ship the *Kristianiafjord*. And many are the tales which officers of the
Blockade still relate of the efforts to hoodwink.

During the first part of this autumn it took a little time to
appreciate all the tricks, and note which were the suspects ;
but, however skilfully the *Bergensfjord* had played her part
in the preceding weeks, she was from this date onwards suspected. Now what, if any, was the benefit to the blockaders
in stopping her that October night ? Apart from having
inculcated a useful lesson that Germany's neighbours could
help on the high seas only with grave risk to themselves,
there accrued more than one satisfactory result. For among
the passengers was the German Consul-General from Korea,
who would not be allowed to see his fatherland till many
months had elapsed. Six German stowaways were also removed. Another three hours, and they would have been able
to begin passing through Scandinavia, then Denmark, into
their native country. Among the cargo there was also plenty
of crude rubber and coffee. Was the *Bergensfjord* carrying
contraband destined ultimately for the enemy ? Admiral
de Chair sent her into Kirkwall to have her properly
examined, so a prize crew was put aboard and the *Endymion*

escorted her till she arrived at the Orkneys anchorage that evening.

A President of the Norwegian Parliament chanced to be travelling in the *Bergensfjord*, and he protested strongly against this delay. To him Admiral de Chair expressed regret for the inconvenience caused, but the orders of the British Government had to be obeyed. The *Bergensfjord's* Master requested permission to wireless his owners that the ship had been boarded by a man-of-war and detained : the Admiral again replied that he was sorry no wireless signals could be allowed, but on arrival in Kirkwall the Master should request the sending of a cable.

After this little affair the cruisers returned to their Muckle Flugga patrol, spreading out to the N.N.W., but they had been properly shaken up by all this flurry : not for years had they been asked to develop such wild energy, and the excitement had been too much for their internals. First the *Theseus* reported that bilge water was leaking into her feed tanks and the density of her boilers was rapidly increasing, so at midnight she had to be sent into harbour for repairs. A few hours later the *Endymion* had to start remedying serious defects to her machinery, so she also was out of action ; and in the meanwhile *Crescent* developed a leaky condenser. It began to be evident that these fragile vessels would never endure the severe speed test : obviously a Squadron that instantly became distressed whenever called upon to pursue was an indifferent instrument of blockade. The fast neutrals would be able to run their contraband and laugh with scorn at these ancients. Something would have to be done about the problem, yet whence could other cruisers be obtained ? The Grand Fleet could not spare any ; whilst overseas there were so many German raiders prowling about the Atlantic, Pacific, and Indian Ocean looking for Allied merchantmen that it would have been impossible to weaken the trade routes any further ; so the "Edgars" patched their defects and got back to work as soon as they could.

October had shown how essential this northern examination was about to become, and no fewer than fifty steamers, schooners, sailing ships, trawlers, had this month been stopped, the greater part having been boarded, and a few sent in either

CAPTAIN (NOW VICE-ADMIRAL) T. E. WARDLE, R.N.

to Lerwick or Kirkwall. Quite apart from the problem of contraband, which would wax greater as the war became prolonged, this policing of the seas was the only method by which German patriots from North and South America could be prevented from reaching our enemy's forces. Concerning the ingenuity and daring of the Kaiser's couriers and agents, who travelled by this route, we shall have much to say in a later chapter.

There were many reasons just now for any lack of happiness in the Squadron at the general outlook. The isolation from the rest of Europe ; the lack of congenial environment on coming ashore for a few hours at some rather dull Scottish harbour ; the dirty weather and ugly seas ; the bad news from the Western Front ; and those painful telegrams which occasionally arrived in the wireless room announcing a brother's death in action—all this kept patrol life in sombrest tones. Then it was always disheartening, after having intercepted with difficulty a Scandinavian full of rye, meal, or other commodity obviously destined for the enemy, though consigned to a neutral nominee, only to receive orders from London that the ship must be released. "Where is the sense of all this red tape ? Why are we wasting our time knocking about up here, if our efforts are to be negatived by a bunch of clerks sitting in comfortable Whitehall ?" That was the kind of question that officers and men asked themselves.

But Admiral de Chair was careful to maintain the Squadron's spirits always at a high level, well knowing that this was the very basis of success. "It is an old maxim," he reminded his Captains, "and one well worth remembering, that three-fourths of the chances of success depend on morale and a confident spirit, and only one-fourth upon material conditions ; and I wish to bring this point strongly before the Captains of the Tenth Cruiser Squadron, so that no effort may be spared to raise the hopes and wishes of every officer and man in the Squadron to the belief that we are bound to be successful, and that every action we enter into will be pursued with relentless vigour and fought to a finish."

But a great trial of endurance arrived on November 11 this first year. The weather had degenerated from trying conditions, with an unpleasant sea, to a full gale. There are but two seasons in those high latitudes, winter and summer, with precious little of the latter. The abnormal currents which sweep past coast and outlying islands helped to kick up most monstrous waves in no time, and on November 9, when the patrol had been shifted temporarily to the south of Shetlands, there began a time of anxiety. The reader is aware that during the first period of the war German surface ships laid minefields off Southwold, the Humber, and Tyne; so, frequently, scares startled alert intelligence with the warning that more minelayers were on their way to ambush the approaches of Scapa Flow. That was why the *Crescent* and *Edgar* were steaming to the south-west of Foula Island in order to watch the Fair Island Channel which extends from Shetlands to the Orkneys.

At first it was possible to bear the heavy sea and strong wind with hope and patience, though the *Crescent's* engines had to be eased till the speed was nominally eight knots. Actually she was making good not more than four knots. By nine p.m. it was impossible for even this rate, and both cruisers were ordered to heave-to. On the morrow the south-westerly gale, which came sweeping without interruption all the way from America till it struck these outlying rocks, was still bad yet tolerable, and speed was again eight knots; yet on the 11th every limit of endurance was reached. The *Edgar* developed such serious engine trouble that she was ordered into harbour, but the weather was too impossible for that to be attempted. The minelayers having proved a mere fiction, Admiral de Chair was about to leave the Fair Island Channel, when the gale decided otherwise.

In accordance with the usual working of these storms, the wind veered from S.W. to W. and finally N.W., when it blew harder than ever, so once more both ships hove-to. Nor did that suffice, for the enemy of all sailormen was in no mood to be disarmed. "I must say", remarks Admiral de Chair, "that the sea we encountered that day was the worst storm I have ever experienced." It leapt irresistibly over the fo'c'sle, wrecked the forebridge, swept overboard the Admiral's sea cabin, carried away the ventilating cowl of the foremost stoke-hold, so that a considerable amount of water got below and put out the fires. Hammock nettings were broken, the port cutter (which was not swinging outboard, but turned in) was damaged beyond repair, a whaler was removed bodily from its davits, hawser reels and other fittings were torn away from the deck, every officer's cabin in the ship, together with the wardroom, was awash, "and", adds the Admiral, "we rather feared that she would go down".

Captain (now Vice-Admiral) T. E. Wardle, who was then in command of the *Crescent*, has been good enough to give me his version : "I was aft, smoking a pipe on deck after breakfast, when we felt the whole ship shudder as a sea struck her right ahead. I started to run forward, and was met by a sea about two feet deep coming along the battery deck. I well remember, because I fell down and got my sea-boots full up. Getting forward, I found that both ladders to the bridge had been washed away, the people on the bridge being marooned, and the sea had struck the chart-house, breaking the glass. Just abaft the bridge we had rigged up a substantial shelter with battens and canvas for the Admiral, and also for a decoding officer, fitted with armchair and table. The whole thing disappeared overboard, though luckily no one was in it. Then I found that the two foremost cowls, very big ones, had been washed away, and that a lot of water had gone down into the foremost stokehold. I got the collision mat over these two holes, in case further seas came over."

The *Crescent's* wireless had been carried away, but just before that incident a signal from Admiral Jellicoe had come in ordering them to run for shelter. That being out of the question, the two ships could only heave-to a little longer, and then, fortunately, the wind veered still further, till it blew from the north-east. This somewhat calmed the sea, since the Shetlands acted as a breakwater, so that both ships could now carry on for Busta Voe and thence into Scapa Flow, where they arrived in a parlous plight. The *Edgar* crawled in, battered and torn, having lost one able seaman overboard, and immediately it was decided by the Commander-in-Chief to send half the 10th Cruiser Squadron south to the Clyde shipyards for a thorough refit. However, on reaching Clyde-bank after steaming through snowstorms and further bad weather, the experts made a thorough inspection, and reported so unfavourably that on November 20 the Admiralty ordered the seven "Edgars" to be paid off; so the old Training Squadron came to a sudden end, Admiral de Chair hauling down his flag in the *Crescent* on December 3.

It was the only wise course. "These ships", one of their officers informed me, "could neither steam nor fight." Nor could they carry enough coal. The result was that either for necessary repairs, or through need of refuelling, they were frequently compelled to leave their patrol area and return into harbour. Admiral Jellicoe described them as unseaworthy, and totally ill suited for blockade work in the winter gales, which were the normal conditions between Iceland and the Scottish coast. Gales or no gales, winter or summer, fog or sunshine, day or night, vessels entrusted with the responsibility of preventing contraband could not in these modern times go into temporary shelter as the Brest blockaders during the era of sail were wont to withdraw into Torbay. The twentieth-century tramp steamer lacks the fine lines, the speed, and many other features of the nineteenth-century light cruiser, yet can, and does, keep the ocean in all weathers with an economical use of coal.

The *Crescent* had once been the pride of His Majesty the King when, as a Prince, he was in command of her : but to-day her ironwork was so rusty, her decks so billowy, her machinery such a lot of scrap metal, that she was a source of mirth to the Navy and of derision to the storms. Practical experience had demonstrated that the Blockade required only vessels that could possess the following features :

(1) Ability to remain on patrol with safety during the worst possible weather.

(2) Ability to continue at sea with enough stores and coal, so that in spite of perpetual patrolling they need not enter harbour for a month or two at a time.

And in looking round for such vessels the strange truth emanated that a combination existed not in the Royal Navy but in the Company-owned fleets of merchant-ships, and these happily possessed a further advantage :

(3) Ability to steam, when required, at such a speed that no Scandinavian or Danish liner would ever get clear away when the chase began.

Thus once more it was manifested, as it had been during the days of Anglo-French, Anglo-Dutch, and even Anglo-Spanish Wars, that the strength of a maritime nation is embodied in its ships of commerce not less than its men-of-war. One month before war broke out Britain owned (including her Dominions and Colonies) 47.9 per cent of the world's steamship tonnage, whilst Germany came next with only 11.9. That of the combined countries Norway, Sweden, and Denmark amounted to only 8.4, whilst the United States (excluding vessels trading on the Northern Lakes) claimed 4.6 per cent. The interesting point is that whilst 60 per cent of British tonnage consisted of tramp steamers and 40 per cent of liners, yet 35 per cent of the two combined represented vessels who could maintain at sea a speed of at least 12 knots. There was, accordingly, a high average standard, and this was accentuated when it was revealed that about 11 per cent of the whole British Merchant Navy comprised vessels having a sea speed of 15 to 20 knots, which was far in excess of that which characterized neutral steamers. Even three years before the European crisis there existed a hundred excellent liners, owned by the principal British corporations, of 10,000 registered tons upwards, with a speed in some cases of 27 knots, in many others of 18 knots, whilst a few could do 13 knots.

From this big pool of efficient steamships, after making allowance for the demands of other squadrons, for transports, and so on, there still remained a wide selection available. Far and away the biggest and fastest were the passenger mail-carriers, but the usual traffic under this category had been so drastically cut down since August 4 that these first-grade vessels could be taken over by the Admiralty without causing trade interference. Already a very few had been employed off Northern Scotland for some weeks and performed such reliable service that there was no question about their superiority over such units as the "Edgars". The Allan liner *Alsatian*, the White Star *Oceanic* and *Teutonic*, the P. & O. *Mantua*, had all done well with the exception of *Oceanic*, which stranded in a fog at Foula Island on September 8, 1914, but eventually broke up; so the resolve now was to develop and extend this merchant cruiser idea till it became a fleet, though still retaining the old title. Thus the above three liners formed a nucleus, and others were soon added, of which the Orient *Otway*, the White Star *Cedric*, and the Allan Line *Virginian* came first. Speaking generally, they were manned by the crews of the "Edgars", but there joined also many ratings who had come straight from the Merchant Marine. Even if the liner's peace-time commanding officer remained and was given a commission in the Royal Naval Reserve, a Captain of the Royal Navy took over command. It was reverting only to the seventeenth-century practice, when a British man-of-war would be commanded by a Captain and the Master continued his duties connected with the ship's navigation and handling.

Whilst the designation "10th Cruiser Squadron" was handed on to the newly created group, there was a great advance towards efficiency which had never been possible hitherto. Armed with 6-inch and 4.7-inch guns, these first-class ocean queens comprised a novel armada that was quite startling in its originality and required a vast organization both afloat and ashore. If we frequently speak of it as a Fleet, rather than a Squadron, it is because in numbers, tonnage, and independence it was worthy of comparison with the Grand Fleet. No longer was it to be a weak collection of worn-out hulls, but an up-to-date cohesion with everything of the best, a most formidable barrier that would make its massed power felt, if only the bureaucrats would let it alone.

But before seven "Edgars" passed into the limbo of forgotten ships Admiral Jellicoe did not hesitate to send Admiral de Chair the following message

I take this opportunity of expressing to you my high appreciation of the work carried out by the ships of your Squadron. The work of intercepting and examining Neutral vessels has been most successfully carried out, and the ships have kept the sea in spite of their age and the difficulty which I know has existed in keeping the machinery efficient. I desire that you will make known to the captains and men my keen appreciation of their efforts, and congratulate them on the success which has attended them.

And under this promising encouragement the new phase against contraband began.

CHAPTER IV

WHILST the 10th Cruiser Squadron is being reorganized let us take a glance at what was effected ashore.

The British Government's policy, being to use rather the weapon of stopping contraband than a blockade, created in August 1914 a Contraband Committee of the Foreign Office as a central controlling authority over the Northern Patrol's inspection. Some of the ablest critics regarded the Declaration of London as a pernicious entanglement, and there were others who saw in this novel restraining body a dangerous precedent. Why not let the Navy alone to carry out its duties in accordance with the Law of Nations unmodified ? The most far-sighted perceived that lack of clear thinking and of firm principle must assuredly, in time, cause grave situations. But the fact is that the War had burst with such suddenness, the country's national mind was so startled by the European outlook, and the average citizen was so concerned with re-cruiting, Red Cross work, and a hundred other details that he had little opportunity to criticize. Even the Press was too full of patriotism, and too eager in keeping up a spirit of optimism, to interfere.

The Contraband Committee, containing representatives of the Foreign Office, the Admiralty, and the Board of Trade, was set up in order to decide whether ship or cargo should be sent into the Prize Court for adjudication. Thus, instead of one resolute guiding rule dominating, each case was decided on its merits, which allowed private judgment and the weight of special circumstances to possess considerable influence. The lurking danger consisted in the effect such uncertainty of purpose might have on neutrals, but especially on the United States of America.

This "hitherto unheard-of jurisdiction", writes one caustic critic,[1] "consisted, not, of course, in any form of open Court, but in a strange and suddenly invented Committee of persons nominated for the purpose by the officials concerned. . . . It acted, deliberated, and decided in secret. It was in continuous touch with Foreign Office opinion. It was bound by no law, custom, precedent, treaty, rules of evidence, rules of procedure, or legal restraint. . . . It maintained upon the seas, against the rule of the Law of Nations, the rule of that Department; and it was used by that Department to ensure the prompt execution of its wishes in cases in which the Prize Courts of England could not be trusted to carry them out." So "every ship and cargo sent in to an English port by the unwearying activity of the English seamen" could be kept out of the Prize Court, and the fate determined by the newly invented Committee. The result was twofold: it allowed cargoes (obviously intended for Germany) to continue to their destination, whereas the Blockaders had no sort of doubt, and the Prize Courts would certainly have condemned such cargoes; on the other hand, the Committee, by occasionally causing to be issued a new Order-in-Council, a fresh list of contraband, was the authority which detained some ship or cargo (against which there was no justifiable evidence) on the curious understanding that at the end of the War these should, in part at least, be returned to the neutral owners.

Here, then, was a most perilous procedure, perilous because it permitted neutrals to pass their goods into Germany on the basis of obtaining from neutral countries some commercial advantage in return, perilous because the illegality of the whole system was bound to cause friction with at least the most powerful neutral State, who, incidentally, might complain in jealousy against preferential treatment. And to-day we know all too well how this misguided rule of allowing supplies to reach the enemy had the effect of prolonging the War.

The fruits of the "rule by Committee" were not long in maturing: they were of the kind already prophesied. The United States, on October 22, 1914, declined to respect such

---

[1] G. F. S. Bowles in *The Strength of England*, p. 179.

H.M.S. "ALSATIAN"
View showing forebridge.

H.M.S. "ALSATIAN"
Showing forward 6-inch guns on port side.

Departmental Control. "This Government", she affirmed, "will insist that the rights and duties of the United States and its citizens in the present war be defined by the existing rules of International Law and the Treaties of the United States, irrespective of the provisions of the Declaration of London." Now the immediate sequel was that the British Foreign Office, having committed itself to an erroneous policy, and being fearful lest the United States might be turned into an enemy, climbed down and modified its previous rule. On October 29—only a week after the American protest—was issued a new Order-in-Council revising the contraband list of August 20, resigning, in reply to transatlantic pressure, some of the previously claimed rights ; and thus a rake's progress towards complete muddle went gaily forward. For the modification produced in Scandinavia and the Netherlands so many dummy neutral consignees that foodstuffs and cotton still continued to reach Germany but with even greater regularity. This, indeed, went on till another Order-in-Council had to be issued in March of the following year ; meanwhile the first winter under the influence of a variable policy satisfied no one except the enemy and the enemy's representatives.

The United States objected against the Allies' claim to seize neutral cargoes on passage from an American to a Scandinavian or Dutch port, and in December we had begun the experiment of allowing imports into Holland only under strict guarantees from an association of Dutch traders, which pledged itself to receive guarantees from individuals as to each consignment, through the "Netherlands Overseas Trust" ; yet America was still unsatisfied, and all the time such ports as Rotterdam and Copenhagen became mere commercial centres from which the goods were reshipped to Teutonic firms. Conditional Contraband—according to Article 33 of the Declaration of London—included such items as foodstuffs and cotton, which could be captured, by the Order-in-Council of October 29, if consigned "to Order", or if the ship's papers did not indicate to whom the goods were to be delivered. The temptation of high prices and enormous profits was to North European neutrals so tempting that this ambiguity of consignation had been a large loophole which must be stopped by the Allies.

Such, then, was the atmosphere at the time when the new 10th Cruiser Squadron was being prepared for fresh duties in the north. The vessel chosen for Admiral de Chair's flagship was the *Alsatian*. Inasmuch as she will, during the rest of our story, represent the General Headquarters of what, in effect (though not in name), became the Blockading Fleet, let us next first admire this magnificent creature. Owned by the Allan Line, she had been running across the Atlantic as one of the finest mail-and-passenger steamers for not many months before the War started. With a cruiser-stern, two enormous funnels and masts, quadruple-screws and turbine engines, and a full speed of 23 knots, she possessed the invaluable patrol virtue of endurance. It was found that by clearing her holds she could carry the phenomenal amount of 6,000 tons of coal, which, at the steady rate of 13.5 knots, enabled her to keep steaming for 42 days. Here, then, was an ideal ship for blockade work, and her 18,000 tons gave her a size which made the "Edgars" look ridiculous. "It was found," Admiral de Chair tells me, "that the battle-cruisers, or indeed any other cruiser, could not stand up to the work or do the job as well as Atlantic liners armed for the occasion." The *Alsatian* suggested sea-independence, for she could chase and hold up any neutral during even the roughest weather, and she was given an armament powerful enough to fight German raider or submarine to a finish. It was the wisdom and advice of Admiral Jellicoe and Admiral de Chair which prevailed on the Admiralty to make such excellent choice of the best liners, just as in the bygone days the fine old East Indiamen during time of war were so valuable in supplementing the fleet.

By the end of December 1914 the Squadron already comprised 18 of the 24 units, and a large proportion both of men and officers belonged to the Merchant Navy. At the Battle of Jutland (omitting battle-cruisers, cruisers, and small craft) there were but 24 line-of-battle ships : at Trafalgar Nelson's fleet consisted of only 27 capital ships, besides a few frigates and small craft. Therefore it is not without justification that one may speak of Admiral de Chair's force as a fleet likewise. The shore organization was left in his hands to create, and the immensity of such an improvisation has never been equalled. First of all there must be suitable bases whither these ships might come for coal, repairs, and redocking. Now it is a considerable job to keep one great liner always in condition, fuelled, stored, manned, officered. It demands, indeed, a big staff and huge establishment to run a number of these in peace-time along the regular trade routes. But here were the crack steamers from all the best lines under one flag, and their maintenance alone demanded a kind of Admiralty in itself.

Not one of the three naval bases, Portsmouth, Chatham, or Devonport, could cope with such a care : there was more work at these dockyards than they were able to finish. So Liverpool became the Portsmouth for the liner fleet, where Rear-Admiral H. H. Stileman was the hard-worked officer-in-charge, responsible for sending each unit to sea by scheduled time, notwithstanding tides unsuitable for coming out of dock, problems of engineering, labour troubles, strikes, and a thousand other details.

The red-funnelled *Alsatian* had been taken over early in August and painted a dull grey. An important feature in each ship presently was to have the crow's-nest fitted on the foremast well above the height of the funnels, the intention being not merely that the usual excellent liner look-out should continue, but that a means should be afforded for sighting the smoke of any blockade-runner before the latter should espy the patrol. It was on August 11 that the *Alsatian* was commissioned as a warship by Captain Valentine Phillimore, R.N., who had won his D.S.O. years previously during the Boxer campaign.

That first week of the War turned Liverpool into a naval beehive, and one marvels that so much was done well, yet so quickly. Her peace-time Master, Captain E. Outram, remained in her as Commander R.N.R., and his experience of having been accustomed to handle her was very welcome. So, too, the Chief Engineer, Robert Wilson, who knew her machinery intimately, was given a commission as Engineer-Commander, R.N.R., and continued at his post. "The commissioning of these ships, with their raw crews of Merchant Service seamen and Newfoundland fishermen, who very quickly became the smartest and most efficient of seamen," says

Captain J. W. Williams, R.N.R., now Marine Superintendent of the White Star Line, who served as Gunnery Lieutenant when *Alsatian* first flew the White Ensign, "was a great credit to the untiring energy of a few naval officers, supported by officers of the Royal Naval Reserve. Whilst First-Lieutenants —usually Lieut.-Commanders—were scouring the naval depots for the best officers and men, and using every known trick to influence Drafting Officers, guns were being mounted.

"Eventually the crews were entrained at the Depot, and it was not unknown for zealous officers to have increased their numbers considerably by insisting that every seaman they saw should be packed into the train—lest anyone should be lost whilst the train stopped at stations. All the seamen were R.N.R. ratings. The stokers, however, consisted of the ships' original Merchant Service firemen, who quickly became amenable to discipline; and I have known instances of their wives coming down to the ship at 7 a.m. with their men, to make sure they did not overstep their leave and so have it stopped altogether. Picture the ship putting to sea with an untrained crew, and ammunition dumped into the bottom of a hold. There was no time to wash, shave, or sleep during these first days. I know of one instance when two live shells tipped out of the loading tray into the bottom of a hold and fell a distance of forty feet, yet with no worse result than slight palpitation of the heart to myself and the few men around. I am sure the firemen were more afraid of the fierce discipline and the threats of the Articles of War than of meeting the whole German Fleet."

The *Alsatian*, armed with some old 4.7's, sailed from Liverpool at the same time as that other armed merchant cruiser *Carmania* was going forth to earn fame during the cruise when she was to sink the *Cap Trafalgar* in the Pacific. By August 18 *Alsatian* reached Lerwick and came under Admiral de Chair's orders, who sent her off on patrol. A few days later arrived the *Mantua*, which Captain Charles Tibbits had just commissioned in a similar manner; so this P. & O. liner was also dismissed to watch the northern area; and presently there came also the *Oceanic* and *Teutonic*, both well-known vessels of the White Star Line. Of the latter's loss we have already made mention, but *Alsatian*, *Mantua*, and *Oceanic*, with very raw crews and somewhat crude methods, began stopping neutral ships, though sometimes getting into strange dilemmas.

"We were not then an organized squadron," says Captain Williams, "and we were sent to all parts of the northern part of the North Sea to patrol, and constantly fell foul of our own squadrons, who did not know us, so that we frequently stood a good chance of being blown out of the water by our own vessels. On one occasion a battleship from a British squadron that was visible on the horizon had been detailed to investigate us, and I most vividly remember her pair of turrets trained on us like two evil eyes. When one pair got off the target, through swinging, the other pair got on, and, needless to say, it was a great relief when the battleship was satisfied with our identity."

This incident occurred on September 18, and the scrutinizer was H.M.S. *Britannia*. The *Alsatian* had that day passed the sad sight of the wrecked *Oceanic* lying low in the water with her back buckled, and then the patrol had been carried out between Fair Island and the Orkneys, stopping and boarding several steamers, when all of a sudden she was herself stopped by a blank shot fired from the *Britannia*, who circled around with guns trained and hoses already playing on deck— so sure was she that *Alsatian* was a German raider or mine-layer. The episode had arisen through some failure to answer correctly the battleship's challenge; but those early weeks were full of events which kept everyone in a condition of suspense.

It was during the dark hours of September 23–24 that the *Alsatian* had a further thrill, for about midnight she passed through part of the Grand Fleet and nearly ran into a battleship. Steaming about, showing no lights, these dark shapes of sea warriors were not easy to discern in the region of damp mists. A week later occurred another proof that it was imperative for the northern waters to be combed with regularity. A fine foreign two-funnelled steamer from New York was intercepted with most beneficial result. She turned out to be the Danish twin-screw *Frederik VIII* (7,555 registered tons), owned by the Scandinavian Line running to Copenhagen. In accordance with the recognized legal right which a belligerent warship may exercise, the *Alsatian* stopped and boarded her. Half a dozen German stowaways were discovered and, to their intense annoyance, removed, of whom one caused no little trouble for some days until the party were sent ashore as prisoners. Nor was this the last occasion when the two liners were to meet under war rules. She will be noticed in the photograph facing page 64 hove-to for the boarding party.

The prevailing rumours at this time were of the kind which the battle-cruiser *Invincible* signalled to *Alsatian* when they passed during the following morning of October 3. "Possible that strong force of enemy may try and break through in next few days," she warned. Then came the likelihood of submarines, so the *Alsatian's* boats were swung out in readiness for any torpedo bringing sudden disaster. Nerves were thus for ever under a heavy strain, when on October 16, the day following the loss of *Hawke*, orders were wirelessed that *Alsatian* should steer to the N.E. of Muckle Flugga. "Things were very lively," says Captain Williams, "and we were expecting to be 'mopped up' at any time, our old 4.7's being nothing to boast about. It was a typical North Sea night— Scotch mist, very dark, and drizzly rain—and we were all very uneasy, spending most of the dark hours at action stations. Round about 10 p.m., in the first watch, the Captain, First Lieutenant, and myself (the Gunnery Officer) were on the bridge with the officer-of-the-watch, when a searchlight from a ship (which we had not the faintest notion was anywhere near us) suddenly shone down on the bridge. It appeared from a very high angle, and the glare was naturally intensified by the darkness of the night". A big warship, obviously ! Was she one of the enemy's strong force about which the warning had been sent ? This was (as to-day we know) just the position where a German might be expected to attempt a break-through, since the *Berlin* veritably passed pretty close hereabouts, after forsaking the Norwegian coast and heading for Iceland, on her way to lay her mines off Tory Island. Indeed, it so happens that the *Berlin* (of whom nothing had been heard or suspected at that date) was remarkably lucky not to have run right into the 2nd Battle Squadron that night. The latter force, which included the *Audacious*, was so well placed, and not many miles of undulating waves can have separated the ex-German liner from the British battleship which, with her consorts, was steaming backwards and forwards, but by a curious twist of history they were not destined quite to meet, though their fates were intimately linked. As to the *Alsatian*, she was keyed up for action and longing to use her newly mounted guns with firm purpose.

"Our R.N.V.R. signalman [continues Captain Williams] made frantic attempts to give the 'flag of the day' by semaphore. The First Lieutenant, ever ready to fight anything or anybody, ordered me to train the guns on our unwelcome visitor, but succumbed to my earnest persuasion 'not to make "him" mad'. The searchlight switched off as quickly as it had appeared, and we were left in comparative peace, with a feeling of what a gift we should be to the enemy when the latter did come."

Now the sequel is this. The vessel with the searchlight was H.M.S. *Audacious*. Six nights later did the *Berlin* lay her minefield off the north of Ireland, and then five days later still (October 27) who should run right into the minefield and founder ? It was the same *Audacious* which, on October 16, by the merest chance, might have illumined the German rather than the British liner. Such was the fortune of war !

Then for the *Alsatian* would follow a series of anxious hours not far from Bergen, still trying to intercept a German armed merchant cruiser which was expected to appear at any moment. Along came the interrupted procession of neutrals, so far as ensigns indicated nationality, yet the enemy would be sure to be disguised as either Scandinavian or Dane. Now which of these could be the suspect ? "We did not get her," says the Gunnery Officer, "but I am afraid we stirred up the neutrals a bit. We had a photograph of the vessel we were seeking, and made some nasty *faux pas* with Danish, Swedish, and Norwegian ships of similar build, careering towards them at about 20 knots, with imperious signals flying to 'stop at once and show your flag', and firing erratic shots across their bows, which I, personally, was not too sure would drop in the right place."

Then one morning, when day was just breaking over a smooth sea, "not a sound on board, and everyone tense at action stations, as we bore down at full speed on this vessel which would not show her flag, Captain Phillimore mentioned casually to me : 'Can you sink her, Williams ?' I, of course, assured him that nothing was easier. However, he didn't seem to have much confidence in our guns, with crews that most evidently hadn't been trained at Whale Island,[1] and his reply was : 'I think we'll ram her, to make sure she doesn't get away.'" What a change had come over seafaring life that Merchant Service officers, brought up always to avoid collisions, should share in driving a wonderful 18,000-tons mail steamer into the sides of another vessel ! It was difficult to readjust one's mind to the new commands.

Fortunately or unfortunately, the crisis never came. The stranger watched the oncoming fine bows and massive hull, perceived that a terrific impact of steel versus steel was about to work devastation ; but then, just as panic-stricken passengers and crew began making determined efforts to clear away the boats, up went the Swedish flag barely in time. The leisurely neutral had narrowly escaped destruction from a very determined Captain.

Interludes of this nature were not without value. If they broke the monotony of dull patrol, they also were helping to smarten raw crews that had only recently been serving aboard tramp steamers or in Newfoundland sailing craft. The material was of the finest, but a considerable need for patient training exhibited itself too clearly. And there must be no silly mistakes through carelessness, such as that which happened one Friday morning when a rating, whilst busily engaged polishing some brasswork, to the amazement of himself and everybody else, suddenly found all hands rushing to action stations. The bell, which was pressed only when General Headquarters should be sounded, had most certainly functioned, though it was the brass-cleaner's hand which had been the unwitting cause of so much rushing hither and thither.

But this preliminary phase in *Alsatian's* early career as a warship concluded at noon of December 1, 1914 when, after entering the Mersey, she secured in the Canada Dock. That same day Admiral de Chair with his staff came on board before

---

[1] The British Navy's well-known gunnery school at Portsmouth.

H.M.S. "BRITANNIA"
With guns trained ready to open fire.

H.M.S. "OCEANIC"
Wrecked early in the War.

DANISH S.S. FREDERIK VIII
Hove-to for the boarding party.

settling in the ship permanently. There was still much to be done until he was entirely free after the closing down of the "Edgars' " books, so that same night he took train with his Secretary (Fleet-Paymaster Vincent Lawford) back to Glasgow, hauled down his flag on the 3rd, and on the following day returned to Liverpool, where his flag now flew from the *Alsatian's* masthead.

Ten days of keen activity ensued for all concerned, and every effort was made to expedite the jobs, but it was no easy matter. Apart from other details for improvement this flagship had to be rearmed, the old-fashioned guns being taken out and eight 6-inch placed in their stead. On December 15 the *Alsatian* steamed a few miles beyond the Mersey Bar to test her new mountings; unfortunately these were far from satisfactory. Three of the for'ard guns, when fired, started five of their rivets, whilst the two after guns started twenty-three and twenty-seven respectively; so back she came into Liverpool for another week.

The truth is that, owing to the inferior quality of labour, which was now being felt in all trades, owing, also, to a feeling of unrest which at this date was permeating some of the less patriotic workmen, contractors found it most difficult to obtain the necessary number of skilled hands, and continuity of purpose was impossible. At Liverpool, additional to the *Alsatian*, the following considerable-sized steamers had been taken up and were refitting : *Cedric, Virginian, Caribbean, Oropesa, Hilary, Hildebrand, Ambrose,* and *Eskimo*; at the port of London were being fitted out the *Orotava, Digby, Otway,* and *Clan McNaughton* ; at Avonmouth the *Patia, Patuca, Motagua, Changuinola,* and *Bayono* ; at Hull the *Calyx* (changing her name from *Calypso*) ; on the Clyde the *Columbella* (late *Columbia*) ; on the Tyne the *Viknor* (changing her name from the *Viking*). The *Teutonic* and *Mantua* were already at sea on the Northern Patrol.

These were twenty-three of the twenty-four excellent steamers of various sizes which, as soon as practicable, were to form the new blockade force. The same labour delays were met with at all fitting-out ports, and it was only the perpetual hastening, encouraging, tact, and driving ability of the commanding officers which enabled their ships to become ready

E

for service : by mid-January no fewer than 21 had been completed, and were either at sea or coaling. Four days before
Christmas, when the *Alsatian* was nearly but not quite ready,
Admiral de Chair proceeded overland to Scapa Flow, where
an important conference was held with Admiral Jellicoe in
the *Iron Duke*. The Commander-in-Chief was much concerned with the problem of creating a real blockade bulwark
between Germany and the outer seas, yet he was still being
hampered by the vagaries of Whitehall, and made anxious
by the increasing submarine threat.

In order to cover efficiently the immense area whose northern
limits ended only where Arctic ice began, a most careful
organization, not merely ashore but afloat, was essential.
These two distinguished Admirals, as we have seen, were
friends of many years standing, who understood each other's
personality and had worked together previously. Moreover,
every ship's Captain had been hand-picked for this duty,
the Executive Officer and Gunner in each case coming from
the Royal Navy ; whilst most of the other officers were hard-
bitten, vigorous seafarers who had spent their whole career
in merchant vessels, and their expert knowledge of Atlantic
shipping was to be invaluable. Many of these keen, eye-
puckered Royal Naval Reservists had been brought up in the
severe school of sailing craft before spending years on some
liner's bridge. Some had undergone a period of naval training
before the War ; others were now holding temporary com-
missions. The crews were composed of men from the Royal
Fleet Reserve, Royal Naval Reserve, Royal Naval Volunteer
Reserve, and Mercantile ratings who had never been aboard
a warship in their lives. This scratch fleet was therefore the
most representative body of British seamanhood which any
circumstances could produce. Before August 1914 one
might have doubted where the special skill of Newfoundland
fishermen could be relied upon under modern conditions
of naval warfare. Readers who are familiar with Kipling's
celebrated novel *Captains Courageous* will remember the class
of work which is done in open boats off the Newfoundland
Banks, and it was just this boatmanship, allied with the seamanship of the armed liners, that was to be the crux of the whole
blockade at sea.

There were no trades unions between the Orkneys and the Arctic Circle, no labour troubles—just blizzards of snow and hail, mountainous waves towering everywhere, a succession of wintry gales, and such rolling about through boisterous weather that, as Admiral de Chair remarked, officers and men "often found it impossible to obtain sleep or rest when off watch". It "brought out high qualities of seamanship and navigation on the part of Captains, officers, and seamen", and in spite of all this arduous experience there was no denying the remarkable discipline, devotion to duty, and firm resolve on the part of everyone. Had Nelson or Collingwood come back to inspect this fleet, they would certainly have said to Admiral de Chair: "Your ships are more seaworthy, your officers are more skilled, your men are happier, and your patrol more continuous than could have been possible when we blockaded the French."

And this would have been the best reply to those pessimists who loved to declaim that all seamanship vanished when sail passed away from the Navy.

To sum up, then: the original squadron of "Edgars", ill-fitted as they were in nearly all respects, had done their best during the first weeks intercepting, boarding, and examining for contraband many vessels which passed between the Shetlands and Norway, whether outward or inward bound. Charged also with the duty of destroying any German man-of-war that should attempt breaking through; ordered, further, to deny the Shetlands' anchorages to the enemy, the worn-out cruisers had never been given the opportunity for going into action, though several of them had accompanied the Grand Fleet when a sweep was being made in the direction of the enemy's waters. The weak feature, hitherto, had been the lack of continuity in its main purpose, owing to the demand of temporary phases during a period when the war strategy at sea had not yet become stabilized. At the end of August the 10th Cruiser Squadron had been moved from the north down to the area between Kinnaird Head and Norway, with orders more comprehensive than those of stopping contraband.

The inspecting of neutral shipping, instead of being the exclusive task, was just one of several. The "Edgars" were to deal with enemy minelayers and submarines before the latter could foul the approaches to the Grand Fleet's bases; areas had to be searched where alleged mines or suspicious objects had been reported, and timely notice be wirelessed to the *Iron Duke* that enemy cruisers were coming. Indeed, the "Edgars" were definitely to engage and fight them when encountered. There would assuredly have been a mighty heavy loss if our old Training Squadron had met any of Germany's modern cruisers on the way to succour her raiders still operating off the South American coasts; but, with any luck and the absence of fog, the Grand Fleet would soon have avenged the loss of a few units.

For one period, then, Admiral de Chair's force was being used defensively as a protective outpost for Scapa Flow and Cromarty. Again, when it was moved back north after the *Hawke* episode, this also was merely a defensive measure, though the position was better suited for trade interception. Finally the November gales had brought about yet another necessity for self-protection, leaving only the three armed merchant cruisers *Alsatian*, *Mantua*, and *Teutonic* to carry on; so that when the first-mentioned was summoned into Liverpool the commercial blockade did not really exist.

The time for a complete transformation of the Northern Blockade was therefore considerably overdue; nor was it fair to the Allied soldiers that this Scottish gateway should be left open and unguarded for German supplies which would ere long be used against the Western front. From the end of 1914 a quite different aspect quickly developed from the highest to the lowest, and it was all for the best. Typical of this change was that which came over the *Alsatian*. "Until Admiral de Chair took over", says Captain Williams (previously quoted), "we were not to any extent organized, and our discipline on board was 'rough and efficient', but in no way on the lines of a first-class battleship. We were unshaven, unkempt, generally short of sleep, and in all led a very hard and comfortless life. We soon began to feel the benefit of the steadying hand of the Admiral. Organized gunnery and training took the place of our very rough methods. A Padre appeared, and regular services and Sunday divisions were soon part of the routine." But there was an amusing side also.

"It was not unusual to see a whole division of men, with their officer, go sliding into the lee scuppers in rough weather during the Captain's inspection; and the Commander's language on such occasions was not always fit for print! Sample: "Call yourselves *sailors*? At the order 'Pace forward— march' you push your adjectival guts out and then fall head over tip into the scuppers.' In order to guard against that soul-destroying monotony which is the greatest enemy of moral at sea, sports, boxing matches, bayonet-fighting contests, concerts, theatricals, were now held on board, and the result soon manifested itself. The seven weeks at sea passed more quickly, and with greater cheeriness. "We all took more pride in ourselves and ships, and soon felt like competing with the Grand Fleet in the smartness of our vessels, as our pride in our glorious squadron increased. Under the influence of Admiral de Chair we had developed from a few hurriedly armed merchant ships to the important Squadron whose tenacious stranglehold on the enemy was to prove one of the greatest factors in bringing the War to a satisfactory conclusion."

The splendid work of Captain Phillimore, a most popular skipper, was not forgotten. He it was who had so quickly got his ship on patrol immediately after the war started, but now, since the Admiral was bringing his own Flag-Captain with him, Captain Phillimore was given command of another vessel. Officers such as he had been pioneers, and had demonstrated the immense capabilities which a big mail steamer could possess as a warship. It is a matter for perpetual regret that the *Alsatian* never had the good fortune that October night of trying conclusions with the *Berlin* north-east of Muckle Flugga. A glorious page in naval history still remains unwritten.

SHIP	REG. TONAGE	FULL PATROL SPEED KNOTS	BUILT IN	OWNERS	NAVAL OFFICER COMMANDING
Alsatian .	18,485	19.5	1913	Allan Line	Capt. V. E. B. Phillimore, M.V.O. (1)
					Capt. G. Trewby (2)
Teutonic .	9,984	19	1889	White Star Line	Capt. H. Chatterton (1)
				,, ,,	Capt. G. P. Ross (2)
Cedric .	21,040	16.5	1903		Capt. R. E. R. Benson
Otway .	12,077	18	1909	Orient Line	Capt. E. L. Booty, M.V.O.
Columbella[1]	8,292	17	1902	Anchor Line	Capt. H. L. P. Heard
Patia .	6,103	16	1913	Elders & Fyffes	Capt. G. W. Vivian
Patuca .	,,	16	,,	,, ,,	Commdr. C. H. France-Hayhurst (died) (1)
					Commdr. P. G. Brown (2)
Bayano .	5,948	14	,,	,, ,,	Capt. H. C. Carr
Motagua .	5,977	14	1912	,, ,,	Capt. V. E. B. Phillimore, M.V.O. (1)
					Capt. J. A. Webster, M.V.O. (2)
Changuinola	5,978	14	,,	,, ,,	Commdr. H. C. R. Brocklebank
Mantua .	10,885	17.5	1909	P. & O. Line	Capt. C. Tibbits, M.V.O.
Hildebrand	6,991	14.5	1911	Booth Line	Capt. H. Edwards
Hilary .	6,329	14	1908	,, ,,	Commdr. R. H. Bather
Ambrose .	4,595	14	1903	,, ,,	Commdr. C. W. Bruton (1)
					Commdr. V. L. Bowring (2)
Virginian	10,757	17	1905	Allan Line	Capt. H. N. Garnett (1)
					Commdr. H. H. Smith (2)
Caribbean, (ex-Dunnottar Castle)	5,824	14	1890	Royal Mail Line	Commdr. F. H. Walter
Orotava .	5,980	14	1899	,, ,,	Commdr. G. E. Corbett
Oropesa .	5,364	13	1895	Pacific Steam Navgn. Co.	Commdr. N. L. Stanley
Eskimo .	3,326	—	1910	Wilson Line	Commdr. C. W. Trousdale
Calyx[2] .	2,876	12	1904	,, ,,	Commdr. T. E. Wardle
Digby .	3,966	14.5	1913	Furness, Withy	Commdr. R. F. H. H. Mahon
Clan Mac-naughton	4,985	11	1911	Clan Line	Commdr. R. Jeffreys
Viknor[3] .	5,386	—	1888	Viking Cruising Co. Ltd.	Commdr. E. O. Ballantyne

[1] Columbella's peace-time name was Columbia.
[2] Calyx's peace-time name was Calypso.
[3] Viknor's peace-time name was Viking (ex-Atranto).
NOTE : Where one commanding officer was succeeded by another, both names are given. It should be noted also that at different periods the numbers of the 10th Cruiser Squadron varied. The above list, which totals 23, shows the strength on January 24, 1915, by which date the Squadron had settled down to its respective patrols. But the loss of three units on January 25, February 3, and March 11, respectively, the commissioning of six other steamers to replace the lost, besides others which had been paid off as unsuitable, had already modified the Squadron's composition by the beginning of May 1915.

CHAPTER V

A LIST of the ships in the reconstituted Squadron will be found on the opposite page, from which it will be observed that there was no homogeneity. Some were passenger ships from the P. &. O., White Star, Allan, Royal Mail, Orient, and other lines; some were freight ships from the Clan Line; some had been used in the banana trade; one vessel had long been employed taking tourists to see the midnight sun.

The largest unit was not the flagship, but that well known *Cedric* which for years had been running across the Atlantic. She was of 21,040 tons. But the smallest was the *Calyx*, 2,876 tons, which in pre-war days was known as the *Calypso*, owned by the Wilson Line. Of this single-screw steamer we shall have more to say presently. It will be noticed, further, that whilst half the Squadron comprised over a dozen vessels of five to six thousand tons, there were half a dozen more ranging from approximately 10,000 tons upwards, whilst only that other Wilson Liner *Eskimo* (3,326 tons) could be placed with *Calyx* in the small class.

The victualling and coaling of twenty-four ships, so as to make them independent of the shore for six or seven weeks, signified so obvious and gigantic an effort throughout the next few years that it need not further be stressed. "As the ships were so large, and as the submarines had made several raids on the Shetlands," says Admiral de Chair, "the Commander-in-Chief thought it better at first to have our bases at Liverpool and the Clyde, so 12 of these liners were berthed on the Mersey and 12 at Glasgow." The difficulty was that in either case each armed merchantman on her way to coal, water, and provision must pass through the North Channel which divides Ireland from the Mull of Cantyre. Now this narrow strait was an ideal spot for submarines to occupy stealthily : they had only to wait a while before targets came along. It is true that anti-submarine measures a little later were taken by the employment of net-drifters and patrols, but right till the close of war this North Channel continued to be a zone of imminent peril.

Another drawback to Liverpool was that the base was about 600 miles, or two days' steaming, from the middle of the patrol line. Thus four days were lost every time a unit came south, and she might be torpedoed just before visiting Liverpool or just after ; but, also, the prevailing westerly gales had the effect of scattering the terrible mines which the *Berlin* had laid north of Tory Island, drifting them across the tracks which these vessels must surely pass. Such risks were both appreciated and accepted as part of the problem.

The new commanding officer in *Alsatian* was Captain (now Vice-Admiral) George Trewby; and Commander John Kiddle, R.N., from the *Crescent* had joined, having come back to the Navy from retirement. It was the latter who was faced with the responsibility of getting *Alsatian* refitted with her 6-inch guns and in all respects suitable as a flagship. I am thus all the more pleased to have this officer's personal account of how the new regime began.

"*Alsatian* was in the course of being fitted with 6-inch guns in lieu of 4.7's when I joined, and there was therefore plenty of time to look round and see what could be done to make things comfortable for the officers and men in view of our lengthy periods at sea. The ship had, of course, been practically gutted in parts, and the Allan Line were busy erecting cabins for the many officers (88, I think there were) borne, the original cabins, as far as possible, also being put back. The First Class dining-saloon, which had been stripped, was divided off with matchboarding into an Admiral's, Ward-Room, and Gun-Room messes ; whilst the space where the library had been was also matchboarded to form a smoking-room.

"A Warrant Officers', Chief Petty Officers', and Stewards' messes were also erected abaft the galley in the second-class saloon. As regards the men, a smoking-room was made for the chief petty officers on the starboard side forward, where some third-class cabins used to be ; whilst the men had the use of the old first-class smoking-room abaft the lounge, this lounge itself being used as the quarter-deck. During the first month or two all the men (seamen and stokers) used this smoking-room, but, friction arising, the latter asked if they could have one of their own, so the old second-class smoking-room aft was divided into two with matchboarding and canvas.

"You will hardly believe it, but the stokers' smoking-room was one of the cleanest and best run of the lot in all the crew's section, the men taking a great pride in it, and having their own rules about using it, and that no man should do so unless properly dressed in the rig of the day. This question of dress with the stokers was, at first, one of the problems to be overcome, as, of course, being unused to discipline and "rigs of the day", they were always about in all sorts of rigs. They were allowed to use their own dress when below, but after their watch was over and they cleaned they had to get into Service dress. It took them quite a long time to become accustomed to that sort of routine.

"As regards the men's quarters, the seamen used the third-class saloon and the surrounding cabins, whilst the stokers were taken out of their 'dogs'-hole' forward and given the lower second-class saloon aft, together with the adjoining cabins. I use the word 'dogs'-hole', as regards the original quarters used when *Alsatian* was running in her own service, since it was the expression used by Captain Trewby when first going round the ship on joining. It was an appalling place ; and how anyone was expected to live and be healthy in it passes my understanding. I've often read books describing 'Life in the Fo'c'sle', and I can assure you it made me realize that the description given in those books did not tell one half the discomforts an average merchant seaman had to put up with. All the men seemed to take a great pride in their quarters, especially the stokers, and I have often wondered what the latter thought when they had to go back to their 'dogs'-hole' on being paid off."

Such was the interesting modification brought about when

the Navy engrafted its traditional routine on the Merchant Service and a liner became the Admiral's flagship. The usual three watches (red, white, and blue) were in force, and altogether the mingling of old ideas with new worked uncommonly well. This cohesion of methods, the raising of standards, were even more beneficial than might be immediately apparent, and much the same improvements were instituted aboard the other converted steamers. The Blockade Fleet thus became not a collection of entities, each working along its own individual lines, but one compact whole, efficient, happy, justly conscious of its worth, glad to be doing a most responsible duty, with everyone, so to speak, pulling on the same rope and tugging his hardest till the end.

Two days before Christmas the *Alsatian* again tested her new guns, so, everything being now satisfactory, she waited till after sunset before getting under way, and used the cover of darkness as a protection against possible submarines, the North Channel off the Mull of Cantyre being negotiated with safety. By breakfast-time on Christmas Day she reached Scapa Flow, took aboard the Admiral, and left that same afternoon for the north, where she joined the *Teutonic, Cedric, Columbella, Mantua,* and *Virginian,* who were already looking after what was known as "A" Patrol. As in the course of our story we shall have occasion to mention these area-lines, it may be well here to explain that "A" was a line which stretched away north from the Faroes, and was thus athwart the track of any vessels bound to or from Scandinavia and Denmark, no matter whether they came north or just south of Iceland. This line may be regarded as a movable bulwark, so placed as to stop the more elusive blockade-runners, such as German raiders anxious to reach the Atlantic under the disguise of neutral traders.

Patrol "B" was a line running north from the Shetlands. It was therefore well east of "A", but, whilst supplementing the latter, was in a position to entrap artful steamers of the *Bergensfjord* character which might choose the route between the Shetlands and Faroes. At present this line was unoccupied. Patrol "C", which became much strengthened later on, was just now under the care of *Otway, Oropesa,* and *Hilary.* It lay between the southern end of the Faroes and the northern approaches to the Hebrides. Thus these three strategically placed patrols were like mobile booms barring that vast watery expanse which must be traversed by shipping when using the northern route between Europe and the oceans beyond.

But there was also a fourth line, Patrol "D", which lay west of the Hebrides, and supplemented "C". The former was in effect an Atlantic outpost and a warning to the latter. At this date "D" was being patrolled by those four smaller vessels *Hildebrand*, *Ambrose*, *Patuca*, and *Calyx*. This four-lined super-scheme, which had been so cleverly worked out by Sir John Jellicoe and Admiral de Chair, was the only practicable means of covering such a colossal area. It was impossible to be strong at every spot, so the key situations were chosen. No screen of destroyers could be vouchsafed, as in the case of the Grand Fleet, but it was at least hoped this very remote northern sphere might be unvisited by submarines, who would prefer to operate rather in the coastal waters. So little was the ambition of U-boat warfare at this time understood !

It was a strange and chilly coincidence that *Alsatian's* first Christmas Day as a flagship should be spent in the loneliest and most cheerless portion of the British Isles, yet the years of food shortage were still uncontemplated, and there was plenty of good cheer below that night. All the culinary resources of the liner which so recently had advertised herself as the "largest and fastest" steamer running to Canada were available, and a glance at the dinner menu reminds one of those immense meals our forefathers used to consume—but never aboard the frigates whilst blockading Brest. Historians have frequently omitted the very human items of information which to-day we should much like to be told. Some of us have often wondered, for example, what Howard or Drake had to eat and drink on those hot July days when they were pursuing the Spanish Armada up the English Channel. It would be interesting likewise to know how Nelson breakfasted on his last morning in the *Victory*.

Therefore, in our quickly changing age, one need scarcely apologize if, for the perusal of posterity, a selection from the

Alsatian's officers' Christmas dinner be appended. It included Russian caviare, clear turtle soup, two kinds of fish, calf's head, roast beef, York ham, roast turkey, roast grouse, plum pudding, ices, trifle, mince pies. Contrasted with this pleasant picture arrived the next day, as many of us still remember, a typical Christmas gale from the S.W., just as the flagship arrived on her station and learned from *Teutonic* that very few ships up till now had been intercepted north of the Faroes. Perhaps as yet this track was too far north to suit the blockade-runners ; but equally likely they were using this route during the night hours, though it was difficult during long dark nights to say definitely how much traffic there really was.

The *Alsatian*, in spite of her size and fittings, could not conceal from her own personnel the damp penetrating cold of such latitudes, the ferocity of wind, the turbulence of sea. She was rolling quite a lot, for all her 18,000 tons, and the doctors were being kept busy with men in the sick bay suffering from chest complaints, or requiring simple surgery. But right away to the westward beyond the Hebrides those smaller ships of "D" Patrol were having a terrible time. Captain Wardle, who had been in command of the *Crescent* last November, when everyone aboard from Admiral downwards felt sure the ship would founder, was now destined to undergo an experience equally bad if not worse. After the "Edgars" were paid off he had been given the *Calyx*. As can be observed from the accompanying photograph, this two-funnelled Wilson steamer was of less than 3,000 tons—far too small for a region where the Atlantic fury first spends itself on its way towards Scotland. Forty miles out in the ocean west of the Outer Hebrides stands that far-away island of St. Kilda fenced round, except at one landing-place, by a precipice of rock. In those days there was still a small community who tended their cattle, wove their tweed, and lived a precarious existence.

Already this month the *Calyx* had been ordered to St. Kilda to inquire how they were getting on there with the new wireless station. "A dreadful thing has happened," was the greeting : "the Minister's cow has had a dead calf !" It seemed strange that such a minor event during the greatest of wars

H.M.S. CALYX

This Ex-Wilson liner narrowly escaped foundering in the Atlantic.

should be worth bothering about, yet even St. Kilda had its local crises. One day whilst patrolling off here Captain Wardle received a wireless signal from another of the Squadron : "Suspicious vessel near St. Kilda." Having regard to all the mysterious happenings (some well substantiated, others mere inventions) associated with German raiders, minelayers, spies, alleged submarine bases and depot-ships, it seemed not unlikely that St. Kilda might have been specially chosen by the enemy as a rendezvous. So here was the opportunity which *Calyx* yearned to possess.

"Full of beans," says Captain Wardle, "I was on the look-out for this vessel. It was a moonlight night, but with heavy squalls of rain." All of a sudden, sure enough a ship did then loom up, and the *Calyx* had just begun making the challenge, when the stranger fired a live shell. Luckily the aim was very poor, else Captain Wardle's ship would have been mortally wounded, but before it was too late there came a pause. It turned out that the stranger was another patrol unit on her way north to join the 10th Cruiser Squadron. Both ships had received the wireless warning, yet neither had been informed of the other's presence in the same vicinity. The small *Calyx* with her two funnels might quite easily have been a German ; indeed she was in appearance almost identical with the *Königin Luise*, which had been sighted in August and sunk by British destroyers just after the German had laid off Orfordness the first (Southwold) minefield.

The north-bound stranger off St. Kilda had turned from her course to seek the supposedly suspicious ship, and it was the sudden squall which prevented her from observing the challenge lights of *Calyx*. Such incidents were bound to occur when so many ships of all sorts were scouring the sea ; and, certainly, wireless played some amusing pranks. It was about this time that one day during a fog the *Calyx* intercepted the following signal : "Passed between two battle-cruisers. Think they were British, as I heard the order to 'close watertight doors'." The message was like the bleating of a strayed sheep, for the *Duncan* was as one crying in the wilderness of fog, having lost her own Squadron but very nearly had run into another.

Of the *Calyx's* experience during the dreadful night of

December 26, Captain Wardle's brief account suffices to quicken our imagination as to how the wintry Atlantic can murder small ships. "We were to the westward of St. Kilda," he has told me, "and never thought we should live through it. We had only a single screw, which of course raced as we pitched—always a sickening sensation—and I dared not go any speed. I tried to keep her with the wind on the bow— if we had got her beam-on, the water would have poured down the accommodation hatches, for she was only a small passenger-ship. Luckily I found that when she fell off a bit she was able to get a little steerage way on, so I could bring her up more to the wind again, when, of course, she lost headway once more. We were rolling 30° each way, and all one could do was to hang on to lifelines on the bridge. I was indeed thankful when with daylight it eased up. I know Admiral de Chair was very anxious about us. The *Calyx* was in commission for only a few months, and I was glad to see the last of her."

During these few days each of the patrols was having a trying time, with driving snow and hail to increase the gale's bitterness. Many of the units were compelled either to ease down or lie-to, nor did the *Alsatian*, with her great freeboard and cruiser-stern, make light of the weather. Several neutral steamers were intercepted, but it was too rough for the Squadron to board in the open, so they were taken under the lee of the Shetlands, where prize crews came aboard, who brought them into Kirkwall for examination. Throughout the night of December 29-30 the flagship was standing by a small tramp, but even after the dawn there was still such a heavy sea that she had to be dismissed. A further anxiety arrived when the wireless reported that one of *Berlin's* Tory Island mines had now been sighted adrift west of the Hebrides. The south-west gales had not been over long in scattering the death-dealing black eggs, so *Calyx* was sent to make a search in her area. On New Year's Day the *Alsatian* was caught in another heavy gale, with a sea which the Admiral reported as "very heavy". "Glad we are not in *Crescent*", wrote one of his officers to-day; whilst another recorded a few hours later that the seas actually came washing aboard *Alsatian's* C-deck. "She took quite a lot of water over here, and pitched tremendously during the night." It was more than unpleasant for those who were fit and able to get about, but it was anxious work for the ship's doctors, who, during the intervals of being seasick, were doing their best for a fireman critically ill of pneumonia.

So just now—as became the Squadron's almost regular experience during the ensuing months up north—there was to be fought an enemy more powerful than Germany could ever pretend. Brutal and merciless to ships and men, the gales scarcely blew themselves out before another series followed with greater force. Down dropped the glass to 28.50, up rose the waves into the sky, and it was under these conditions that the 10,757-tons *Virginian* was sent off to patrol beyond the north of Iceland for the purpose of ascertaining if neutral shipping were passing that way, also to report if the ocean there was blocked by ice. Meanwhile the *Hilary* began standing by a Norwegian barque named the *Marietta*, which had become dismasted in the gale, and presently took her in tow. But a pathetic disaster happened an hour after midnight on Saturday, January 2.

The wind had backed to S.E., then it increased to force 9 (i.e. nearly 60 miles an hour), and the glass fell still lower, being now 28.10. Through this turmoil the *Hilary* was towing slowly and painfully the unfortunate *Marietta*, hoping to get her safe in port. At 1.10 a.m. the much tried barque could endure the gale's punishment no longer, and, springing a leak, foundered. The Norwegians took to their boats, but it is scarcely surprising that under the prevailing conditions one boat capsized and only six men were saved. The *Hilary* managed to pick up the survivors, whom she landed at Kirkwall, but among those who had perished were two of her own people : Sub-Lieutenant O. E. Miles, R.N.R., and Signalman F. Scott.

Such sorrowful incidents did not relieve the drabness of this northern life, and each unit had its own domestic tribulations. Thus, only a week later, the fireman in *Alsatian's* sick bay, who had hovered between life and death whilst his ship contended with weather, succumbed to his pneumonia and was committed to the sea this same afternoon. A couple of days previously the *Cedric*, whilst hoisting in her boat after boarding, had an unfortunate accident which caused injury to four seamen and the abandonment of the boat as a total wreck. The wonder is that, with all those steamer patrols so frequently engaged inspecting vessels, the losses of personnel were not heavier.

There is something awe-inspiring both for onlookers and the handful of men as the boarding party puts off from one tall ship's side to another, over steep green, white-topped hills, rushing down terrible declivities of an unstable switch-back. Man's utter impotence at the hands of wild nature seems at such times so severely stressed. One flick of a wave at any moment could send boat with crew to the bottom : one scend of the sea could hurl the wooden craft against the neutral's steel hull and strew the water with splinters ; one error of judgment in coming alongside would mean broken limbs if not instant death. But this was all in the wintry game, and the daily gamble with destiny went on.

As the fresh patrol vessels kept arriving from their respective ports, it was found necessary for the Admiral to meet them, instruct them, put them through their paces, and send them off on their lines of interception, these lines being so carefully placed that if a neutral should have passed unnoticed by night through one line she would be caught by another during the next daylight. Every unit in each patrol was to keep herself informed concerning the locality of her sister ships, and as to what the latter were doing at any given time. It was a triumph of organization that at last the blockading fleet, with its four lines, each of six ships steaming at 13 knots thirty miles apart, and all turning together at a fixed time, was established in such a manner that on a clear day it was quite impossible for enemy or neutral to pass through the line unseen.

Never was wireless ever more usefully employed ; yet drastic measures had to be taken lest there should be unnecessary signalling and the ether become a chaos. On the other hand, there were occasions when it was necessary to jam all wireless messages which some Scandinavian liner might be emitting for a suspicious purpose. It was nearly always possible for the Admiral to keep in touch with his Captains, however far apart they happened to be ; and, contrariwise, the latter could always refer some difficult case for his special judgment.

H.M.S. "ALSATIAN" IN DRY DOCK

H.M.S. "ALSATIAN'S" SEA-BOAT
hoisted out ready for
boarding a neutral ship.

Thus distance was annihilated, central control was rendered possible, and the flagship became likewise a general clearing-station for intelligence. If, for example, Whitehall had information that a certain notorious steamer was to leave New York on a certain date and must be stopped before reaching Bergen, it was only necessary to get in telegraphic communication with Sir John Jellicoe's *Iron Duke* in Scapa Flow, who in turn would send a wireless warning to Admiral de Chair at sea. The latter, with a mental picture before his eyes of this huge spider's web, could issue special orders to whatever patrols were watching athwart the particular tracks.

It was found that the four patrol lines were most successful when drawn at right angles to the courses of expected blockade-runners. Whenever one of the squadron sighted a suspect, she immediately gave chase, but informed the next-in-line what she was doing, and even calling up the latter for help if required. But it was part of the technique always to keep 4,000 yards outside the stranger, lest the latter should be a raider in disguise and fire a torpedo.

On another page we alluded to the indignation, the bitter disappointment, felt by the Squadron at the way in which the Foreign Office negatived the stern efforts which boarding parties, carried in open boats, had been making. Here is one flagrant instance which Admiral de Chair has given me.

In January 1915 the *Greenbrier*, a ship from the U.S.A., was caught by *Cedric*, and as her cargo was of a very suspicious nature (including contraband and 14 Germans) she was sent into Kirkwall under an armed guard. There, however, she was presently released by order of the Foreign Office, much to the surprise of *Greenbrier's* Captain and crew, who thought they would certainly be detained and the cargo put into the Prize Court : in fact, when the news reached America, there was a good deal of contempt and amusement at our leniency, and it only encouraged neutral merchants to try the game again.

But this month there was a most interesting capture, which not even the Foreign Office's various Committees frustrated, and this episode has in it the stuff out of which good detective stories are fashioned. Let us start from the beginning.

CHAPTER VI

DISASTERS BEGIN

DURING the first autumn of the War strenuous efforts were made by Germany's diplomatic staff in the United States to aid our enemy by every legitimate and illegitimate method which was practicable.

Two categories were especially important. Every able-bodied German man should be smuggled across to the Fatherland somehow ; but, also, accurate and regular American news must be sent in regard to such matters as the true feeling of United States citizens concerning the War, and especially the disposition of merchants in regard to the British Blockade. A further requisite was that German agents, despatched west across the Atlantic for the purpose of fixing up big contracts, should be able to travel backwards and forwards unhindered. This could be done only by trickery, lying, and abuse of neutrality.

Large quantities of false passports had to be issued, so that Germans could travel as Americans, and an office for this purpose was opened by Lieutenant Hans von Wedell in Bridge Street, New York. This super-spy was working under the instructions of that notorious Captain von Papen,[1] the Military Attaché, whom the United States Government eventually caused Germany to recall ; and von Papen, in turn, was a colleague of the Ambassador Count Bernstorff. It was important that the latter should keep in close touch with Berlin by means of couriers, and already von Wedell had made one return trip as such when, in November 1914, von Papen similarly despatched him.

---

[1] Destined subsequently, in 1932, to take a prominent part in Germany's politics.

Von Wedell, who at one time was a New York newspaper reporter but subsequently a lawyer, was married to a charming German baroness, who, on December 22 of that year, was given by von Papen the sum of 800 dollars (£160 at par) for certain services rendered. That is to say, she was one of those who played their part as courier between Europe and America. The schemes to which her husband descended in order to get passports for German patriots included the bribing of tramps and people of New York's underworld to obtain and deliver up to him these documents at anything from 15 to 20 dollars a time. A certain amount of faking was done to complete any requisite modification.

But towards the approach of Christmas New York was becoming too unhealthy for von Wedell, and it would be better if he faded away. The forged passport industry was about to be revealed, and trouble was within sight. Von Papen firmly advised him to disappear, so Christmas Day was spent in hiding, and von Wedell was succeeded by Carl Ruroede. On December 26 von Wedell wrote his farewell letter to Bernstorff, and a few days later went down to the New York dock, where the Scandinavian liner S.S. *Bergensfjord* (twice previously mentioned) was ready for sailing. Accompanying him came Carl Ruroede, together with four other Germans, of whom one was an officer. They had furnished themselves with passports made out for citizens of American names. At this stage, just when it seemed certain that all six would soon be on the high seas heading for Bergen *en route* for Berlin, there came a dramatic interruption. Federal agents of the United States arrived on board, lined up the wanted men with the other passengers, identified Ruroede and his four friends, arrested them and took them ashore, where in due course the former was sentenced to three years' imprisonment on account of his fraudulence, whilst each of the four had to pay a fine of 200 dollars.

But, unhappily, though the officials expected also to find von Wedell, they had no description of him, and failed to identify him, so presently the *Bergensfjord* cast off and steamed away. It had been a singularly narrow escape, but at last he was able to breathe freely as the Statue of Liberty vanished in the background. He was no longer von Wedell, but a

"Mr. Spero, American citizen". How he must have laughed
that night in his cabin, and congratulated himself on his
freedom ! And with this ends Act I of the drama.

Act II opens with a complicating occurrence. Intelligence
has been flashed over his head across the Atlantic into Whitehall
that this Norwegian mail steamer has sailed ; that she is
expected to pass through the Blockade at some date between
January 9 and 13 ; and that it is reported she carries a number
of German Reservists travelling under neutral passports.
This intriguing news next comes across England, Scotland,
Scapa Flow, and thence to the *Alsatian*. The orders are that
Bergensfjord is to be intercepted. The various Captains are
informed accordingly, and, in order that the patrol may be
the better directed, Admiral de Chair keeps his flagship south of
the Faroes. For these armed merchant cruisers at that time were
fitted only with a Marconi apparatus of short range and small
power, which sometimes made it a little difficult, when north
of the Faroes, to maintain touch between flagship and patrols.

As to the setting of the picture, it suffices to say that the
patrols were arranged as on the accompanying plan. The
Alsatian was to the east of line "B", so as to cut across the
Faroes-Bergen track. This "B" line stretching north of the
Shetlands included the following : *Cedric, Patia, Teutonic,
Orotava,* and *Viknor*. In "C" Patrol were *Otway, Bayano,
Oropesa, Hilary,* and *Digby* ; whilst in "D" were *Hildebrand,
Patuca,* and *Clan MacNaughton*. Others were either away
coaling, on passage, or specially employed. Picture the fourteen
ships steaming at right angles to their respective lines, now
turning east, now steering west. A glance at the plan at once
reveals the effective design of so disposing these barriers that,
day or night, it would be most difficult for the most astute
neutral skipper not to be encountered in at least one area.

Knowing the characteristic elusiveness of *Bergensfjord*, it
was to be expected that at this period of the year, when the
dark nights are long, she would make the best use of the
loneliest track; it seemed unlikely that she would pass between
the Shetlands and Orkneys, more possible that she would come
between the Shetlands and Faroes, yet far more probable she
would go north of the Faroes before altering course towards

Bergen.   Hence the importance of Patrol "B".   Particular
note should be taken of the *Viknor*, which was the oldest ship
of all.   There must to-day still be many passengers who

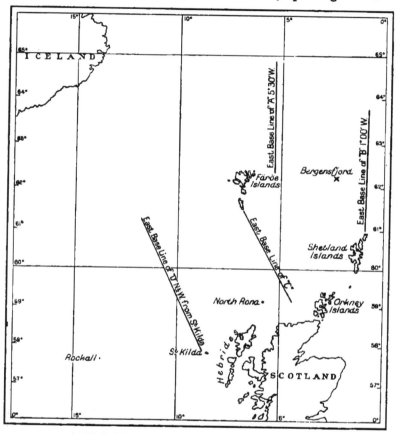

PATROL LINES OF BLOCKADE IN JANUARY 1915.
THE POSITION WHERE S.S. "BERGENSFJORD" WAS INTERCEPTED IS
INDICATED BY A CROSS.

remember touring the Norwegian Fjords in the *Viking*,
which was made to change her appellation as a warship because
already there was a British destroyer of the latter name.
But the *Viknor* was twenty-seven years old and not classed as

A1 at Lloyd's : you will not find her in *Lloyd's Register* of 1914. In spite of her 5,386 tons, she was a poor seaboat, yet for all that she was destined to play a conspicuous part during her short period in the Royal Navy.

She had taken some time to fit out on the Tyne, so she did not sail from there to join Admiral de Chair's flag until three days after Christmas, and on New Year's Day began her duties on Patrol "B". But this ex-pleasure steamer was unaccustomed to wild wintry gales, and she received so much damage that she must needs seek shelter in Burra Sound. However, that embarrassment passed, she was able to rejoin her sisters and remain extra vigilant for the oncoming Norwegian.

We are still in Act II, and the suspense is suddenly quickened at 6.30 a.m. on January 10, when the *Oropesa* on Patrol "C" hears *Bergensfjord's* wireless talking to Bergen. The Norwegian is some hundreds of miles away, and her signals are faint, yet it is she herself. We pass over another day of waiting until 8.30 a.m. of January 11, when one of Patrol "B" units flashes the good news that she has intercepted and stopped the *Bergensfjord*, the position (lat. 62°10′ N; long. 2°24′ W.) being just as one might expect—well to the eastward of the Faroes, which the *Bergensfjord* had left to the northward, and on the track which would soon take her into territorial waters of Norway whilst giving British islands a wide berth. But it is *Viknor*, that old tourist visitor of Norway's bracing coast, which has had the fine opportunity of halting the far newer and faster ship.

Having heard the news, Admiral de Chair hurries to the position and there finds the *Viknor* standing by the *Bergensfjord*. The latter has failed to rush the blockade, and besides *Alsatian* there has arrived *Patia*, together with *Teutonic*; but the services of these two are immediately required for chasing an oil steamer which *Viknor* has also reported. In the meanwhile the climax of this sea drama develops when the *Viknor's* boat is lowered and comes alongside *Bergensfjord*. You can imagine the feelings of Hans von Wedell as he hears the Norwegian engines slow down to stop; perceives that almost within sight of the neutral coast his escape is suddenly checked; and that just over there, rolling to the swell, is an old ship wearing the British White

Ensign. Not a pleasant outlook for a fugitive to contemplate on awaking from slumber !

Up the steep steel side climbs the boarding party, and then they come tramping along the wooden deck. The examination of ships' papers and passenger-lists begins.

"Passenger travelling under the name of Spero, with a neutral passport ?"

"Spero—yes. There he is."

The *Alsatian* directs Spero, and any German Reservists, to be arrested and taken aboard the *Viknor*.

Von Wedell may have been a punster as well as an optimist when he chose the Latin word meaning "I hope". But "Spero" quickly changed to despair when he saw that the game was up and he could not bluff as he had been doing ever since the War started. Just as the time had long since departed for passport-faking, so an end had now come to his trans-atlantic trips on behalf of Germany.

"I own to being von Wedell, but I claim American citizenship."

The matter could be thrashed out better ashore, and doubtless the United States authorities would illumine the question ; so the lawyer-defrauder was put into the boat and removed to *Viknor*. Six stowaways—how stereotyped had this number become !—and one sexagenarian passenger, all reputed to be German Reservists (though they stoutly denied it), were also removed and placed under arrest aboard the *Viknor*. No documents could be discovered, but it was reported that they had been destroyed by a German doctor. A prize crew was placed in charge of *Bergensfjord*, as it was perfectly clear she had no intention of calling at Kirkwall, and now she was sent into that port for further examination.

The final episodes of Act II conclude with the usual display of annoyance, indignation, and anger on the part of *Bergensfjord's* Master, an attitude which one can well under-stand; but this was the time of war, and he must have known that it was impossible to fool part of the British Navy *all* the time. On the way south towards the Orkneys port he protests this afternoon that he is carrying international mails, and refuses to give any assistance in the ship's navigation. However, the presence of the prize crew on board, together with the

Alsatian and *Viknor* steaming on either beam, soon overcomes any truculence, and the Norwegian reaches Fair Island Channel, where she is handed over to the destroyer *Garry*. The last phase comes when she is again released, and on January 14 a wireless message is picked up from *Bergensfjord* to Bergen suggesting that the route of her sister ship *Kristianiafjord* (of the same Company), due about February 7, should be altered. The intention was to avoid British patrols for the most obvious of reasons.

Now Act III is as short and surprising as it is replete with irony and sudden change of fortune. A great Greek dramatist would have recognized here the just reward of the spy villain, the fugitive from justice, the forger of official documents. The *Viknor* was ordered to Liverpool, where she was to land her prisoners, and to coal, but by the end of the week came the disquieting news that she had failed to arrive. There can be no doubt that she steamed safely down the west coast of Scotland, and on Wednesday, January 13, was in communication with Malin Head signal station, which is on the north Irish coast, roughly midway between Tory Island on the west and Giant's Causeway on the east. That is the last which was ever heard of her ; although wireless messages were sent to the *Viknor* and ships searched, she was not seen again. But within a week bodies and wreckage were washed ashore at Portrush (to the west of Giant's Causeway), and there can be little doubt to-day as to what happened. She must have struck one or more of those mines which were the cause of H.M.S. *Audacious* having foundered. The recent heavy Atlantic gales and seas, sweeping eastward along the Irish coast, had plucked mines from their moorings and sent the dangerous black "eggs" drifting. It was sad to think that every officer and man perished, and it was hard lines on the prisoners ; yet how strange was this ending to a spy story, how notable the sudden twist, that von Wedell, after eluding the American police and voyaging many hundreds of miles, should in the final scene go to his doom on a German mine ! He had set out from New York for Berlin, and it was the *Berlin* which caused his death.

Commander Ballantyne was thus destined to enjoy only the briefest period in command of the ex-cruising yacht.

Just before the War he had been living abroad studying foreign languages, afterwards served in *Royal Arthur* of the original Training Squadron, and then had been joined as second-in-command in the *Viknor* by another interpreter, Lieutenant-Commander H. L. Shephard, who came from *Grafton* after the "Edgars" were paid off.

This situation of Tory Island minefield, to windward of the track which must be used by vessels of the 10th Cruiser Squadron when bound in or out of Liverpool, was an additional risk. Although minesweeping trawlers were sent to clear, it was a long while before the area could be cleaned up, for the weather and high seas were a perpetual hindrance. But the submarine menace was growing, and this was capable of becoming to the blockaders as great an enemy as the gales of winds. During November 1914 the more enterprising U-boats had been operating not merely up the North Sea but well down the English Channel. Lieut.-Commander Hersing in U-21, who had shown himself one of the most daring of Germany's officers, on the night of September 2 crept right up to the Forth Bridge, and then emerged, sinking H.M.S. *Pathfinder* ten miles south-east of May Island. On November 22, U-18 got so nearly into Scapa Flow that she was rammed off Hoxa Head by a patrol trawler, and received such injuries that this submarine foundered and the German crew surrendered. But the uncomfortable fact remained that enemy submarines were now violating such northern latitudes.

During that same month Hersing, in the English Channel, inaugurated the procedure of sinking ships by gunfire rather than torpedo. But the torpedoing of the battleship *Formidable* west of Portland on January 1, 1915, was another reminder that this undersea warfare might have serious results for the Blockading Fleet. Still more deeply was it felt by a peculiar coincidence. On January 5, Admiral de Chair had shifted the Patrol lines "B" and "C" twenty miles further west, warning them of submarines said to be off the Shetlands. As an additional precaution the patrols were now ordered by day and during moonlit nights to zigzag. From this date comes the first actual relation between submarine cause and effect. For the *Hildebrand*, which was taking a steamer into Kirkwall for examination, could not enter because of the submarine scare, so destroyers finished the escorting. A still sharper instance occurred at the month's end, when the *Alsatian* was due to spend some days in Liverpool, coaling and revictualling.

On January 31 she had completed taking in stores and was ready for sea, when she was held up in the Mersey for another week. It was Hersing again. He had created a submarine record, taking U-21 down the English Channel into the Irish Sea, being sighted off Bardsey Island on January 28, after which he bombarded Barrow and remained some time off the Mersey approaches, here sinking three ships before returning safely to Germany, where he received the Kaiser's congratulations for the longest trip a submarine had hitherto attempted.

For Liverpool it was a sensational development that its very exit should be threatened, and for the 10th Cruiser Squadron flagship the delay was serious. Not until the nights were less flooded by the moon was *Alsatian* allowed to proceed, and in the meanwhile other units had to get their coal either in the Clyde or Loch Ewe. When, at length, on the evening of February 6, *Alsatian* did steam down the Mersey, four others, *Caribbean*, *Bayano*, *Oropesa*, and *Calyx*, likewise put to sea after being denied egress by Hersing. But confirmatory evidence now came that *Viknor's* death must certainly have been mine-caused; for to-day the *Virginian* exploded a mine in a position (lat. 56°25′ N., long. 73°5′ W.) south of Barra Head (Hebrides). The S.W. gales and tides had unquestionably, as to-day we know quite definitely, driven it to the north-east from Tory Island area. Next day (February 7) the *Alsatian* sighted another mine in much the same area, and the *Bayano*, who was following astern, spotted two more to the south-east. Owing to sea and heavy mist it was not possible to sink these lurking dangers.

It was lucky that all five units from Liverpool returned to their stations in safety, but there is still to be recorded another of those sea mysteries which are really simple disasters. What had happened to the *Clan Macnaughton* ? The Admiral had heard nothing of that Patrol "D" vessel since the early morning of February 3. Her colleagues, *Hildebrand* and *Patuca*, searched for her in vain; but when, on February 9, the *Alsatian* met *Hildebrand*, the latter informed the Admiral that wreckage (supposed to be portions of the missing ship) had been seen. There can be no doubt that the Clan liner perished in just the same manner as the *Viknor*. She struck a mine during a gale of wind, so that she went down with all her 284 officers and crew. She was commanded by Commander Robert Jeffreys, who formerly had the *Grafton* in the old 10th Cruiser Squadron, and had commissioned the liner during the first week of December at Tilbury; so two months were the limit of this ship's war work.

The evil which a mine-layer achieves lives long after her. The *Berlin* did not dare to try reaching Germany after her deed, and interned herself at the Norwegian port of Trondhjem on November 17; so it was impossible for the Squadron to avenge itself. But from the position (lat. 58°47′, N., long. 9°27′ W.) whence the *Clan Macnaughton* last communicated, being well west of the Hebrides, it is by no means taxing the imagination to suppose that a mine was the primary cause of disaster. Hatchway cover, griping spar, door, battens, lifebelts, were found, but never a body.

Accidents happen in the best of ships, though at first this improvised fleet with its untrained crews certainly incurred risks that rarely happened elsewhere ; but it must be recollected that there never was a squadron of steamships which, collectively or individually, put in so much continuous time at sea. Therefore the opportunities for trouble were magnified. The *Teutonic*, as an instance, had an experience which might have meant serious loss. She was patrolling, when a heavy sea unshipped a six-inch shell from the ready-use rack on deck, causing the shell to explode against the bulwarks and doing a certain amount of damage to the ship. That was repaired by the *Teutonic's* artificers, and fortunately no one was injured.

CHAPTER VII

THE COUNTER-BLOCKADE

BEFORE the first winter was over it became very clear that two highly important developments, hitherto rather menaces than controlling factors, were to manifest themselves prominently. And both were intimately related to the Blockade operations. The first was the submarine problem, and the second was how to keep in a state of friendship with the United States whilst doing our best to prevent her produce from reaching Germany. As the months passed, these two considerations became increasingly grave, but they were further complicated in that Germany herself was not less anxious to retain the United States' favour, whilst the American cotton exporters, meat packers, and other traders were making such handsome profits that they would resist, and continue to resist, every British effort to stop contraband.

Looking back on those events and surveying the whole view unrestrictedly, as to-day we are fully able, the subject becomes intensely entertaining. It is an established truth that the Great War would never have occurred except that Germany's leaders believed a victory would be snatched quickly without the intervention of Britain. The Teutonic military mind sought to perform its work without troubling much either about its own Navy or the naval forces of the Allies. "You leave this war business to the Army, and we'll see the job through." That was why the Germany Navy were not even asked by their sister service, during those first weeks of war, to make raids down the English Channel and sink transports that carried the British Expeditionary Force across to France. Then, as we have observed, not till late that autumn did Germany wake up and begin timidly sending a submarine or two to shell or torpedo steamers off Havre.

That which Germany could not nationally endure was firm economic pressure exerted from the sea. This fact has not been quite fully appreciated in Britain, because we have been too self-conscious that our own great danger lay in being cut off from overseas supplies. One of the last incidents that immediately preceded the War was the visit to England of Prince Henry, the Kaiser's Admiral brother. The object of his mission was to ascertain whether Britain would come in or keep out of the War ; and he went back with a report that Britain had no intention but to remain outside the impending European trouble.

During the two decades of 1894–1914 Germany had undergone the transformation which came over England at the beginning of the nineteenth century : she had changed from being a self-supporting agricultural country into a nation of industrials who depended for their supplies largely on the outer world. The same exodus of country workers to settle in the towns and toil in factories took place through these latter years in Germany as it had a century earlier in England. And the notable corollary must be mentioned that, whilst the German agricultural production became insufficient for the nourishment of a rapidly increasing population, thereby demanding bigger importations of food, Germany's manufacturers were compelled to find an adequate outlet only by extending their markets abroad. Thus in a comparatively brief period Germany, notwithstanding that she was a continental country, had taken on the attributes of an island nation, but especially its vulnerability through economic pressure. A Blockade must cut off her lifeblood.

What were the raw products which Germany had accustomed herself to rely upon from overseas ? The answer includes the following : cotton, wool, copper, lead, rubber, paraffin, nickel, oils, fats, wheat, rye, barley, cattle. Stop these from entering the country, and you would begin her starvation, for in 1914 she had the huge population of 70 millions. Therefore the very last thing which Germany desired was that Britain should join with France, should take charge of the naval pressure, should close the eastern end of the English Channel and the Scotland-Norway gate against the above commodities. And, remembering this, we can well appreciate the bitter disappointment, disillusion, and indignant anger which Germany felt when at midnight on August 4 Britain no longer stood aloof, and Prince Henry of Prussia was found to have been misinformed.

The man who, more than any other individual, built up the German Navy was the late Grand-Admiral von Tirpitz, who survived the war long enough to set down his reminiscences, which are most illuminative of the months leading up to Germany's counter-Blockade operations. In an earlier chapter we called attention to the great American Admiral Mahan's remarks on the strategically favourable position which nature has given the British Isles, and Admiral Tirpitz emphasized the same truth. "England did not fear an attack from us," he wrote;[1] "she had a guarantee against this in our unfavourable strategical situation in the 'wet triangle' . . . which limited the effectiveness of our fleet." Conversely, the position of the Grand Fleet and the 10th Cruiser Squadron in their capacity as keepers of the northern door were now causing such genuine anxiety that Germany had to think of some antidote against a closure which must eventually shut off her supplies. Here history proves once again that events do not always follow in natural sequence according to the dictates of logic. Up to the end of January 1915 Admiral de Chair's Squadron, though now in thorough working order and, in spite of the dark hours as well as the gales which hindered boarding for days at a time, intercepting and sending into harbour for examination an increasingly large number of ships, was still being hindered from performing its task fully. Its efforts were limited, frustrated, and even negatived by Foreign Office principles and interference; yet enough evidence had been allowed Germany that if this strong arm of the sea were only given free play it would crush the life and spirit of the Kaiser's people. Starvation! That was the inevitable result.

Now Germany realized at the beginning of 1915 that there was only one way of preventing such a possibility: she must

---

[1] *My Memoirs.* By Grand-Admiral von Tirpitz. London, 1919. Vol. I, p. 239.

bring the war to a victorious conclusion in the quickest time. But stalemate set in on the Western Front, trench life took the place of progress, so the idea of a short sharp campaign was out of the question. The High Sea Fleet never got over the shock which it received at the Battle of Heligoland on August 28, 1914. This is not an opinion but an historical fact, even better appreciated in Germany than in England. The future defensive policy of the German Admiralty was not very helpful as a reply to the British Blockade. It was at this stage, then, that the submarine was taken in hand to be used as a means of striking Britain in the same manner that she was hitting Germany; that is, attacking her through her seaborne commerce.

"The most effective weapon that we possessed", wrote Admiral Tirpitz,[1] "against England's commerce was the submarine. . . . The main difficulty was to be expected in our relations with America, especially since this country, contrary to the whole spirit of neutrality, had developed shortly after the outbreak of war into an enemy arsenal." Now before the War many Admirals, both British and German, had found it difficult to accept the claims which keen, ardent young officers enthusiastically put forward on behalf of their underwater craft. But within the first few months of hostilities actual experience had taught that the new school had not exaggerated their capabilities. In Germany there had been as much elation as surprise that the three "Cressys" had been sent to the bottom by one U-boat without difficulty, that submarines could sink a battleship (H.M.S. *Formidable*, on January 1); cruisers (H.M.S. *Niger, Hawke, Pathfinder*); and by the end of January have performed such lengthy voyages as to the Orkneys on one side and right up the Irish Sea on the other. Such achievements fired the imagination, and provided Germany with an adequate answer to the Blockade problem.

At the beginning of November 1914 was inaugurated by the leading naval authorities in Germany a series of discussions concerning the possibilities of a U-boat campaign. In the following January occurred a conference which included

---

[1] *Ibid.*, p. 390.

Admiral Tirpitz, the Chancellor, and the responsible heads. The historic result was that on February 4, Admiral von Pohl, Chief of the Admiralty Staff, declared by a notice in the official *Reichsanzeiger* that the waters around the British Isles, including the English Channel, herewith became a war zone, and that from February 18 every merchant ship met with in that zone would be destroyed.

Admiral Tirpitz wanted only a blockade of the Thames. He and his friends were opposed to the larger declaration, because Germany at that date owned so few submarines and her officers lacked enough experience : the declaration was too ambitious and premature. It was, he affirmed, "not effective, and lacked reality, thus encouraging objections. It injured the credit of our declarations, and thus in a sense damaged the prestige of the German Navy." His brother officer, Admiral Scheer, has also left it on record that a blockade was not proclaimed, because the lack of U-boats prevented such a possibility of it being effective. Thus the curious situation arose in those days of Britain and Germany carrying on against each other a blockade which neither party chose to designate by that name. More accurately than Germany could the British conscience claim that the enemy was truly being hemmed in, yet Admiral Pohl's "paper" blockade was to have curious repercussions.

We now have the information that only 23 U-boats existed ready for enforcing this new move ; and if one considers the hundreds of watery square miles around Great Britain and Ireland, the large proportion of submarines which must at any given date be in dock for repairs, destroyed in action, or on passage to the distant patrol areas several days from the base, the suggestion of any effective blockade was farcical. But the threat annoyed no nation more than it irritated the United States, and thus began a series of incidents which deflected much of America's wrath hitherto concentrated against Britain. By a serious error of judgment, by the folly of an impulsive declaration, Germany took the first step of a rake's progress. With incredible tactlessness and lack of prevision she went on adding pain to American sensitiveness, torpedoing the *Lusitania* and *Sussex*, committing one foolishness after another, until finally the United States for its own

THE LIGHTER SIDE OF BLOCKADING

OFFICERS PLAYING HOCKEY ABOARD H.M.S. "ALSATIAN"

"NOTHING DOING"
A Revue produced aboard H.M.S. *Alsatian* whilst on patrol.

self-respect had no other choice than to enter the contest against Germany.

But more than two years had to pass before the final crisis of April 1917 occurred. The immediate consequence of the declaration on February 4 was that the United States Government on February 12, 1915, despatched its first Note to Germany protesting against this submarine intention. The United States, at least, could not allow its merchant ships to be sunk whilst on passage to the British Isles ; so Germany had to instruct her U-boat officers to spare whatever neutral vessels might be found within the barred zone. And once more the "paper" blockade became wanting in substance, for the doors to British ports would still be open to vessels flying the neutral flag.

What resulted ? To the great embarrassment of our enemy, British merchant ships were officially advised to adopt the time-honoured ruse of flying neutral colours. If this procedure seems to us suggestive of trickery, it was justified by the situation ; and in the meanwhile Germany, within a fortnight of her declaration to the world, was made to look somewhat foolish. On February 17 she sent America what Tirpitz regarded as "our altogether too humble answer", and the threatened submarine blockade did not actually begin till the 18th. "The submarine warfare", records the Grand-Admiral, "now became . . . of no effect in securing the ultimate victory of the German people, but still had material enough to create incidents and quarrels with the Americans."

Nor did the initial mistake end at this. By a curious mental process both Tirpitz and other leaders of German opinion now formed a conclusion that at least this U-boat menace might be used as an instrument for bargaining. To what intent ? If only Britain would modify her attitude, make certain concessions, and abide by the Declaration of London, then Germany would abandon her submarine campaign. Our enemy was seriously convinced that within six weeks the British Government would now have to yield thus far. Never was made such a mistake in estimating the psychology of a rival.

The United States Ambassador, Mr. Gerard, had been instructed to remind Germany that the sole right of a belligerent in dealing with neutral shipping on the high seas was limited to visit and search, *unless* a blockade had been proclaimed and was being effectively maintained. But to attack vessels entering the prescribed area without first determining their belligerent character, their nationality, and the character of their cargo was unprecedented in naval warfare. When Count Bernstorff, the German Ambassador in America, now informed the United States Government that his nation was ready to consider abandoning her attack on British merchantmen provided Britain ceased preventing foodstuffs being conveyed to German civilians, it was tantamount to an admission that Admiral de Chair's Squadron was definitely tightening up the commercial pressure.

Nevertheless, the international situation by the month of March was not a little complicated and delicate. It may be at once stated that the united efforts of three distinguished diplomatists were fully required if a grave peril was to be avoided. Sir Edward Grey, and the American Ambassador, Mr. W. H. Page, in London, together with Sir Cecil Spring-Rice, the British Ambassador in Washington, between them did wonders. The German statement that the submarine effort had been decided on merely as a measure of self-defence was an attitude requesting pity. The citizens of the United States contained many families of German or Irish descent whose influence in the Senate and finance could not be denied, and it was weighed against any sympathy with Britain. For President Wilson the task of keeping an even balance became increasingly difficult : yet just as water will find its own level when freed from interference, so men's actions will regulate themselves according to the instincts of primitive humanity if let alone. The United States "respectfully suggests" that Britain should not interfere with foodstuffs destined from America to Germany, and further suggested that if Britain refused to purchase immunity from submarine attack by allowing the foodstuffs to reach Germany, then the United States might place an embargo on the export of food, together with those other supplies which were being sent across the Atlantic to the Allies.

At first consideration this announcement seemed fraught with disaster ; yet here entered the human factor. Tirpitz was not wholly inaccurate when he stated America had become an "arsenal" for the Allies. If some traders had lost their normal markets to Hamburg, others were making fortunes in sending munitions and supplies of many sorts to British or French ports. The last thing that these providers wished was a rupture, so the Anglo-American rope of diplomacy was subjected to varying strains, sometimes reaching tenuity, at other periods becoming quite slack and then tightening with a jerk—but it never snapped altogether.

Germany's offer to bargain was received in England with contempt, and the sequence is worth noting. On the first day of March, Mr. Asquith announced in the House of Commons that in consequence of the "campaign of piracy and pillage" we were driven to frame against the enemy retaliatory measures so as "to prevent commodities of any kind from entering or leaving Germany. These measures will, however, be enforced by the British and French Governments without risk to neutral ships, or to neutral or non-combatant lives." These two Governments would, none the less, hold themselves free to detain and take into port all ships carrying goods of presumed enemy destination, ownership, or origin. "It is not intended to confiscate such vessels or cargoes, unless they would be otherwise liable to confiscation."

This was a bold standpoint, but it was not welcomed in America with enthusiasm ; nor was President Wilson inclined to accept the new theory of a "long-distance blockade", or the seizure *on suspicion* of neutral vessels bound for neutral ports. The President's attitude can be summed up briefly in an anxiety to persuade both belligerents to recognize the rules laid down in (1) the Declaration of Paris, (2) the Declaration of London. In plain language it amounted to this : "If you must fight between yourselves, kindly keep within the rules of boxing."

Those early weeks of 1915, with all their contradictions, their patchwork policy, their continual retrimming of purpose, were typical of the chaos which was overcoming the world, and only to-day can we see the results with painful clarity. Whilst, strictly speaking, the British Prime Minister, in foretelling that Britain would prevent goods of any kind from entering or leaving Germany, certainly claimed an ability that was beyond our power, and public opinion in America generally was against recognizing a long-distance blockade as one accepted by International Law, yet even now the issue was not so simple.   For some American merchants argued that their commerce would suffer less injury if this policy of isolation were carried out than if an "effective" blockade were maintained.   Why ?   Because under the latter every neutral vessel trading with the enemy was subject to seizure from the moment it left port, and the cargo liable to forfeiture ; whereas Mr. Asquith had plainly announced that, whilst cargoes of neutral vessels would not be allowed to reach their destination, they would not be forfeited.

The Prime Minister's statement was followed by another Order-in-Council, dated March 11, 1915, and it marked a new chapter.   It was a "reprisals" Order, issued as a firm reply to the German submarine declaration of February 4, the general aim now being to shut Germany off from ocean-borne commerce, whether as regards exports or imports.   Sea-borne trade as confined to the Baltic could not be controlled by the British Navy.   The iron-ore steamers, for instance, which came down from northern Sweden via the Gulf of Bothnia, remained untouched except for a sharp but brief period when British submarines created havoc.   But from March 11 there would be an end to those Atlantic vessels and freights of German destination or origin.   Contraband would be condemned ; non-contraband would be either requisitioned or returned to the owner.   The neutral importer would be made to give his individual guarantee for the innocent destination of each consignment ; and the Contraband Committee, instead of treating all non-contraband goods with equal severity, now concentrated on a select list of articles, especially foodstuffs, fodder, and raw materials.

Under this new Order-in-Council the Big Blockade really begins, but not till then.   From Admiral de Chair's fleet even greater pressure would be requisite, and the aim now was that in making a few severe examples of delinquent neutral blockade-runners their owners would presently learn how inconvenient and unprofitable were the delays when ships were caught carrying cargoes for the enemy.   So successful became this scheme that even by July 1915 not one neutral shipping line would knowingly accept a German cargo. At least one well-known American authority on International Law (Mr. F. R. Condert) asserted in the *New York Herald* that it was not an illegitimate interference with neutral commerce, but permissible under the rules of International Law as practised by the U.S.A., and he cited precedents arising out of the American Civil War. Nevertheless, the tone of the American Press as a whole resented this latest Order-in-Council, and called upon their Government to maintain American rights. Nor would the British claim be accepted of interfering arbitrarily with neutral shipments to neutral ports, even when suspected of ultimate enemy destination.

Now just when signs indicated that Anglo-British differences once more seemed to reach danger-point, another strange thing happened. On March 11—the very date of the "reprisals" Order-in-Council—there steamed into the American harbour of Newport News the armed merchant cruiser *Prinz Eitel Friedrich*, a German raider which had come all the way from Tsingtau and had been very active in her operations against shipping. She effected some repairs and was allowed to go into dry-dock until March 14; but she created an atmosphere suggestive of trickery, and some uneasiness was caused when her Captain professed his determination of putting to sea. Finally, however, on April 8, he handed the United States Collector at Newport News an application for internment. But already she had roused American indignation, for there landed from her the crew of an American four-masted sailing ship, *William P. Frye*.

That vessel had been captured by the *Prinz Eitel Friedrich* at the end of January in the South Atlantic off the South American coast. She was bound from Seattle for Queenstown with a cargo of wheat. Notwithstanding that the *William P. Frye* was American-owned, the German raider jettisoned part of the grain and then sent her to the bottom. It was an illegal act, yet eventually (and only after pressure) Germany was compelled to pay heavy recompense. There were two other aspects of this case. The first was to emphasize the contrast between the methods of the British Blockade (which sent suspected ships into port and there examined for contraband) on the one hand, and the ruthless behaviour by German cruisers on the other. But, secondly, the American public were so enraged because United States citizens had been taken prisoners and detained for six weeks that the anger against Britain's policy lost no little virulence.

The United States Government were hurt that Germany did not offer to indemnify the *William P. Frye's* owners, and sent a Note to the Kaiser's Government suggesting as reparation the sum of 228,060 dollars plus interest from the date of sinking. But, indeed, the whole transatlantic situation was now so completely muddled that the 10th Cruiser Squadron was less interfered with than might otherwise have been logically expected. For consider the following additional complications.

The United States was dependent on Germany for the supply of dye-stuffs, and was thus inconvenienced by the British Blockade. Conversely, Germany depended on the United States for cotton, out of which her propulsive ammunition was made. But on March 11, also, no less influential a person than Sir William Ramsay, supported by eleven other eminent chemists, began putting pressure on the British authorities to exclude all cotton from reaching the enemy. America insisted that since Britain had not declared a blockade, she could not capture cotton or any other goods in neutral ships destined for neutral territory. Did the belligerents rely upon the rules governing a blockade, or the rules which obtain when no blockade exists? And four days after March 11, Sir Edward Grey informed Ambassador Page that in order to alleviate the burden on neutral countries Britain would refrain from exercising the right to confiscate ships or cargoes which belligerents always had claimed in respect of the breaches of blockade. We would now stop only those cargoes which were destined to or from the enemy's country.

Nor was this three-sided international dispute made more simple when German-Americans suggested an astute scheme for defeating the blockade by sending food across the Atlantic into Germany through the Parcels Post. It was hoped that if the Allies interfered with the U.S.A. mails a *casus belli* would follow and at last President Wilson's nation would enter the War. Next came a protest from Count Bernstorff that the

United States Government had done nothing to enable American exporters to ship foodstuffs into Germany, yet still permitted arms and ammunition to reach the Allies. Surely, argued the Ambassador, that was a violation of any neutral spirit?

The American Government replied, this same April, that it had acknowledged the right of "visit and search", as well as of applying the rules of contraband to articles of commerce: in fact the U.S.A. had insisted on the use of "visit and search" as an essential safeguard against mistaking neutral vessels for those owned by the enemy. It had likewise admitted the right of blockade if actually exercised and effectively maintained; but nothing beyond these points had been conceded. And the munitions? Ah! The United States considered that the placing of an embargo on the trade in arms at the present time would constitute a change in America's laws of neutrality, and would be a direct violation of such neutrality.

One may admire the casuistry of all this, whilst reminding ourselves that at this date a number of submarines, many submarine-chasers, immense quantities of ammunition, were being fashioned (whole or in sections) by American labour for delivery to Britain's fighting forces. The honest verdict of posterity must be that each of the three parties was trying to square his conduct with principle, whilst finding that amid all this conflict of purpose a compromise was really impossible. And, with persistent Teutonic tactlessness, our late enemies seemed determined to prevent the United States from ever becoming their friends.

Late in this same April did Germany annoy America by the new Prize rules, which virtually meant the suppression of neutral trade in all seas where German warships could operate. "This exceeds anything attempted by the British Orders-in-Council." So the net result of the whole international imbroglio was that America continued to be kept aloof from belligerence, and financially it was to her advantage. If the big steel works were obtaining handsome contracts from the Allies, other American firms were doing more business with Germany and Austria than at any previous date—though indirectly and circuitously. I have refrained in these chapters from parading dull statistics, but the following comparison of figures eloquently shows that whilst £3,131 represents the value of American goods which reached Germany during March 1915 *direct*, vast quantities must have travelled indirectly via Germany's neighbours.

COMPARATIVE TABLE SHOWING AMERICAN EXPORTS TO GERMANY'S NEIGHBOURS DURING MARCH 1914 AND MARCH 1915.

EXPORTED TO WHICH COUNTRY	DURING MARCH 1914	DURING MARCH 1915
Netherlands . .	£898,240	£1,922,263
Sweden . . .	£128,815	£1,544,371
Norway . . .	£108,270	£548,017
Denmark . . .	£93,302	£1,084,292

We mentioned on a previous page how essential American cotton was for the manufacture of Germany's explosives ; but it was needed for a dozen other purposes besides. In that vast national effort of German Armies, their transport, equipment, and so forth, it were easier to show where this transatlantic thread was not used than to total the numerous categories under which it continued indispensable. Cotton was required for the air-brakes of German railways' rolling stock, for the manufacture of motor-car tyres, for agricultural machinery, for the leather driving-belts in the factories, for the insulating cables which carried electric power. Cotton was as much part of the asbestos, which covered boilers, as it was an essential part in the manufacture of Army clothing, bedding, ground-sheets, tents, mackintoshes, tarpaulins, trench waders, and even the very linings of soldiers' boots. But, in spite of all this, so fearful were we of causing offence to America that we had expressed our intention of not placing cotton in the list of contraband.

The Southern States, where this commodity was grown, waxed indignant when any suggestion showed itself in the Press or Parliament that cotton trade through the Blockade ought to be thwarted. We were accused of being over-cautious and nervous, yet it is quite evident from the following figures that European neutrals must suddenly have discovered a much greater need for cotton lately, unless they were acting as the intermediaries of Austria and Germany.

COMPARATIVE TABLE SHOWING AMOUNT OF AMERICAN COTTON EXPORTED
TO GERMANY'S NEIGHBOURS DURING, RESPECTIVELY, THE FIRST NINE
MONTHS OF WAR AND THE PRECEDING TWELVE MONTHS.

EXPORTED TO WHAT COUNTRY	TOTAL BALES OF COTTON FROM AUGUST, 1914, TO APRIL 30, 1915	TOTAL BALES DURING PRECEDING TWELVE MONTHS
Netherlands . .	419,370	105,000
Sweden . . .	747,630	100,000
Norway . . .	125,510	13,689
Denmark . . .	65,830	27,500

That is to say, these four countries in nine months had imported over a million bales of cotton more than they had consumed during the whole previous year. Need we any stronger evidence as to how the endeavours of our Blockading Fleet were being limited at this date ?

CHAPTER VIII

ONE of the earliest effects of the War's outbreak was the determination of certain German shipowners to carry on business as usual by changing the registry of their vessels. And at one time it looked as if the chance had returned to America of acquiring that unique position among the world's Merchant Navies which she had possessed at the outbreak of her Civil War.

Under an Act of August 1914 no fewer than 111 foreign vessels, representing 400,000 tons, were admitted to United States registry. Among them was the S.S. *Dacia*, which had been owned by the Hamburg-Amerika Line and was formerly engaged carrying cotton from New Orleans and the Gulf ports to Bremen ; but, seeing the approaching trouble that was overcoming Europe, she sought the security of American jurisdiction and was interned at Port Arthur, Texas, where she remained during the first five months. She was then purchased by a Mr. Edward N. Breitung, an American citizen of Michigan, the son of a German who was once a member of Congress. The family fortune had been made out of copper mining, and this was the first venture in ocean shipping.

The *Dacia*, having changed her nationality and flag, was sent forth on what must become a unique trial voyage. She carried a cargo of cotton intended for Bremen ; but would the Allies permit her to reach that port ? The Government of the United States fully realized the delicate problem which such a voyage would create, yet the President and his advisers were not unwilling to have the validity of American registry law tested, and to see exactly the status which belonged to that considerable number of German merchant ships now interned at American ports.

There was no secrecy about *Dacia's* departure, nor had public opinion the slightest doubt that she would never reach the North Sea ; long before that was sighted she would have been held up by a patrol, conducted into a British port, and then placed in the Prize Court. If, however, the *Dacia* did get through, she would be only the first of many. A syndicate of American bankers and shipping men were prepared to purchase and transfer to this neutral flag other interned German steamers and send them to Bremen also with cotton. The whole civilized world stood by expectant. If the British patrols should detain her at this critical period of American sentiment, then who could say what serious sequel might not speedily follow ? One thing was very certain, and the British Government made it plain : they declined to recognize the validity of this transfer.

It was on February 1 that *Dacia* sailed from Galveston with 11,000 bales valued at £176,000, and it was consigned for reshipment at Rotterdam for Bremen. Such a large cargo of cotton would receive the heartiest welcome in Germany, as may be gathered from the expense that was being risked. The freight rate was $3.50 per bale—the highest rate that had ever been paid—and the American State Insurance Department had been cautious enough not to accept such a risk as *Dacia* indicated. For Britain was not alone : both France and Russia had intimated their opposition to the transfer of belligerent-owned ships from their original registry to American. As early in the War as November 9 Britain and France had signed a convention regarding the subject of prizes which might be seized, so there was complete unanimity among the Allies.

The patrols were warned, both north and south. As to the latter, we may conveniently refer at this stage to the excellent work which was being done at the eastern end of the English Channel. This bottle-neck is naturally restricted by Nature having presented us with the Goodwin Sands, but at the beginning of the War a British minefield had also been laid and announced. The latter was really inefficient ; the mines soon got adrift and scattered themselves along the

Dutch coast, where seaside residents found that by cutting them in two these dark "eggs" became useful for growing plants. But the moral effect of the alleged danger area survived for many a long day, and neutral vessels were easily shepherded into the Downs, where the search for contraband was carried on vigorously.

The Drifters of the Downs Boarding Flotilla certainly had a busy time, frequently examining eighty vessels a day, but this was under conditions far more comfortable than would have been possible at sea to the north of Scotland. For centuries the Downs had owned a reputation as an anchorage for sailing ships, nor was a neutral steamer under the conditions of modern warfare unduly endangered, except when U-boats lurked. This southern counterpart of the Northern Blockade was very thorough, and experts went very carefully through passengers' luggage, the cargoes, and even the coalbunkers (where more than one German stowaway was discovered). The examining officers were in close touch by telegraph with the Contraband Committee in London, who were able to make quick decisions after details as to cargo, consignor, and consignee had been flashed up to London. Most of the principal neutral shipowners by March, at least, had agreed to call either at the Downs or at Kirkwall; for such a proceeding was to their own advantage: it prevented the delay of having to be fetched in from some distant point of their course, it saved waste of coal, and, in the case of any vessel not trying to deceive, it all tended to smooth working. Some of the more elusive and notorious liners up north were not over-conscientious in respecting such an undertaking; but in the Dover Straits there were too many torpedo craft and armed units of the Auxiliary Patrol for any evasiveness to be tolerated through the narrow sea.

In the Foreign Office, by the creation of various new committees, whose fingers were always in touch with a comprehensive card-index system of facts, there was now in existence a vast Blockade bureau which had to be satisfied before an intercepted neutral could pass. Thus from early in 1915 a careful account was kept of the important commodities which were being sent into neutral countries; and if these figures rose well above the normal, then there was cause for confiscation. The War Trade Statistical Department, an Intelligence Department, an Enemy Exports Committee, were but the forerunners of other highly specialized sections.

By mid-February the *Dacia* suspense was becoming acute, and it was not known whether she would prefer to attempt the English Channel route rather than the north-about passage. But suddenly it became apparent that more than one of these ex-enemy steamers was trying the same experiment. On February 16 the 10th Cruiser Squadron encountered the first, when *Changuinola* intercepted the American oil-tanker *Pioneer* of New York. The latter's Captain, a United States citizen, did his best to rush Patrol "C", but the *Changuinola* was too vigilant for him and sent off a boarding party. The result of that visit was to provide the following interesting facts. The *Pioneer's* present owners were the Standard Oil Company ; she was carrying a cargo of petrol to Gothenburg (Sweden) and Copenhagen ; but this steamer until recently had been the German *Kiow* of Hamburg, and she was making her first voyage under the American flag, having changed her registry since the outbreak of the war. So she was taken into Kirkwall with a prize crew.

Five days after this incident came another episode, when the *Hilary* (also of Patrol "C") intercepted the American S.S. *Cushing* carrying petroleum. Now the *Cushing* was a German vessel down to October 14 last, and, in accordance with the Allied policy just mentioned, the transfer of registry could not be recognized, so into Kirkwall she went likewise. The next of these events occurred on February 25, when the *Ambrose* on Patrol "D" stopped the American S.S. *Denver*, which was carrying a cargo of cotton from Norfolk (Virginia) for Bremen, and we have here a perfect example of the anomalous condition in affairs. The *Denver* had reason to consider herself treated with harshness ; for Britain had not yet dared to designate cotton as contraband. Furthermore, she had been given a certificate from the British Consul, before leaving Norfolk, stating that of contraband she carried none.

Nevertheless, every British subject outside the Foreign

Office, seaman or scientist, business man or munition-maker, saw the utter folly and lack of logic in allowing Bremen to receive all these bales that would presently be used against the Allied armies. There have been occasions in history when naval officers have, either literally or metaphorically, turned a blind eye. Admiral de Chair with his great fleet was charged with the duty of exerting commercial pressure on the enemy. Then, of all products, why should he give facilities for the passage of cotton ? He acted precisely as Nelson would have done under the circumstances : ignored the seals and consular certificates, and made no exception to the rule that all vessels using the north-about route must call at Kirkwall, either voluntarily, or with prize crews. One may argue that this was irregular procedure, and no doubt it was ; yet the 10th Cruiser Squadron had been from the first committed by the force of circumstances to unprecedented practices.

Here was the greatest of all blockades, yet officially it was not a blockade. Here were ships being rightly subject to "visit and search", and no neutral could object, no international lawyer could cavil up to that point. In previous wars, however, this had been always done at sea. Strictly, and legally speaking, we had no right to send neutrals for that purpose into Kirkwall, or any other harbour ; yet it was so justified on the basis of practical common sense that this precedent will be adopted in future naval wars. But why ? Because a modern cargo or passenger steamer is a much bigger and more complicated affair than one of the old sailing ships. If, for example, you wanted to see the contents of a 900-ton three-master in the olden days, it was a fairly straightforward job. In the twentieth-century war there was a great diversity of cargo ; much of it would have to be brought up on deck for closer examination, and steam winches used. If there were any sea running, and the ship rolling about, these cotton bales or packages must incur damage. The inspection can be better made to the satisfaction of everyone if that ship is anchored within some sheltered harbour.

Moreover, a ship's papers have become more detailed nowadays, and need longer time for checking. And how are you going to search effectively among the bunkers for stowaways, or make sure that some German Reservist is not hiding in an oil tank, with only his head showing because he can hold his breath no longer ?   If passengers and crew are to be lined up and checked according to the lists, their baggage gone through, and the secret recesses of the steamer rummaged conscientiously, can it be done elsewhere than at anchor ?   Surely, if the principle of "visit and search" be once conceded, there can be little reasonable objection to this being executed under the convenience which is provided only by a port ?   And there was yet another justification for the Kirkwall requirement.   At any moment out of the mist might burst a German raider having the general appearance, the markings, the flag, of a neutral.   Down would fall flaps, flag, and external disguise ; shells and torpedoes would endanger examiners and examinees.   Or from out of the sea would poke a periscope's head, and the same kind of slaughter would ensue.

So Kirkwall continued to become the chief clearing-station of the Blockade, and Stornoway was used at this period only when west-bound ships were suspected of being minelayers or acting as tenders to U-boats.

Now whilst the *Denver* imparted the news that *Dacia* was only 200 miles astern of her, and our Northern Patrols were most carefully formed so that this much desired steamer should not get through our lines, the ex-German was to rob the 10th Cruiser Squadron of her presence.   The Press and public opinion on both sides of the Atlantic had become so worked up as to what Britain would do to *Dacia* that the above-mentioned recently registered steamers would have demanded little attention had the popular mind known of their existence.   And then followed the big joke, which in one action took away all possibility of an Anglo-American crisis, disappointed the sensationalists, but settled the problem definitely without international offence.   For it was to the English Channel that *Dacia* steamed, and, with clever prudence, the British authorities arranged with France that one of her warships should be the interceptor.   So the cotton never reached Germany after all, the *Dacia* was taken into a French port, and without waste of time a commission tried the case.   On March 23, 1915, the verdict came that the seizure of *Dacia* was valid.   Another crisis thus vanished, and the Big Blockade got on with its work.

For the ships of the 10th Cruiser Squadron it was always a grave inconvenience when a prize crew had to be provided. During the month of February it was not exceptional if 18 prize crews were away at one particular time, and this absence meant a serious depletion.   Some would be from one ship, some from another, yet not necessarily from the same patrol line.   The difficulty was to collect all these officers and men after their arrival in the Orkneys and redistribute them back to their respective vessels ; the problem was intensified not only by the long distances but by the intolerable weather. When the Armed Boarding Steamer *Caesarea* was now allotted this job, a long-felt want became filled, yet not even she could perform impossibilities, and sometimes it was days before this vessel could leave port.   At last she would brave the conditions, reach the rendezvous, find the seas so bad that no boat could be lowered, and then back she must steam to port.

In the meanwhile perhaps temporarily the gales would ease up and the waves die down enough to allow boarding to be resumed, so the same work had to be done with fewer men.   But there could be no relaxation of vigilance, for the Norske Amerika liners were still doing their best to slip through with contraband, and the S.S. *Trondhjemsfjord*, on February 13, did her best to avoid our patrols by passing north of the Faroes, with not the slightest intention of calling into Kirkwall. However, she was intercepted, and it was found that the cargo which she was bringing from America included fuses as well as detonators.   Needless to say, she was now sent into Kirkwall with a prize crew.   A careful look-out was also being kept for the Danish *Oscar II*.   This twin-screw liner of 9,996 tons, owned at Copenhagen, must not be confused with the single-screw Swedish *Oscar II* of 3,403 tons, owned at Stockholm, that will be duly mentioned.

Now the Danish *Oscar II* had left New York on February 4 bound for Norway and Copenhagen, and the 10th Cruiser Squadron had reasons for making a more intimate acquaintance with her.   The strategical scheme to entrap her is interesting and illuminative ; for, as she came within that

BOARDING A BARQUE IN FINE WEATHER

BOARDING ON XMAS DAY

area between the north of Scotland and south of the Faroes, she began sending wireless messages across to Norway, which also were picked up by the Blockaders. From these radiograms Admiral de Chair rather gathered that she had succeeded in slipping through Patrol "C". He accordingly shifted Patrol "B" during the night of Saturday-Sunday (February 13–14) some forty miles to the eastward. This had a most satisfactory result, for the *Cedric* sighted the *Oscar* in the distance, chased her, and after four hours captured the Dane at 3 a.m. in lat. 61° N., long. 1°20' W., that is to say, north-east of the Shetlands.

Although this steamer belonged to one of the lines which were to use the north-about route on the understanding that their vessels would call at Kirkwall first, it was quite obvious that she had not the slightest intention of so complying. She was thus taken into that anchorage for compulsory examination, although her Master made a protest in writing. Among the many passengers on board were several who were supposed to be travelling under assumed names lest their identity as German Reservists might be revealed. The expert searchers got to work, did their job with thoroughness, and after a few days she was allowed to proceed, finally reaching Copenhagen on February 20.

This necessary interference of neutrals, and their temporary detention in Kirkwall, continued to irritate America considerably. Perhaps the ablest expression of this feeling is to be found in a volume published that year in New York and entitled *American Rights and British Pretensions*, a well-documented expression of contemporary indignation ; but it is necessary to quote only one passage to show how deeply the United States were moved. "The Government of Great Britain", declared the writer, "has virtually set up in the midst of the busy seas an arbitrary court, claiming unheard-of powers and exercising the most tyrannous police functions".[1] But, for all that, these high sea "police functions" were indispensable, unless the Blockade was to be the farce which in the beginning it threatened to become. Of the *Oscar's* further evasiveness we shall have something to add later,

---

[1] *American Rights and British Pretensions on the Seas.* By W. B. Hayle. New York, 1915.

H

but on that same Sunday just mentioned came a small incident demonstrating that only by means of stopping, boarding, and subsequent examination in quiet waters could the enemy be deprived of men or goods.

During the afternoon it fell to the lot of *Alsatian* that she should sight in a position between the Faroes and Shetlands a Norwegian sailing ship named *Olav*, of 1,576 tons. She had left Rosario on November 21 with 1,672 tons of bran made up in bags, bound for the two Danish ports of Aarhus and Aalborg, though there could be little doubt that the ultimate destination was German; and, indeed, her Norwegian Master was quite sure such was the case. Ocean sailing vessels at this date were steadily becoming more rare, and the *Olav*, with her weather-stained canvas, and her fore topmast split through banging about against the lower topsail yard, was a picturesque if pathetic sight. But she must certainly be sent into Kirkwall—there could be no alternative. Her second mate, Herman Voigt, turned out to be a German, and was just the fine type of sailor whom the U-boats, or the raiders, would soon be delighted to welcome. So he, at least, was stopped from reaching his country. Two young Austrians were also found, and they, of course, had to be removed.

It was on the following day that the *Bayano*, whilst patrolling north-west of the Hebrides, sighted a ship's grey-painted lifeboat, and, though the name was missing, it seems pretty certain this once belonged to the unfortunate *Clan Macnaughton*. Nor did the winter gales, with snow and hail and white-crested wave-tops, exhibit any mercy. On one of these naval occasions the *Caribbean* rolled so heavily that her foremost funnel shifted. The extent of her oscillation was something quite remarkable, and by means of a pendulum on board she registered 50° with her lee roll, which actually brought her gunwale under, and this, it will be remembered, was a vessel of more than 8,000 tons. How much more than 50° she swung backwards and forwards cannot be ascertained, for that figure was as far as the instrument registered; but, whilst the ship recovered quickly each time this alarming list ended, it was quite serious enough. Nor was the weather content with its influence on ships themselves. Officers and men, however much they sought to disguise the fact, undeniably began to feel the strain of vigilance, the penalty of nursing their vessels through persistent cold and wet. Thus it chanced that the *Patuca's* Captain, Commander France-Hayhurst, R.N., had to enter hospital when his ship came into the Clyde, and he died in Glasgow before the end of February.

There was no small moral courage shown by everyone during those dark, cheerless days and unending nights in maintaining a will to win. Yet not all the discouragement came from sea and sky. Did those people in their well-warmed Whitehall offices, who never went afloat throughout the whole War, but smoked their pipes and sat in comfortable chairs, ever realize the moral effect of hindering rather than encouraging this silent Squadron of the icy north? Did they appreciate how dispiriting it was that after the *Teutonic* had intercepted a Danish steamer from New York, with 99 German passengers on board, including a judge and a Governor from New Guinea, the bureaucrats negatived the patrol's efforts and allowed the Dane to proceed? And, as if all this was not bad enough, there was a coal strike in Liverpool whilst the *Cedric* was in for refuelling, so she had to leave for her patrol with 800 tons of coal short.

Three days after the death of Commander France-Hayhurst his former shipmates were having a busy and anxious time. *Patuca* was out on that wild Patrol "D", which at this period stretched away from St. Kilda's lonely isle in a north-westerly direction. It was just before 2.30 a.m. on a bitter February night when she sighted the American S.S. *Navahoe* bound from Bremen for Norfolk (Virginia), steering west. The *Navahoe's* Master was just as skilful in the art of blockade-running as were the Scandinavians or Danes. He knew their technique, but he had one or two methods that were all his own. One consisted in the use of lights. Every landsman knows that in addition to her starboard and port sidelights a steamer under way must exhibit a white light on her fore-mast, and, if she is not less than 150 feet in length, a second white light as well. A sailing ship under way exhibits only sidelights. Now when the *Patuca* first sighted *Navahoe*, the latter was showing her sidelights, but none other : she was pretending to be a sailing ship. For her own self-preservation against collision she was indicating her presence though falsifying her character. However, if she liked to take such a risk and disregard the international regulations, she might have some difficulty in settling matters with the insurance company should an accident occur.

On the other hand, *Navahoe* was nearly through the last Blockade line, and with a little more luck she might have got clear. When *Patuca* loomed up, *Navahoe* swung round 16 points and headed back eastward. But the patrol gave chase, overhauled and stopped her. The Atlantic was in one of its ugly moods, and would not allow a boat to be lowered, so *Patuca* signalled the stranger to follow under the lee of St. Kilda, where examination of papers might be transacted. Curiously, just at this moment the *Navahoe* reported that her condenser was broken and would need three hours for repair, but presently she made a more defiant signal, which read thus : "Condenser ready. No contraband. Refuse to follow you."

Patuca was not to be put off, and the Admiral wirelessed her to hold the *Navahoe* until the weather moderated, to board and examine her when possible. The dreary day drew towards its close, the north-west gale had no inclination to die down, the waves were still terrible, when at 5 p.m. the *Navahoe* deemed it better to submit to examination and not roll about here any longer ; so she made the signal "Lead", and the *Patuca* now led her to St. Kilda. This is not much of an anchorage, but a limited amount of shelter was possible from the gale, and *Patuca* lowered away her boat. The latter safely reached the *Navahoe's* side, when there exploded a very heavy squall, so that the boat was swamped and had to be cut adrift, though the Boarding Officers and crew managed to climb aboard the steamer. No lives had been lost.

The *Patuca* then took *Navahoe* 33 miles north of St. Kilda and there hove-to, but an examination under those conditions was impossible, and proved the wisdom of the practice already introduced during this present war, of exercising the right of "visit and search" within harbour. The gale and spray prevented the hatches being lifted for inspection of cargo, and the American would shortly require both drinking and boiler water ; so the incident concluded with both ships steaming to Stornoway, where the examination was made conveniently in shelter.   Her suspicious character, suggested by the irregular behaviour at first meeting, was not confirmed : she was neither a minelayer, nor an oil-carrier for U-boats, but was in ballast. So that affair passed with no further advantage except the important result that neutrals were now appreciating a powerful factor : the Blockade was a reality which had to be faced, and no amount of bluff could avail.

It was rough on the boarding parties' uniforms when these open-sea visitations had to be made, and the Admiral asked the Admiralty that a special hard-lying allowance might be made on that account.   These boatloads were the people who came in personal contact with non-belligerents and brought to neutrals the individual application of the Orders-in-Council.

The eternal wonder is that so few boats and lives were lost even during the worst months of winter.   Next to these specialists must be mentioned the wireless operators and the coding staff, whose work was as important as it was onerous. For the Blockading Fleet was akin to a vast spider's web extending from Iceland north and south, east and west. Each unit had to keep listening-in, not merely to the Admiral, but to each other and to approaching neutral steamers.   The Navy could not afford to lend its own wireless personnel, so young Marconi operators had joined up, and soon became invaluable.

From time to time the wireless signals of neutrals eastward bound, and talking between themselves, were intercepted by the Blockaders with no little satisfaction.   The Americans were especially communicative in giving across the ether their position and destination, such valuable data generally leading to their capture. The Danish S.S. *Frederik VIII*, a fine new 11,850-tons American liner owned by the same firm to which the *Oscar II* belonged, gave herself away badly on March 5 when homeward-bound. She was heard, twenty-four hours before being met with, calling up her owners, so the patrols were ready waiting, and at 3.15 a.m. of the following day the *Virginian* went off in pursuit. After less than two hours' steaming she brought *Frederik VIII* to a halt. The latter was at once boarded and examined. Nor was the visit altogether useless.

The neighbourhood of the Faroes on a cold, leaden March morning at five o'clock is not the cheeriest environment for passengers to change their habitation ; but war is war, and far too many Teutons had been allowed to reach Europe from America. In the course of the *Virginian's* inspection one obvious German who answered to the name of Schmidt, aged 65, was arrested and removed. With him also was brought a passenger who said his name was Lang and claimed to be a Russian Finn. Unfortunately for him he had no passport, was unable to speak any Russian, but what he did say was uttered with a strong German accent, so it was better that his voyage should end right now.[1]

At this date Kirkwall, which was of increasing importance to the Blockade, remained under the care of a retired naval officer. Commander W. L. Down, nominally, was King's Harbour Master, but in addition exercised the functions of Examining Officer, Senior Naval Officer, Censor, and Referee in all international disputes. Probably not even Lord Stowell ever possessed a wider practical knowledge of Prizes. It was a busy life working from 7 a.m. till 2 a.m. the next day, and sometimes even longer, but with very little assistance. Whilst the number of detained vessels not rarely amounted to 18, representing some 40,000 tons, yet there was a steady coming and going : it was not exceptional for 14 to be cleared and seven more arrive in the same day.

Each of these neutrals would be personally visited by him and details telegraphed, followed by a fuller report. Two keen, hard-working, experienced Customs Officers performed the actual examination work, and they came alongside in drifters. But the drawback was that all control was centred in London. Neither Commander Down nor the Customs Officers had their hands free : at best their work was that of registrars and superficial detectives. The cargoes could not be examined with thoroughness, though crews and passengers

---

[1] The reader is reminded that a photograph of *Frederik VIII* appears in Chapter IV.

were interrogated. Time was short, neutral steamers must not be delayed unreasonably ; yet in the Scandinavian or Danish liners carrying 600 or 800 passengers there was opportunity to select only the suspicious cases, to obtain the assistance of friendly people in tracing those who spoke German or had distinct national characteristics. At least a couple of days were needed for such inspection, and twice that period would not have been excessive ; yet Whitehall was so fearful of offending neutral feelings, and wires came pouring in that Kirkwall was to hurry up the steamers' departures. Why so very few of the latter were not put into the Prize Court, complained one officer, "is a mystery to me and to the men who command them". Then Whitehall would defend its own action by declaring that no such vessel had been suffered to proceed until stringent guarantees had been received that the cargoes were not intended for Germany. It was very difficult to convince those who went aboard oil-tankers, and such steamers as the *Trondhjemsfjord* (carrying a million detonators), that Germany was not the ultimate destination.

Such was the typical British muddling-through method as applied to the Blockade in its first phases, so the patrols went on with their jobs, pitching and rolling to the gales. The *Alsatian* would notice one of her sisters, such as the *Digby*, jumping about so skittishly as to reveal alternately forefoot and propellers. Medium-sized Norwegian tramps would be encountered bucketing into the waves, and then would appear a British steam trawler white with frozen spray bound back to Grimsby from the Iceland fishing grounds, and hoping not to be torpedoed before gaining the Humber. On the last night of February even the stately *Alsatian* rolled across the stars 25° each way, so that the contents of most cabins were continuously on the move and no one got much chance of sleep.

No wonder that the Lords Commissioners of the Admiralty and the Commander-in-Chief of the Grand Fleet now expressed their appreciation of the work which the 10th Cruiser Squadron was performing in spite of the arduous conditions. In one month out of 122 ships intercepted, of which 43 had been sent into Kirkwall, and 79 allowed to proceed, there had been not a single instance of any vessel being missed by the patrol when such a stranger's interception was desired. And when one thinks of all the northern sea expanse covered during most of the twenty-four hours by darkness or mist, one may well say that in the annals of naval warfare there never was a blockade like this.

CHAPTER IX

By the time Germany inaugurated her Submarine Blockade in February the more enterprising of the U-Boat Captains had realized that the British Dover minefield and the line of drifters' nets need not be taken too seriously. With just reasonable care the Dover Straits could be safely negotiated. For those mines which still survived were generally visible on the surface, their firing mechanism was defective, and in any case these dark objects could be avoided. As to the nets, there was always a sag rather than a rigid line, and they had a tendency to become tangled up at the change of the tidal stream which runs pretty strongly in the Straits; so a determined submarine officer had only to lie on the sea-bed north of the Ruytingen Bank till dark, and then cross the nets. He would so time his attempt that the first of the down-Channel tide coincided with midnight or the early hours before sunrise.

There were periods, however, when the Straits rather frightened the enemy. On March 4, for example, U-8, after successfully passing through the defile whilst westward-bound, got tangled up in the drifter *Robur's* nets, and was hunted by Dover destroyers till the German crew were compelled to surrender and the submarine sank. During this same spring drifters were towing their nets also across the North Channel, that narrow neck between Ireland and Scotland which Admiral de Chair's vessels had to negotiate before or after reaching Liverpool.

But the North Sea was much simpler for enemy submarines, and their activities were less restricted. On March 10, U-12 was rammed and sunk by the destroyer *Ariel* outside the Firth of Forth, after the former had been operating as far north as Peterhead. That month also saw a visit up the North Sea by Commander Weddigen, Germany's greatest submarine hero. It was he who last autumn had in U-9 sunk the three "Cressys", and now was in command of U-29. But his career was quickly ended when H.M.S. *Dreadnought* sent his craft with all hands to the bottom.

The unsettling truth had to be faced that German submersibles were now coming with their torpedoes to most parts of the British Isles. U-34 and U-35 had penetrated the Dover Straits, and not even were the seas around Ireland to be regarded as beyond the limits of the enemy's radius. Thus double-handed destiny was creeping towards the Blockade, up and up on the east as well as on the west side of Great Britain. Could it be that within a short time the Blockade lines would find themselves wiped out by the invisible U-boats and the northern seas made so dangerous that no patrols could hinder contraband from reaching Germany's ports?

The first shock occurred on March 11—that important date of the "reprisals" Order-in-Council which was to tighten up the British Blockade by way of reply to Germany's submarine campaign. Admiral de Chair had brought the *Alsatian* through the North Channel into Liverpool three days previously. The flagship was now giving leave and coaling, when the startling news came that the *Bayano*, which had left the Clyde the previous night, had been sunk this morning at 5.15, ten miles S.E. by E. of Corsewall Point. This locality is at the southern end of the Firth of Clyde; but on the Scottish side of the North Channel where those straits are but 25 miles wide.

H.M.S. *Bayano* was the first of the new 10th Cruiser Squadron of armed merchantmen to be lost in the same manner as H.M.S. *Hawke*. Steaming from her base with lights out, this ex-Elders & Fyffes steamer went down with nearly all hands. Her second-in-command, Lieut.-Commander K. A. F. Guy, who previously had similarly served in the *Hawke's* sister *Edgar*, was fortunately saved, together with seven other officers and men; they were picked up and landed by the auxiliary cruiser *Tara*. Eighteen petty officers and men were picked up by the S.S. *Balmerino* and landed at Ayr, but about 200 lives perished that night.

The *Bayano* was proceeding slowly, yet the night was so dark that one could not see across the deck. Thus it was impossible to discern the submarine which was lying on the surface, stopped and waiting. All that the German had to do was simple : she just remained till the dark mass of 5,948 tons steamed alongside, and then the target was so easy that the *Bayano* was torpedoed amidships and went down in four minutes. The same morning the S.S. *Castlereagh*, of Belfast, steamed through quantities of wreckage and dead sailormen still floating in their lifebelts. Captain McGarrick took the *Castlereagh* for some time out of her course, hoping in his search to find some poor fellow clinging to life ; but the U-boat was still on the spot, and now for twenty minutes chased the *Castlereagh* away. On this same March 11, H.M.S. *Ambrose*, another of the Squadron, was on her way towards Liverpool, when she had an exciting encounter off Oversay Island.

Commander Bruton found himself attacked by at least one submarine, if not two. One torpedo was followed by another, and then 400 yards on the port quarter appeared a U-boat's conning-tower. Fire was at once opened from the *Ambrose's* guns, and after eight or nine rounds it seemed as if the enemy were hit, but nothing more was observed other than a thick oily spray which seemed to indicate that she had been wounded. The *Ambrose* had escaped death only by skilful ship-handling, for the Booth liner could do no better than 14 knots at her best ; but luckily the weather happened to be favourable for good steaming, and she came safely up the Mersey the following day.

The enemy's submarines had wasted no time in answering the Order-in-Council. Not merely was the Blockade definitely weakened by the loss of a unit, but temporarily by the detention of four others. In consequence of the danger that waited off the Firth, orders were given that the *Digby*, *Hildebrand*, *Changuinola*, and *Patia* (who had all accumulated up the Clyde) must not come out till the Admiralty allowed. By the 15th all danger appeared to have passed, and the *Digby* steamed out to resume her patrol. She got clear of the North

Channel, carried on to the north-west beyond the coast, and everything seemed good, when suddenly a submarine showed itself. The position was 25 miles south of that lonely Skerryvore Rock which lies south-west of the Inner Hebrides, and the German had chosen her outpost with ability. It was well placed for entrapping both those vessels which were using the Clyde and those which would be bound via the Minch. Admiralty colliers, store-ships, men-of-war on their way to Scapa Flow, units of the Blockading Fleet returning from their coaling bases—in fact all sorts of types and sizes might be expected as targets.

The *Digby* (14.5 knots) managed to escape by firing with her gun, and took temporary refuge in Tobermory Harbour, whither a destroyer escort was sent from Larne, so that on the following day this Furness-Withy steamer got back on her patrol. Similarly, when the *Alsatian* came out of Liverpool at midnight a week later, and went hurrying along at 18 knots, she was met by the destroyer *Dove*, who escorted her through the North Channel till well past Rathlin Island. Some officers who had possessed themselves, whilst on leave, of a patent life-saving waistcoat now thought this opportunity for wearing it should not be missed, But, fortunately, the flagship got back to her northern mists uneventfully. Now to-day we can piece together some of the details as seen from the other side, and it is worth noting that already two of the most enterprising German young officers had between them put a girdle round Great Britain. It was on February 25 that U-20 (Lieut.-Commander Schweiger) and U-27 (Lieut.-Commander Wegener) both started from the Ems on blockade duty. The former proceeded via Dover Straits, down past Land's End, up the Irish Sea, and thus to west Scottish waters. The latter reached the same area, but by the other route—round the north of Scotland, Cape Wrath, through the Minch—and she it was who torpedoed the *Bayano*.

These two submarines thus became specialists as regards the Irish area, and we may conveniently add by anticipation that U-20 on May 7 (only a few weeks later) sent the *Lusitania* to her doom, whilst on the following August 19, U-27 was sunk off the south Irish coast by the Q-ship *Baralong* in one of the most celebrated duels of all naval history, when Wegener perished[1] together with his crew. Thus was the loss of *Bayano* avenged.

The alarming results of these two submarines' visits during March to an area so far distant from Germany brought to the imagination a probability that this strange contest between the British and German Blockades would presently produce similar disasters. The weakest feature of the whole 10th Cruiser Squadron organization was centralized in that passage between Rathlin Island and the Mull of Cantyre; or, more broadly, the approaches to both the Clyde and Liverpool. If, therefore, some other coaling base could be selected nearer to the patrol areas, these visits to the Mersey and Clyde would be only rare occasions. The question was now examined, and with what conclusion we shall presently observe.

But, before we pass on, there is still one more incident which belongs to that couple of anxious days March 11–12, and it illustrates another of the difficulties which had to be faced. The Danish S.S. *Canadia,* on her voyage from Galveston, Texas, with a cargo of cotton and flour, *nominally* for Christiania and Gothenburg, was stopped by the *Hilary* on March 11. A prize crew, consisting of Lieut. Herbert Spencer, R.N.R., and six men, were sent on board to take her into Kirkwall, and for that reason a course was first set to the east until the north of Fair Island should be sighted, whence a southerly course would bring the *Canadia* off the Orkneys. Unfortunately the weather became thick on the 12th, but at 7.10 p.m. Lieut. Spencer reckoned that he must have passed Fair Island, so altered course to the south-east. Navigation was always difficult in those waters, and I have before me a letter from the Captain of a ship in the 10th Cruiser Squadron (now an Admiral) who from the time he was Sub-Lieutenant till he was promoted Captain was a navigating specialist; yet he experienced great difficulty during the Blockade. "We found ourselves nearer the shore than we thought we were more than once. I remember one nasty night in the neighbourhood of Greenland during a snowstorm, not too sure of our position and sounding as a precaution, although I knew it was

---

[1] For full details see Chapter VIII of my *Gallant Gentlemen.*

practically of no use. I was very glad when I could turn away from the land again !"

So it was with Lieut. Spencer in the *Canadia*. He took soundings, but, owing to the nature of the sea-bed, they were of little value, and suddenly, at 8.45 p.m., the land revealed itself so close ahead that the ship struck. It was still Fair Island ; he had not yet cleared the latter. The net result was that *Canadia* became a total loss, but, thanks to Lieut. Spencer's seamanship and coolness in danger, both the ship's crew and the prize crew were saved. It should be added that the only chart on board was a small-scale one which the Danish Master had been using. The Prize Officer had to rely on the ship's dead reckoning, and the Master's statement that the *Canadia* was doing 9$\frac{1}{2}$ knots. As a matter of fact she was doing about 7 knots, so that when the turn was made to the south-east she must needs hit the very land she had sought to avoid. Spencer was a very able officer, and this accident did not prevent his receiving the Distinguished Service Cross a few weeks later ; but a curious situation arose legally. The *Canadia* became a total loss, the case went into the Prize Court, and judgment was not delivered until April 1922, when Lord Phillimore declared that after all the *Canadia's* cargo did not consist of contraband !

The increasing number of vessels now being sent into Kirkwall as a result of the Order-in-Council of March 11 caused a serious depletion in the ships' companies, so that prize crews had sometimes to be provided by units not actually taking part in the capture. On Lady Day no fewer than eleven steamers were intercepted, of which seven were sent into Kirkwall. The loss of *Bayano* was not the only weakening of cruiser strength, for now it was decided to pay off both the *Calyx* and *Eskimo*, neither of which had been man enough for the rough job. That they had survived the worst part of the winter was remarkable, though we have seen from the former's commanding officer how nearly *Calyx* was lost at Christmas-time. But the final scene of *Calyx* was set in extraordinary optimism. On her way south from Rosyth to the Humber, before being handed over to her owners in Hull, Captain Wardle took a pilot. The latter must certainly have been hope personified. Matters were not going too well on the Western Front, the submarine menace was developing ominously, and the general outlook this March was one of apprehension. But that stolid Yorkshire pilot confessed he had taken four tickets at £7 each, entitling him to a tour of the French battlefields, provided the War should finish by August. If hostilities were not over by then, half the money was to be refunded.

Perhaps it was as well that the pilot could not foresee that during the next three and a half years the enemy's Submarine Blockade only just failed to win the War, and that Zeppelins should come over the Humber dropping death into Hull.

The new Order-in-Council on the one hand, and the more daring adventures of U-boats on the other, caused a quickening of pace from this spring : it was to be a fight to a finish, and that finish was starvation. The only question was in regard to the victim's identity. Would Britain really be able to close the door against her enemy ? Or would the latter make it impossible for seaborne supplies to enter British ports ? Looking back on the past, we now realize that in 1915 the full gravity of the submarine threat was never appreciated, but entirely underestimated for another couple of years, until the painful truth could not be concealed any longer.

Admiral de Chair's fleet, in spite of the greater responsibility which devolved upon it from March 11, was still scandalously hampered by bureaucracy, so that it is difficult to write of the facts impartially. One hesitates to have any belief in such ugly ideas as "defeatism" and "the hidden hand". In those days the British public was too busy with the details of war, and their own personal duties, really to entertain suspicions of other people ; but to-day it can look back more critically over certain aspects, with a firm resolve that in any future war the Navy at least must not be hampered from exercising its complete duty. Notwithstanding that all neutral ships were now boarded, their papers scrutinized, and, if any suspicious circumstances suggested themselves, such vessels were immediately sent into port for a thorough inspection, yet Whitehall officials could still spoil such efforts.

The information obtained by the Customs representatives was telegraphed to the Foreign Office, where east-bound ships were dealt with by the Contraband Committee, and west-bound by the Enemy Exports Committee. No vessel now was to be allowed to reach a German port ; all vessels from German ports must hand over to the Allies the goods embarked in such ports ; cargoes with an enemy destination must be discharged in an Allied port ; and vessels which should proceed to an enemy port after being allowed to pass—ostensibly for a neutral destination—would be liable to capture on any subsequent voyage.

Now towards the end of March the notorious *Bergensfjord* was approaching Europe from New York again. Patrols were arranged for her interception, and on the 29th she was stopped by the *Otway*, who sent her into Kirkwall with a prize crew. The usual strongly expressed protest from the Norwegian Master was written, but this did not make much difference. It was the third occasion when the *Bergensfjord* had been sent into port, and she had always done her best to evade the patrols. But every time she had been released, and now she was released once more. It seems incredible that this liner, which on previous occasions had been so use-ful a link between Germany and America, should be allowed to carry enemy subjects ; yet this time among her passengers were one German officer of Reserve, and 16 other Germans, all of military age. They were travelling with false Norwegian passports, and were permitted to proceed. Great was the indignation of Admiral Jellicoe, Admiral de Chair, every officer and man of the Blockading Fleet, that such wicked folly should have been possible. But she would certainly try so profitable an experiment again.

During all this time German steamers were running cargoes regularly from Copenhagen, Norwegian and Swedish ports, into Bremen via the Kiel Canal, so that when once the goods had crossed the Atlantic, got through the Blockade, and reached neutral Europe the rest was easy and Germany could be sure of her supplies. Hence the slightest weakening of the Northern Barrier, whether by patrols or by procedure in Kirkwall, meant free gifts to our enemies. Another de-velopment now became popular, and was successfully adopted by such ships as the Swedish S.S. *England,* which in spite of her name could scarcely be regarded as the Allies' friend. This steamer, in April 1915, arrived from Rosario and was bound *nominally* for Stockholm, her cargo consisting of maize, wheat, and bran for certain Swedish firms. But it never reached Stockholm. It is true that after unloading part of it at Gothenburg she set off down the Cattegat; yet this did not mean very much, for, by arrangement with our enemy, she allowed herself to be captured by German warships and taken into Stettin, where the remainder of the cargo was sold for German consumption.

Of the big trade which was still being done by Germany with Sweden in respect of magnetic ore some mention has previously been made, and more will follow. The value of this commodity to the enemy increased enormously as the British Blockade became tighter, since to Scandinavia must the German munition-factories look for their supplies of raw material. The source of this ore was a place called Lulea, which is just below the Arctic Circle at the north-west corner of the Bothnia Gulf. Thus steamers could load there and reach German ports after passing through the Baltic. But another route of transportation was to bring the ore from Lulea across Sweden by the most northerly railway in Europe to the Norwegian port of Narvik, which lies at the head of Ofoten Fjord, in the north-east of West Fjord.

To Narvik the German steamers came regularly to load up, and then, by keeping within the three-mile limit of the numerous outlying islands and using the cover of night at open spaces, they had little difficulty in getting south till they hugged Danish or even Dutch waters. Before the War Germany had largely relied on Spanish ores for manufacturing the best qualities of steel, and the British Blockade created great inconvenience by shutting off that source at a time when it was most required. With the advent of spring a decision was now made by Britain to extend its blockading efforts so as to stop the Narvik trade, and early in April Admiral de Chair sent the *Teutonic* to intercept the Swedish S.S. *Sir Ernest Cassel,* which had left Narvik on the night of April 3 for Rotterdam. So successfully did *Teutonic* carry out her orders that on April 6 she found and captured the steamer in lat. 62°3' N., long. 4°42' E. (that is to say, to the south-west of Aalesund, off Norway's coast), and sent her into Kirkwall with a prize crew.

I

It was a useful seizure, for the *Sir Ernest Cassel* was carrying 10,600 tons of this magnetic ore. During the next two days *Teutonic* remained off the Norwegian coast looking for another Swedish steamer, but a mysterious incident occurred on the night of the 8th. A suspicious vessel, thought to be one of the German cruisers, followed *Teutonic* during the darkness, and the British Captain endeavoured to entice the stranger in the direction of Muckle Flugga, where an engagement would have followed. But at 2 a.m. there came a heavy rain squall, and the mystery ship was never seen again.

On that same day, however, occurred the first incident of a case that has now become historic in the annals of International Law. During the previous night a heavy gale was blowing from the W.S.W., with squalls of rain and hail that did not flatten the tremendous waves. The *Alsatian* was on her way from inspecting Loch Roag on the west of the Hebrides, as it had been hoped that this anchorage, with its tortuous and narrow entrance and beautiful scenery, might prove suitable for a coaling base in lieu of Liverpool or the Clyde. She now came upon the Swedish S.S. *Zamora*, bound from New York to Stockholm. As it was still too bad weather for boarding, the flagship kept her company during the night. Even the *Alsatian* rolled so violently that she again prevented many of her people from enjoying their watch below.

But at 9 a.m. on April 8, when in lat. 60°42′ N., long. 5°14′ W. (south-east of the Faroes), the wind and sea having decreased, a boat was lowered and a boarding party went off. She was found to be of 2,375 (Swedish) tons, and her cargo (New York for Stockholm) comprised copper, wheat, and oats. After an hour's examination she was sent into Kirkwall, to the displeasure of her Master, who expressed his regrets that he had not gone farther north to avoid the patrols. The *Zamora* was afterwards placed in the Prize Court for adjudication, but in the meanwhile she was sent round to Barrow, where the copper was requisitioned by the British Government for munitions. The President of the Prize Court at this date was Sir Samuel Evans, and the case came before him two months later; but the chief point of interest was a vindication of that essential principle which we stressed in our first chapter : the independence of the Prize Court as an impartial international tribunal, its freedom of the Orders-in-Council, and its refusal to come under Foreign Office dominion. No history of the Blockade would be complete whilst neglecting the *Zamora* incident, since it was the grand opportunity for vindicating the principles of justice even against the immediate advantages of Britain herself. I shall therefore not need to apologize for the full consideration which follows. The final judgment by the highest Prize Tribunal of this country was a condemnation of the

system set up by the English Foreign Office to secure control of English sea-warfare within its own walls; that part, namely, which consisted in the assumed power of the Foreign Office to give directions to Prize Courts as to the principles of Law upon which their judgments should be founded.[1]

When Sir Samuel Evans delivered his judgment on June 21, 1915, he was connecting the present War with those in the time of Napoleon, and the principles as expounded by the great Lord Stowell. The former stated that

it is not necessary to discuss the question whether this Court is bound to obey an Order-in-Council which may seem to be contrary to the acknowledged law of nations. If that question should arise, I am humbly and fully content to assume the standpoint of Lord Stowell in the case of the *Fox*, in which he had to deal with the Orders-in-Council which were made by way of reprisal after the celebrated Berlin and Milan decrees of Napoleon.

He then quoted with approval this expression :

This Court is bound to administer the Law of Nations to the subjects of other countries in the different relations in which they may be placed towards this country and its Government. This is what other countries have a right to demand for their subjects, and to complain if they receive it not. This is its unwritten law.[2]

The point in the *Zamora* case, so far as the Swedish owners were concerned, consisted of a simple problem. Could the copper be requisitioned by the British Government *before*

[1] *The Strength of England. Vide supra*, p. 205.
[2] *Lloyd's Reports of Prize Cases ... during the European War*. Vol. IV. London, 1917.

being condemned in the Prize Court ? The Swedes now
appealed to the Judicial Committee of the Privy Council,
and in April 1916, exactly a year (to the day) since *Zamora's*
arrest, Lord Parker, when delivering judgment in favour of
the Swedish owners, said :

> The Prize Court Rules derive their force from Orders of His Majesty
> in Council. These Orders are expressed to be made under the powers
> vested in His Majesty by virtue of the Prize Courts Act, 1894, *or
> otherwise.* . . .
> The idea that the King in Council, or, indeed, any branch of the
> Executive, has power to prescribe or alter the law to be administered by
> Courts of Law in this country is out of harmony with the principles of
> our Constitution.   Prior to the Naval Prize Act, 1864, jurisdiction in
> matters of prize was exercised by the High Court of Admiralty by virtue
> of a commission issued by the Crown under the Great Seal at the
> commencement of each war.

And this commission authorized the Court to hear and determine cases "according to the course of Admiralty, and the
Law of Nations".

And then Lord Parker emphasized the universality of
the last mentioned. It was a point particularly worth making,
since it demonstrated the big difference between the British
and the German Prize Courts. The former, not being bound
by Orders-in-Council or similar local instructions, were scrupu-
lously fair and impartial ; whereas the German Prize Courts
based their decisions on their Naval Prize Regulations, i.e.
on orders promulgated by a belligerent Government. And
it was one of the good things which came out of the War that
neutrals did always acknowledge the impartiality of British
Courts.

> The law which the Prize Court is to administer [added Lord Parker]
> is not the national, or, as it is sometimes called, the municipal law, but
> the law of nations—in other words, international law . . . A Court
> which administers international law must ascertain and give effect to a
> law which is not laid down by any particular State, but originates in the
> practice and usage long observed by civilized nations in their relations
> towards each other or in express international agreement. . . . If an
> Order-in-Council were binding on the Prize Court, such Court might
> be compelled to act contrary to the express terms of the commission
> from which it derived its jurisdiction.

The Prize Courts are, in fact, the only channels by which such persons as are aggrieved by the acts of a belligerent Power in time of war can obtain redress.

"According to international law, every belligerent Power must appoint and submit to the jurisdiction of a Prize Court . . . which administers international as opposed to municipal law." Only if there should be a gross miscarriage of justice would there ever be need for diplomatic intervention. If, however, the Prize Court were under the direction of the Foreign Office, it could not more than nominally administer the law of international obligation.

The value of these pronouncements during the War's progress, and as precedents for any future wars, cannot be denied. The United States, with every justification, had complained of the Orders-in-Council as the Blockade basis; and now the supreme Prize Court in Britain had likewise declined to recognize such Orders. But, apart from that, there had been established in an age of steamships, motor submarines, torpedoes, and mines the same fundamental principles which had been laid down in the period of oak and canvas, hemp and muzzle-loaders.

"Plus ça change . . . !"

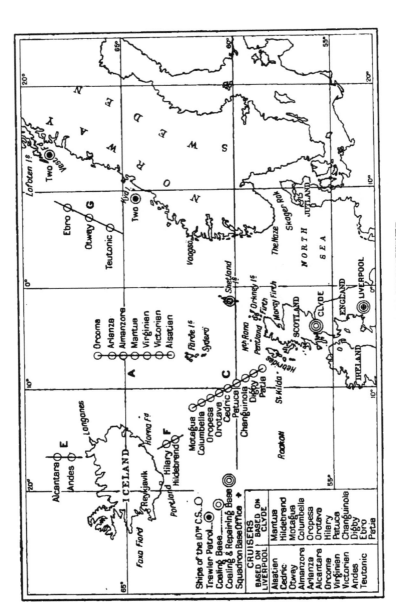

THE BLOCKADE LINES STRENGTHENED

CHAPTER X

It was some relief to the Blockaders that at last the days were getting longer and the dark nights of shorter duration. These altered conditions necessitated a modification of the patrol lines. Thus "B" (running due north from the Shetlands) and "D" (running north-west from St. Kilda) were both abolished. But "A" still stretched north from the Faroes, whilst "C" was a line roughly north and south between the Hebrides and some distance south of Iceland, where a new line "F" was to be introduced. Another new line "E" was to run at right angles from the north of Iceland, whilst yet another interesting patrol was line "G" off the Norwegian coast, so placed on meridian 3° E., between lat. 62° and 63⅓° N., as to intercept any ships which, during the finer weather and absence of ice, might try the dodge of going round the north of Iceland, or be found carrying ore for Germany from Narvik down the Norwegian coast as mentioned. Lines "E" and "F" ought to intercept any blockade-runners which hugged that island's shores.

Such a thorough scheme, with so many mobile barriers at every strategical area, demanded 27 armed merchant cruisers, though at present only 18 were available. Nor could Admiral de Chair retain them in their respective positions during more than a few days at a time ; for the long procession of neutrals did not delay to keep Germany informed as to where and how the Blockading Fleet was disposed, and therefore the submarines would know in what sections of the sea-tracks could the sisters of *Bayano* be located. This U-boat threat was more than a serious nuisance, and there kept accumulating too many scraps of genuine evidence that the north-about route was being more frequently used. On April 14 the Swedish S.S. *Carolina*, coming from Charleston for Gothenburg, reported to *Cedric* that a large U-boat was sighted steering S.W. from a position about midway between the Faroes and Hebrides ; that is to say, within the area of "C" Patrol, which must now be moved further eastward. Five days later the *Oropesa*, whilst returning from the Clyde to her patrol, sighted and shelled perhaps this same submarine in that favourite lurking-area between Skerryvore and the Mull of Cantyre. When the *Alsatian* passed through that spot a few hours later a large patch of oil (which U-boats were wont to discharge after being attacked) was still visible on the surface. The flagship was on her way to Liverpool, and, needless to say, did not waste time hanging about the danger zone. She was doing her 20 knots by the time Mull of Cantyre swept by, and next day was safe in Liverpool.

To-day we know why Scottish waters at the end of April were so visited ; for on the 29th submarines were reported off Ailsa Craig, Barra Head, and St. Kilda. The truth is that the U-boats were going through their periodical hatred of Dover Straits. Early this month U-32, whilst trying to get home, became entangled in the Dover nets. Not liking this, she managed to clear herself, but elected to go all the way back down the English Channel, up the Irish Sea, round the coast of Scotland, and so down the North Sea. U-33 likewise got the notion that Dover mines were more numerous than hitherto. So for a time the Dover Straits became unpopular for the bigger-class U-boats based on Germany, though the Flanders UB and UC class, based on Zeebrugge, were not affected. It so happened that on April 25 there was setting forth from the Ems that same Hersing in command of U-21 whom we mentioned in a previous chapter. It was inconvenient that the Dover defile just now should have been forbidden. He was just beginning the longest voyage which any submarine had yet attempted, being bound for the Mediterranean.

Circumstances compelled her to go right away north past Fair Island, then south to Gibraltar, which she passed about May 6. Within three weeks later she had entered the Dardanelles, torpedoed H.M.S. *Triumph* as well as *Majestic*, before going on to receive an ovation at Constantinople.

Now that practically all the waters navigated by the 10th Cruiser Squadron, whether north or west of Scotland, had become the highways of the bolder and bigger submarines, it was well that half a dozen more fine liners were fitted out, armed, commissioned, and added to Admiral de Chair's existing eighteen. In place of the tender *Calyx* and *Eskimo* now came the much abler vessels *Alcantara* and *Orcoma*, of whom one was destined in due time to become famous in naval history throughout all future years. The remaining four were *Andes*, *Arlanza*, *Ebro*, and *India*, each of which had been commissioned as a man-of-war before the end of April. Their tonnage, owners, and naval commanding officers are as under :

SHIP	REG. TON.	OWNERS	NAVAL OFFICER COMMANDING
Alcantara	15,831	Royal Mail Line	Commdr. T. E. Wardle, R.N.
Andes .	15,620	,, ,, ,,	Commdr. C. W. Trousdale, R.N.
Arlanza .	14,930	,, ,, ,,	Capt. D. T. Norris, R.N.
Ebro .	8,480	Pacific Steam Navig. Co.	Commdr. E. V. F. R. Dugmore, R.N.
India .	7,911	P. & O. Line	Commdr. W. G. A. Kennedy, R.N.
Orcoma .	11,577	Pacific Steam Navig. Co.	Commdr. C. W. Bruton, R.N. (late of *Ambrose*)

The first long winter had brought out the high qualities of navigation, seamanship, and boatmanship in a manner never so thoroughly tested since the advent of steam. All this interception and examination of shipping for the prevention of contraband and enemy Reservists had demanded no little tact and patience. Since December 24 no fewer than 926 vessels had been boarded up to May 5, of which 253 had been sent into port with prize crews, and not one "wanted" neutral had been missed by the patrols. Nevertheless, the 10th Cruiser Squadron had lost by disaster three ships, 80 officers, and 1,185 men in the performance of their duty. These figures were quite serious, having regard to the short period covered.

It is very certain that, unless this 10th Cruiser Squadron

had existed in the north, our late enemies would have continued to receive large numbers of Reservists from all parts of the world by this route. That they had some reason for hoping still to get through, in spite of the Blockade, is evident from those numerous records of interception. We mentioned the American S.S. *Greenbrier* on an earlier page, which in January had been sent into Kirkwall but was afterwards mysteriously released by order of the Foreign Office. Now it was only at the end of April, whilst the *Alsatian* was in Liverpool, that information was obtained from officers of the White Star Line which showed the wicked folly of such release.

The *Greenbrier* reached Bremen, and her Chief Engineer (who happened to be an Englishman) was promptly interned. But the 14 Germans of course stepped ashore in happiness at the kindness of the British Foreign Office in allowing them a safe return. She was full of contraband, and for this arrival the German authorities were not less pleased. It was really too good of the silly English to be so helpful. As to the American Press, they at first expressed indignation that *Greenbrier* should have been sent temporarily into Kirkwall, but when the journals presently learned of the contraband and 14 Germans—all released—they could only marvel at our simplicity : so the *Greenbrier* case became the laughing stock of all the ports in southern United States.

Similarly, three Swedish steamers that had recently been taken into Kirkwall this spring and set free were duly met by German cruisers off Malmo (the extreme southern end of Sweden) and escorted safely into a German port, where the cargoes were discharged, after which the trio continued their voyage into Sweden. On May Day the Danish S.S. *United States* on her voyage from New York was stopped by the *Cedric* and sent into Kirkwall. There were found on board, besides half a dozen German women, one Austrian stowaway, one German Reserve officer (an aviator), and a man with no naturalization papers, though in possession of an American passport.

It will be recollected that, in consequence of the North Channel between Scotland and Ireland having become a submarine zone, the desire for a coaling base instead of the

Mersey and the Clyde had caused Admiral de Chair to examine Loch Roag in the Hebrides. But this was not found perfect, and on May 5 he had taken *Alsatian* at dawn into Busta Voe, Swarbacks Minn. An inspection here showed that Busta Voe was much more suitable as an anchorage : there was room for at least seven of the Squadron, if necessary, to lie at single anchor ; colliers and auxiliaries could be berthed easily close inshore ; there was plenty of drinking-water available ; and there would be no difficulty in the creation of adequate defences. This spot in the Shetlands also seemed particularly convenient because of its central position in regard to the patrols and neutrals' shipping tracks.

Of this convenience there came a sudden proof ; for the Admiral's visit was brought to a sudden close by the wireless report that an oil-tanker had evaded our westward patrols and was steering to the N.E. She must be caught. Her last known position was in lat. 60°30′ N., long. 4°20′ W., that is to say, S.W. of Muckle Flugga. At 18 knots the *Alsatian* therefore proceeded on such a course as might with luck cross the stranger's. It was a long effort ; the flagship came out of Busta Voe at 9.15 a.m., and steamed searching to the northward all day till tea-time. At 3.30 p.m. the oil tanker S.S. *Petrolite* was caught north of Muckle Flugga, yet so reluctant was she to be thwarted that no fewer than four blanks had to be fired in her direction. The *Petrolite* was another of those ex-German steamers which had passed into a new nationality. She was now owned by the Standard Oil Company, but until less than a month ago had been the *Excelsior*, her American registration being dated April 14, 1915. She had 4,300 tons of oil cargo intended for Copenhagen, and had sailed from Philadelphia five days after the registration of her fresh nationality. Only one German, and he already a United States citizen, was found among the crew ; but the *Petrolite* was regarded as suspect, and into Kirkwall she was sent with a prize crew. Two days later our old friend the Danish S.S. *Oscar II* was once more intercepted on her homeward voyage, again sent into port, and more Germans (all provided with American papers) were found among the passengers.

Nor was the change of registry confined to the United States. A steamer named the *Rago* was purchased by Albert

Jensen of Copenhagen and renamed the *Vinland*. Jensen was said to be financed by Hugo Stinnes, the German millionaire; so when the *Vinland* reached the Blockade with a cargo of maize from across the Atlantic, she, too, was sent into Kirkwall. But some of these neutral skippers could neither keep silence on their wireless nor control their tongues. The American S.S. *City of Macon* was stopped coming west with only stone ballast; yet her Master must needs boast that when eastbound he had slipped through our Blockade in thick weather and his cargo reached Germany with safety. He now found his ship being sent into Stornoway for a thorough examination, and he was a marked man for the future. Still, by the end of May, whilst large numbers of vessels, both steam and sail, continued to be encountered, the volume of trade was manifestly decreasing, and the number of ships using this northern route was markedly smaller than formerly.

Thus at last the Blockade Fleet had become known universally among neutral skippers as a barrier almost impenetrable, except on the very rarest of occasions during thick weather, when a sporting risk could be taken. And the most striking evidence of increasing pressure exercised by Admiral de Chair's armed merchantmen was now found, not only in regard to Germany's supplies (which will be discussed later), but in the attitude adopted by the Scandinavian shipping companies. It is no use denying the fact that Britain at this date was not over popular. She was hated by the Germans, who could not get sufficient quantities of essential goods; not merely she had offended the people of America, but, by causing delay and interference with fast Norwegian mail steamers, Swedish passenger ships, cargo vessels as well, she had been a source of considerable annoyance. Such high fares and freights were now obtainable that the waste of two or three days in Kirkwall meant a serious financial loss to neutral shipping lines. Moreover, there was no sign that the Allies' armies on the Western Front would ever become victorious; and on sea there had not been fought some spectacular, decisive battle which neutral maritime nations rather expected the inheritors of Nelson's tradition would provide.

But, in spite of British prestige being far from exalted,

we find the Norske-Amerika Line—owners of those trouble-some steamers *Bergensfjord*, *Kristianiafjord*, and *Drammensfjord* —entering into a most significant agreement with the British Government on May 14, 1915. The conditions were not such as might have been expected from the truculent behaviour of certain Masters : on the contrary, the owners exhibit a sur-prising desire to assist Great Britain. It was agreed to furnish the British Government promptly with such information as the latter desired regarding particular consignments. No German or Austrian Reservists in future were to be carried. "The British Government cannot abandon their right of detention and search." The Norske-Amerika Line would use their utmost endeavours to prevent cargo reaching countries at war with Britain.

On the other hand, the British Government undertook to interfere with the line's ships as little as compatible with the military interests, and to give as rapid clearance as possible from British ports. Agreements were also made with other lines such as the Bergenske Shipping Company, which, *inter alia*, agreed to call when homeward-bound at Ardrossan for inspection ; and it was further agreed that this Company on their bills of lading should insert an instruction that consignees of certain goods were to furnish a guarantee that the goods were "for consumption in the country of destination shown in the bill of lading, and will not be re-exported".

Nevertheless, there was not yet a complete mutual trust, and certainly not a mutual admiration. Perhaps this condition is partly explained on the grounds that it is easier for a tiger to be friendly with a terrier than for the blockader to be on good terms with a blockade-runner. Always in past history the skipper who succeeds in hoodwinking those who seek to stop contraband is regarded as a kind of hero, deserving of praise ; whilst the preventers, on the other hand, are looked upon as the story's villains. The Captain Kettles of real life have not all been blue-eyed angels of innocence.

So when on the next occasion *Drammensfjord* was inter-cepted, not well to the southward, but hugging the southern shore of Iceland, where *Arlanza* of the new "F" Patrol inter-cepted the Norwegian bound from New York to Bergen, there was a certain suspicion. An armed guard brought

Drammensfjord into Kirkwall, where it was noticed that, whilst she carried guarantees against transhipment of the food-stuffs and rubber which formed part of her cargo, the rest of her freight consisted of explosives, copper, and brass, for which no guarantees were presented. That was May 23. About a month later she was again stopped, but this time by the *Alsatian*, and so far N.E. of the Faroes that evidently she was going round the north of Iceland.

It was a lovely June morning, the time 8.30. Five days previously she had left Christiania for Baltimore in ballast. When the boarding party came off, they found the Master, if not sympathetic towards Britain, at least polite and aware of his obligations as required by International Law. Guarded and reserved as to giving any information which did not concern his ship or cargo, his general demeanour was characteristically Norwegian. The Mate, however, was openly pro-German, and, when ordered to conduct the Boarding Officer through the ship, did not make any attempt to hide the fact that such a visit was a gross annoyance. The Mate stated that the Master of *Kristianiafjord* openly boasted he could avoid the patrols whenever he liked, and the Mate further added (with a jest that barely concealed a hope) he would inform the Germans of the patrols' localities, so as to send submarines and attack with torpedoes. The Masters and Mates of Norway in general (indicated the Norwegian) held the greatest contempt for the Blockaders.

There was no question about the U-boat activities, though at present the German policy was rather to do the work of its own Submarine Blockade than destroy the British Northern Blockade, except and unless individual units were met with in those favoured areas off the Clyde and Mersey approaches already mentioned. After the Commanding Officer of the Flanders Submarine Flotilla had in April rescinded the order forbidding the smaller type from negotiating Dover Straits, one craft got entangled in the Folkestone-Gris-Nez boom which was then under construction. She lost her nerve and returned. The ban was again placed on attempting Dover Straits, so that not until late in August did the enemy make further attempts down the English Channel.

But this temporary closure gave a renewed importance to

submarine operations up the North Sea and, after rounding Cape Wrath, down the Minch into Irish waters. Why did they not make more attacks against the 10th Cruiser Squadron ? The answer is that the risk of going so far north beyond the sight of land was not likely to prove so profitable as to choose restricted channels and busy approaches. The area between Scotland and Iceland was so vast, exposed, and lacking landmarks for U-boats of that day. By the time these ever-shifting patrol lines had been located, so much fuel would have been consumed that a sister submarine could have reached the North Channel and remained waiting for certain, instead of possible, targets. Those patrol lines most likely to be hit were (a) one stretching across the Fair Island to Hebrides track, and (b) any line which remained fairly close to the Norwegian isle-dotted coast. In the first case, a U-boat on passage out or home might sink an armed merchantman casually met ; in the second, a submarine would have to be sent out specially to stalk a unit.

That which was alarming consisted of the almost daily reports indicating how varied were the positions. At the end of April U-boats were reported off Ailsa Craig, off St. Kilda, off Fair Island steering west, off the Butt of Lewis, off Skerryvore and the Mull of Cantyre, and elsewhere. Moreover, the sinking of *Lusitania* off the south of Ireland, whilst plunging every officer and man of the Blockading Fleet into a savage gloom, clearly showed that the time was long since past when submarines could be despised. The British Blockading forces owed their immunity to the care which their Admiral took in moving the lines forty miles this way or that, ordering each ship to keep zigzagging at high speed during times of crisis, and to the lack of definite onslaught which might have been made by a German flotilla sent out to wipe out any selected patrol line.

Vessels patrolling north of the Faroes at the beginning of May found it still quite light on deck, in those latitudes, even at 10.45 p.m. ; so that, whilst there was not the same protection of darkness from the underwater craft that must rely on a periscope, at least it would be more difficult for the blockade-runners to evade interception. The institution of two units immediately to the north, and another pair immediately to the south, of Iceland now became most likely traps for the dodgers. Drift ice was coming from Greenland across Denmark Strait to Iceland intermittently, but the north Iceland passage seemed to be practicable by the beginning of May, and thither *Alcantara* was despatched ; for perhaps by this extreme northerly route might come more German mine-layers and raiders.

Soon, however, Commander Wardle wirelessed from *Alcantara* on May 10 that a large field of unnavigable pack ice was closing in and drifting south-eastwards. The former tells me : "Admiral de Chair replied that he would come and see it. I was to rendezvous off Cape Langanaes.[1] On his arrival he said, 'Take me to it !' But when we reached what my navigator thought was the right spot, there was not a sign of ice. Either, of course, the navigator had made an error, or the ice had shifted in the twenty-four hours. So I suggested steering west to look for it. The Admiral was getting dubious of my veracity, and said he must go back if we did not sight ice before midnight. To my joy, about 11.30 p.m. we sighted the ice blink (it was daylight), and soon afterwards the ice."

"We sighted this ice floe", says Admiral de Chair, "while the sun was still high above the horizon and setting behind the ice ; and I must say it was a very beautiful sight as the sun's rays glistened through the icebergs and hummocks, but intensely cold, as the wind was off the ice and the temperature well below zero." The edge was afterwards traced by the *Alcantara* from lat. 66°48′ N., long. 16°12′ W., to lat. 68° N., long. 13°2′ W., and no passage could be discovered. Although the *Alcantara* steamed about 300 miles north up the Arctic Circle, no evidence of a channel was visible, and this was afterwards confirmed by the Captain of a sealer, who stated that no vessels as yet were passing north of Iceland.

It was well to have that point settled, yet it was character-istic of the War's vast scene that patrols should extend so far towards Polar regions that photographs could be taken after 10 p.m., and it was never too dark for reading the seconds of a watch. The *Alcantara* was thus free for another important

---

[1] Cape Langanaes is at the north-east corner of Iceland.

duty, viz. to patrol off the Norwegian coast near Lundo Island, so as to intercept the steamers passing down with ore for Germany via Rotterdam. The *India*, employed on this work, had just sent in to Kirkwall the Swedish steamers *Gotland*, *Volrath Than*, and *Nordland*, bound for Rotterdam from Narvik; and now *Alcantara* similarly captured the Swedish S.S. *Malmland* with ore; after which Commander Wardle returned to examine once more the north Iceland coast. There were signs that the ice was breaking up, though passage to the westward was still not possible.

But this officer, during his short sojourn off Norway, had been able to obtain the valuable information that the ore-ships from Narvik passed inside the islands, coming out near Kya Island, where as many as five steamers were seen keeping within neutral waters. The best position for patrols would be just south of the Lofoten Islands, that is to say, off the West Fjord previously mentioned, and the time was now approaching when something of a climax must develop. For Germany was feeling the grip of the Blockade as never previously, and this question of supplies became increasingly serious. Iron ore was to be obtained at all risks in order to feed the guns. But what about nourishment for her people ? By May 1915 the prices of food in Berlin were already 65% above those of July 1914, and they had risen in Vienna higher still; whereas in England the average prices had increased not more than 30 or 35%.

Very noticeable, however, were the increased exports from Holland to Germany, especially in regard to wheatmeal, cotton, and copra; and this increase was a measure of the straits in which our enemy now found herself, thanks to the Blockade shutting her off from the outer world. It was obvious, however, that, partly through desire of gain, partly through fear, the Dutch were assisting our enemy through a half-opened door to the inner world. The Nederlandsche Overzee Maatschappi had been the first of the guilds or trusts, to be followed by the Danish Industrieraadet and the Swiss Société de Surveillance. But there was no doubt whatsoever that this Netherlands Overseas Trust was not watertight, and before the end of 1915 it had to accept from the Allies a rationing schedule.

We have called attention previously to the inland waterway

K

system which connects Holland so intimately, and this was one of the holes of communication that no amount of agreement could block up satisfactorily.   For instance, by an existing Rhine Navigation Treaty, after the cargoes of Swedish iron ore had reached Rotterdam and been transferred into those great steel barges called *rhineschiffs* before being towed into Germany, no one could interfere—they must pass on, and not even the Dutch Government could obstruct their progress. Furthermore, during the process of reshipment from steamer to barge, it was quite easy to slip in plenty of Dutch goods for Germany, and thus the Nederlandsche Overzee Maatschappi might know nothing about that.   Two things were very certain : that large quantities of goods from Holland did continue to reach our enemy, and that during this year 1915 there entered Germany two million tons of ore in 557 cargoes.   Reckoned in terms of shells, torpedoes, mines, guns, and submarine hulls, this was still a terribly large amount to be permissible, yet the geographical conditions prevented the Blockaders from stopping it utterly and entirely, as they so heartily desired.

In due course we shall see some of the crises which ensued from trying to wipe out the Narvik trade.

CHAPTER XI

ECONOMIC PRESSURE

Submarines continued to be reported off such localities as the Mersey, Barra Head, St. Kilda, and even as far north as latitude 60°, which again caused the Blockade Patrols to be shifted temporarily north and west. The increased range and activity of U-boats had, by the middle of June, become one of the conditions to be expected for the rest of hostilities. But quite a new phase developed, which showed how determined was Germany to get any supplies by bluff and bullying of neutrals.

For east of the Faroes, one cold grey morning this month, the *Alsatian* intercepted the Norwegian barque *Bessfield* (1,235 tons), bound from South America with a cargo of wheat for Bergen "to order". Captain Peter Hassel, her Master, stated that on June 7, when thirty miles off Mizzen Head (S.W. Ireland), he was fired on by U-34, the shell bursting overhead and fragments clattering on deck. The submarine came near, ordered Captain Hassel on board with his papers, and, after examining them, the German commanding officer further ordered him not to call at any British port, but to proceed for Bergen direct, adding that he was reporting the *Bessfield* by wireless to other U-boats round the British Isles, and any attempt to make a British port would result in the barque being sunk without warning. These instructions were given in writing, the document being headed "U-34", and were to be shown to any other German submarine which might stop her.

It is interesting to note that the *Bessfield* was now sent into Kirkwall, and that U-34 never lived to know of this. For later on she was sent this year to operate in the Mediterranean, where she remained until two days before the end of war. On the night of November 8-9, 1918, she was sunk in the Gibraltar area by the combined efforts of ML.155 and the Q-ship *Privet*.

On June 21—the identical day whereon *Alsatian* met the *Bessfield*—another instance of German submarine blockade ruthlessness was exhibited 120 miles east of Aberdeen. The Norwegian S.S. *Venus* was steaming across the North Sea bound for Newcastle with a cargo of Norway's food products, when she was stopped by a U-boat who refused to let her go until many cases of salmon and tinned fish, together with 416 cases of butter to the value of £5,000, were thrown into the sea. The reader will observe that there was no sending the neutral ship into Prize Court, but merely heavy-handed vindictiveness. And by a mere coincidence a further example of Germany's determination to get food (when she could not prevent Britain's supplies) was learned of only five days later.

It was 10.30 on Saturday night, somewhere between Iceland and the Faroes, that the Dutch steam trawler *Ocean III* was boarded. It turned out that she was on her way out from Ymuiden to the Iceland fishing grounds. Unfortunately that morning one of her 15 crew, whilst heaving ashes over the side, had ruptured himself, so Dr. A. C. Roxburgh, the *Alsatian's* temporary surgeon, was able to go aboard, apply a pad and bandage, and advise the Dutch Master to hurry the man into Reykjavik hospital. But this skipper also reported to the *Alsatian* that when fishing near Heligoland at the end of April the *Ocean* had been captured by a German torpedo-boat and taken into Hamburg, the Dutchmen being all kept below whilst passing through the Elbe approaches. It is true that ultimately the trawler was released, but the German authorities had promptly stolen the fish and not taken the trouble to pay one single mark.

Such scraps of intelligence, whilst of limited value in themselves, had a cumulative worth that could not be denied. Nor could the enemy appreciate how useful was this secondary duty of the Blockade Fleet. Scarcely did a Boarding Officer return from the numerous ship visits without bringing back some important data, which, on being sent up to Head-quarters, confirmed other information obtained from totally different sources. Our secret service was assuring us that by June male labour in Germany was already scarce and the British Blockade had created a food shortage. It was therefore illuminating, on the day after meeting with *Ocean*, that the little Norwegian S.S. *Sigvald Martinsen*, of 227 tons, should confirm this news.

She was engaged in the fish-carrying trade, and her Master informed the *Alsatian's* Boarding Officer that on the last voyage she took a cargo of fish from Aalesund to the German Baltic port Stettin. It was noticed that there were very few male labourers on the Stettin docks, most of the work (such as shovelling coal) being done by women ; the prices of everything were very high, and potato bread was in general use.

In England the cry still went up, "Cotton supplies *must* no longer reach Germany" ; but the British Government paid little heed to this obvious demand. Not so, however, in France was the danger callously regarded, for in June there were seized at Marseilles £20,000 worth of cotton in bales that had been consigned to an intermediary firm at Zurich. It was pathetic to know that Germany had obtained practically all she wanted of the last American cotton crop via neutral countries, though we could have stopped almost the whole lot. The new crop would be ready for shipment from the United States in September. Surely we could not be such fools as to let this most essential commodity get through ?

But there could be no question that the information of neutral skippers on the food question was quite accurate. So long as the Blockading Fleet was left alone to do its persistent duties, Germany was doomed. Whether she performed an occasional raid against the North Sea coast or won battles on the Western Front, her expectation of life was limited by the length of her supplies. She had gambled on a short, quick victory—and lost. Nothing could now save her from eventual collapse, except some further folly that might issue from Whitehall.

By June maize in Germany was four times its normal price, petrol double, meat higher by 50 per cent. (The latter would have been considerably more expensive but for the fact that Holland was such a helpful neighbour.) What seems so open to criticism was the vacillating policy of the British

Foreign Office, and an undue nervousness of neutral protests. Sweden, who throughout the War was entirely pro-German and anti-British in her sympathies, now complained of the hindrances caused to her shipping through our Blockade; whereupon British delegates were sent at the end of June to Stockholm to take part in an Anglo-Swedish conference. And the strange result followed that Britain temporarily waived total prohibition of cotton into Sweden by allowing the latter to receive 15,000 bales.

Against the rising tide of public indignation in Britain the Government was finding itself hazardously placed. Lord Robert Cecil, then Secretary for Foreign Affairs, stated in Parliament on July 12 that on the one hand they had to consider America, which produced the cotton, and on the other those countries—Sweden, Norway, Denmark, and Holland—which consumed it. This Minister, after hedging, could only express the fear that if the whole cotton supply to neutrals were cut off, this "would lead us in international difficulties". At this date the price of cotton being sold in Germany was five times that on sale in Liverpool, and there could be no better proof that Germany's demand was much greater than the available supply : in other words, the Blockade was doing well so far as it was permitted, and could do considerably more if only the Foreign Office were a little more courageous. Members of Parliament could not understand this cowardly policy in keeping cotton out of the contraband list. Surely, whilst you are fighting an opponent and your blows are seen to cause serious distress when levelled at one part of his anatomy, you should not stop hitting that target but increase the force of those blows ?

By mid-July, to the great surprise of Germany, the Kaiser's Government decided to assume control of the entire coal industry "for the protection of public interests"; but here was only further evidence of the pressure which was being imposed by sea. Food was rapidly getting scarcer, the consumption of meat was prohibited to two days a week, and the production of beer—without which no German life was tolerable—was reduced 40 per cent. Before the War large quantities of meat had been consigned to Germany from the United States, then (by reason of the Blockade) it was sent via Denmark and Scandinavia, until the amounts attracted such attention that some of the vessels were seized and placed in the Prize Courts.

Now, as time went on and the political influence of American meat-packers made itself felt, there was a peculiar arrangement made whereby cargoes were still brought into the Prize Court, but 90 or even 93 per cent of the value was paid by Britain to the packers. Similarly, the American cotton exporters were made happy by cash payments for detained cotton cargoes. By July 19 nearly £700,000 had been paid in respect of 25 shipments purchased. Thus both the American Meat Packers' Association, which included the big firms of Armour and Swift, and the cotton growers in the south, were placated because Britain became buyers in lieu of Germany. Whilst this was a clever and ingenious measure, it could only be regarded as an expensive postponement of the main issue. "Cotton must be made contraband absolutely!" The bold policy had still to be awaited.

In vain *The Times* of July 21 insisted that cotton ought to be made Absolute Contraband *at once*. At least 1,000 tons of cotton daily were being used in Germany for the manufacture of shells and machine-gun cartridges, and another 500 tons for the military clothing. So long as the merchants in Bremen were willing to pay 2s. 9d. a lb., as against 6d. a lb. in Liverpool, German agents in the United States had every incentive to risk running the Blockade, seeing that they could well afford to lose four out of every ships despatched, provided only one got through.

Throughout these weeks, then, the 10th Cruiser Squadron, with the long daylight hours that were too often cloudy or foggy, but occasionally fine and calm with sunshine, was kept doubly alert. The old offenders were finding the neutral trade so profitable that they could never be trusted. The Danish liner *Frederik VIII*, with a number of Germans among her passengers, was again sent into port under an armed guard. Off the Flannan Islands, that solitary group of seven uninhabited rocks beyond the Outer Hebrides, the *Motagua*, on June 14, was in the act of boarding one steamer, when she observed another being sunk by a large submarine. The patrol proceeded at once towards the stranger, and was able by gun-fire to drive the enemy away, but was not in time to save the German's victim from sinking altogether, though *Motagua* rescued the two boatloads who were pulling for the Flannan Islands. It was lucky that the patrol had intervened, for the survivors would have found nothing on the seven islands apart from eider-duck and gannet. She was able to escort the first steamer till beyond the danger zone.

And still the contraband tried to rush the Blockade. On this same day the *Hilary* stopped the United States S.S. *Sea Connet* bound from New York for Scandinavian ports. Her cargo of rifles, copper, armour-plating, and ammunition obviously could not be passed, and into Kirkwall she had to go. But the submarine peril quickened. In a spot roughly half-way between the Butt of Lewis and the Faroes the *India* was attacked by a U-boat so effectively that the torpedo only just missed the ship. The position was just where a submarine had been seen on a previous occasion, which proved that these dangerous craft, whilst going to or from their Irish operational areas, did not hesitate to try bagging any patrol that came across their track. At this time the *India* was on her way to the Clyde for coaling, but the reader will note on a later page what her subsequent fate was to be at the hands of another U-boat.

There is reason, however, to think that this first attack on *India* may have quickened the submarine's desire to more complete success; for next day (June 15), not very far from the same spot, the *Orotava* sighted a U-boat close to the Danish S.S. *Russ*. The neutral had just been stopped by the German, and the boats were already half lowered for abandoning ship, when the *Orotava* steamed to the rescue and opened fire on the submarine, driving it away. Keeping between enemy and neutral, the *Orotava* escorted the *Russ* out of danger till the latter went off on her north-westerly course for Baltimore, whither she was bound in ballast from Copenhagen. It was a curious situation that the unpopular British patrols should sometimes be the very saviours of neutrals against the nation for whose benefit cargoes from America were being fetched !

North of Iceland the field-ice was still too extensive by mid-June for any navigation yet to be practicable, so at present there was no fear of trouble from that region. But just when scares died away and everything seemed normal, there would come some sudden burst of excitement and the patrols would be even more vigilant than ever. This time it was the notorious *Kristianiafjord* again. She had left Bergen on June 16, and there were secret reasons why she should be intercepted and sent in, but she could be relied upon to slip through if at all possible.

Next day, at 10 a.m., she was heard signalling to Bergen, and so communicating at frequent intervals. The *Alsatian* therefore kept silence and listened. But the Norwegian was subtle and cute, her replies to Bergen were very brief and quickly made, so that it was difficult by means of *Alsatian's* direction-finder to get a bearing of the liner. Throughout the day the latter kept up her conversation, but she had cleverly arranged that the strength of her wireless should not appreciably alter, and the net result was that her approximate position could not be estimated.

Not until another five hours had elapsed could even a rough idea of her position be conjectured, and this was so vague that she might be on the flagship's port bow or even the latter's starboard quarter. Aural vigilance was never relaxed, and at 9.45 p.m. the *Kristianiafjord* gave herself away by informing Bergen she was 370 miles from that port—she must soon cross Patrol line "C" (running N.W. from the Hebrides towards Iceland). Therefore, in order that the Norwegian should have no means of locating the position of ships in that patrol by her direction-finder, Admiral de Chair ordered all the "C" patrols to make no wireless signals. He, however, in *Alsatian*, began signalling on full power, and this scheme was far cleverer than that of *Kristianiafjord* at her best. For the latter now could ascertain where was the *Alsatian*, who thus would be carefully avoided, which the Admiral entirely wished.

We pass over the intervening hours until Friday, the 18th, when the flagship was centrally placed to the north-east of the Faroes. It was another of those grey mornings, when suddenly *Mantua* sighted *Kristianiafjord* hurrying west. The time was 10.30 a.m., the position lat. 60°42′ N., long. 11°37′ W., or roughly half-way between the Hebrides and Iceland. The game was up : the Norwegian had run into the very trap he hoped to avoid. Strongly he protested that it was most unwarrantable his ship and 544 passengers should be detained, but for the best of reasons an armed guard brought the liner into Stornoway.

The fact is that the days were now long past when neutrals could hope to wriggle their way through the British Blockade, either by brilliant navigation or vehement protest. Apart from the submarines, and the uncertain policy of the Foreign Office, the 10th Cruiser Squadron had little to fear nowadays : it was easier for an elephant to go through a cottage doorway than for a "wanted" ship to pass between Norway and the south Iceland coast.

And the moral result of this *effective* blockade would before long become visible among neutrals : indeed, British prestige on the sea was quietly, if unwillingly, recognized in Sweden, notably, as beyond all question. Such control of the maritime communications was in utter contrast with the German Submarine Blockade, which, though quite a threat, was by no means effective. The proof is not difficult, since from the beginning of war down to the end of June 1915 nearly 20,000 voyages of merchant ships had been made in and out of Liverpool alone, and about 99 per cent had been safely accomplished. It followed, consequently, that if a blockade were ineffective, it ceased to exist, and that the rights which pertain to a blockade did not apply. Thus Germany had no justification to inflict on a neutral such treatment as was permissible only during an effective blockade. Had the 10th Cruiser Squadron been less efficient in strategy, tactics, numbers of units, personal devotion to duty, or professional ability, then the Scandinavians, Danes, and the people of the United States might have united in a successful effort to preserve the seas' freedom for their own trade and the lasting benefit of Germany. Nothing is more futile and more fruitful of international irritation than a false, or paper, blockade ; and the debt which the British nation owes to the officers and men of Admiral de Chair's Northern Patrol is equalled only by the general public unawareness of such obligation.

CHAPTER XII

THE STRANGLEHOLD

TOWARDS the end of June the coaling base at Swarbacks Minn was established, so that the ships of the 10th Cruiser Squadron need not visit the Clyde or Mersey except when repairs had to be made. Rear-Admiral W. B. Fawckner was put in charge to organize and superintend, the entrance was protected against submarines by means of a boom and nets, and arrangements were made for coaling 24 units. It was found that water could be taken from the shore by means of hoses, and the ships could moor fairly close.

But obviously this Shetlands base meant a considerable effort ; for the Squadron daily consumed 1,600 tons of coal and 150 tons of water for the boilers. This demanded that four colliers should always be available, and 200 or 300 stokers always ready to assist in coaling these liners whenever they should arrive. H.M.S. *Gibraltar*, one of the "Edgars" mentioned at the beginning of our story, was fitted out as a depot and repair ship. She was sent to this harbour and moored so that her guns could command the boom, and aboard her were berthed the stokers in addition to her own reduced complement. Her wireless enabled Admiral de Chair to keep in touch. Look-out stations were erected and connected by telephone, since it was by no means improbable that the enemy would some day make a raid or, at the very least, send his submarines to foul the entrance with mines.

All this organizing took busy weeks, but when once everything was set going it became manifest that (apart from evading the submarine menace off the Clyde and Mersey) here was an immense saving of time and fuel. The *Patuca* was able to demonstrate this quite early. Within four days she had entered Swarbacks Minn, taken in 1,000 tons of coal, filled up with water and fresh provisions, cleaned her boiler tubes, and was back on her patrol. It was an outlandish place, and there was for the crews neither that sense of security nor the civilization which Liverpool afforded. In course of time the rate of coaling got faster as the facilities improved.

Concerning engineering matters, "the way they have in the Navy" was not identical with the custom aboard liners. The Mercantile Engineer officer had not been wont to do so much refitting as his brothers in the fighting service, so that when the time did come for overhaul these ships of the Blockading Fleet needed rather more attention than had been expected. But an additional reason for extensive repairs was the continuous steaming week after week. It is to be remembered that the genuine man-of-war is designed and built on the assumption that she can refuel at short intervals, whereas the merchant vessel must be able to make trans-oceanic voyages at good speed away from all coaling or oiling facilities. And, indeed, these 10th Cruiser Squadron units proved such capabilities to the full. During the first six months —that is to say from Christmas Day, 1914—the *Alsatian* steamed 35,758 miles, which is the equivalent of having gone right round the world and then crossed the Atlantic again. Such a strain on the machinery and its upkeep, on the engineering staff superintending its wear and tear, nursing this complicated mechanism so as always to be responsive when high speed was suddenly demanded, was a responsibility that had been no sinecure. The resources of the private shipyards were being tried severely, and during the latter part of June every dock on the Clyde from Troon inwards was occupied by one or other of His Majesty's ships. Sometimes it was necessary for one of the latter to wait 24 hours before a dock was vacant.

But the remarkable and meritorious fact must be borne in remembrance that, in spite of all this unprecedented pressure, the system endured it so well that extensions were practicable and unforeseen demands were readily met.

In the meanwhile those neutral ships which were determined to give trouble still maintained their characteristics. On June 20 the *Bergensfjord*, which might have been nicknamed the "German Atlantic ferry", was again stopped on her

way from New York to Bergen, in spite of her Master's
customary and strenuous protests. This was the fourth
time she had been found guilty of unneutral action. Among
her 473 passengers were seven German women, two German
naval officers, and the notorious Dr. Dernburg.[1] That,
surely, was bad enough, but most of her cargo was contraband ;
and, one may well ask, were we not treating this ship with an
indulgence which Germany would never have tolerated had
the conditions been reversed ? Would not our late enemies
have sunk her in exasperation ?

Two days later there was a whiff of excitement on "G"
Patrol, which had been placed off the Norwegian coast ready
for interception of the ore-steamers. Off Kya Island (which
is in lat. 64°28′ N., long. 10°13′ E.), on the flank of that rock-
protected inner passage so frequented by the vessels coming
down from Narvik, the *Teutonic* sighted the German S.S.
Konsul Schultze and immediately gave chase. It was a curious
twist of the War that a former crack Atlantic greyhound should
be pursuing an ore-carrier, but the latter at once altered
course and fled into territorial waters north-eastward of the
island towards Folden Fjord. The greyhound remained on
watch outside, and the *Victorian* was sent to try to drive
the German out. The latter, however, was not seen again by
the watchers, and managed to scurry into Trondhjem.

The problem of dealing with these German and Swedish
ore-vessels was difficult of solution. Thanks to the geographical
protection from the outlying island fringe, it was almost
impossible to make a capture without violating the neutrality
of the waters. It was somewhat risky, also, taking a big ship
such as the *Teutonic* in and out among reefs. Moreover, it
was noticed that when Admiral de Chair wanted to communicate with *Teutonic* by wireless, Bergen set up so persistent

[1] Dr. Bernhard Dernburg, the son of a Jewish journalist, was the German
Colonial Secretary from 1906 to 1910. At the outbreak of war he was sent across
to the United States, where he arrived with Count Bernstorff on August 25, 1914,
the latter having been home on leave. Dr. Dernburg now began a big campaign
to win American sympathies. A Press bureau was established in New York,
whence were published pamphlets and the notorious weekly, *The Fatherland*.
His efforts to convince the United States of Germany's cause, in spite of certain
vicissitudes and exposures, had some success until May 1915, when his attempts
to justify the torpedoing of *Lusitania* so disgusted the American people that
he sailed from New York in the *Bergensfjord* on June 13, 1915.

an interference with her radio that it seemed more intentional than accidental.

How could those Narvik-Rotterdam steamers be enticed forth ?

Finally Admiral Jellicoe sent the armed trawler *Tenby Castle* to assist close in, whilst the *Teutonic* and *Victorian* waited in the offing. It was the method of employing a ferret to force the rabbit into the area of the fast hounds. But consider the circumstances. The commanding officer of the trawler must be one who could think and act quickly ; not be afraid of scraping the mussels off the jagged outlying rocks, nor of undertaking a bold initiative which might end in a court-martial if he made a slight error. Foggy weather was the friend of the foreign skippers, who knew the route almost blindfolded, and under those conditions could lure the patrols on to half-tide dangers.

But the *Tenby Castle* was well chosen, and her commanding officer, Lieut. J. T. Randell, R.N.R., was a real "hard case", one of those genuine "dyed-in-the-wool" seamen who fear nothing except failure. The celebrated affair of the *I'm Alone*, which occurred some years after the War and made him a public hero on the other side of the Atlantic was a typical exposition of his independent spirit.[1]   Give Randell a tough job, and you could be sure that something would soon happen to enliven a dull world. In this particular case it occurred on June 30, 1915, when the *Tenby Castle* was about five miles N.E. of the Kya Island. Just before noon he sighted an ore-steamer coming down from Nero Sound.

It should be mentioned that such vessels were frequently on the very borderline of territorial waters, and it was not possible for a stranger to say accurately whether the Swede or German was just in or just outside neutrality. Only by taking a cross-bearings frequently could it be stated exactly where Norway's rights ended and the open sea beyond the three-mile limit began ; but those of us who have commanded trawlers and drifters, with their not too accurate compass, and know that it is usually somewhat awkwardly placed

---

[1] When in command of the *I'm Alone* off the Atlantic coast, his ship was sunk by gunfire, the American officials having suspected him of rum-running. He was rescued from the sea and put under arrest.

for taking bearings of an isolated pinnacle, can sympathize with Randell. Besides, he was much too interested in the primary duty of stopping the ship.

As the latter closed, it was seen that her name was *Pallas*, and she was flying no colours. The *Tenby Castle* now hoisted the White Ensign and the International Signal to stop immediately. This was ignored, whereupon Randell steamed round and, perceiving that she was a German belonging to the port of Flensburg, fired a shot across the stranger's bows. The *Pallas* stopped engines, but still had enough way on to head shorewards. Randell steamed towards her and ordered the German to show her colours, which she declined. She was next told to steer west, and this she refused likewise. Randell now gave the German five minutes in which to make a decision : either come with the *Tenby Castle* or be sent to the bottom ; and meanwhile Randell sent off a wireless to the *Victorian*.

The German skipper was about as determined as Randell, for the armed trawler was just coming alongside and about to place aboard an armed guard, when the German put his telegraphs for full speed ahead and darted off. *Tenby Castle* therefore fired a couple of shots at the ore-ship's steering gear on the poop and did a certain amount of damage, though there were no casualties, and once more the *Pallas* stopped engines. She had sufficient way on to take her shorewards, and by the time *Victorian* arrived the *Pallas* was about two and a half miles from the land.

It is a nice point as to whether the German was, or just was not, within Norwegian waters when first spoken ; but now there could be no doubt that she was well within neutrality. The incident had been witnessed by a Norwegian patrol vessel, whose Captain came up and insisted that in accordance with International Law the ship must be released, and this was done. The incident ended on July 20, when the British Foreign Office apologized for having thus violated Norway's waters. But before that expression of regret had been made the *Tenby Castle* once more showed her skipper's determination.

It was July 7, just a week had passed, and now Randell was again on the job, but this time he was much nearer the source. The time was 5.50 a.m., it was a thick rainy morning, and he was off the western end of West Fjord. Suddenly out of the mist to the N.N.W. emerged a large steamer, whereupon the *Tenby Castle* went full speed, and ordered the steamer to stop. The latter turned out to be the Swedish S.S. *Malmland*, carrying about 7,000 tons of magnetic ore. She was next told to follow the trawler, but disobeyed and went full speed ahead. Randell then made her keep astern at reduced speed, and just before 8.30 a.m. came up to H.M.S. *India* (previously mentioned), to whom she was handed over. Nor was that all.

Just after the following midnight Randell was again off West Fjord, when he sighted yet another steamer approaching from Narvik. There was still plenty of light in that latitude, and he fired a shot across the foreigner's bows to make her heave-to. Then, steaming under her stern, he read her name and port of registry : FRIEDRICH ARP, HAMBURG.

A German, this time ! But another of the obstinate kind, who refused Randell's orders to follow astern and began steaming in towards the land, whereupon Randell repeated his pet tactics and fired a shot into the enemy's quarter, which infused obedience to some extent, though the *Friedrich Arp* still refused to follow. At length, having given the latter five minutes to consider whether he would come quietly or be sunk, the German once more went full speed shorewards. By this time an hour had passed since first meeting, and no further bluff could be tolerated : the warning had been offered and ignored. The *Tenby Castle* opened fire, and shelled the German ship at the water-line till she sank, the crew of 13 being picked up and four hours later handed over to the *India*. Randell by this drastic procedure prevented 4,000 tons of magnetic ore from being used against our soldiers in France. The incident had taken place four and a half miles from the nearest land, well away from territorial waters.

Lieut. Randell for twenty days, practically unsupported (except at a distance), lay off that coast doing his plucky work until withdrawn. *I'm Alone* was the name of his post-war ship, but it was also expressive of his war service during the time when he sank one enemy steamer, nearly secured a second, and handed a neutral over with her important cargo. He was eventually awarded the Distinguished Service Cross. The *Friedrich Arp* was on her way to Stettin, and had a pilot aboard, and to-day we know that the steamers in Narvik

H.M.S. "OROTAVA" ENTERING BUSTA VOE

BUSTA VOE
Showing some of the Blockade Fleet at anchor

A TRAWLER PATROL

were being kept well informed of the noon positions of our vessels in Patrol "G", so that the only way to catch the ore-ships was by such small craft as the *Tenby Castle,* which could remain well out of sight. Naturally Norwegian pilots, Swedish and German shipmasters, all kept themselves fairly up-to-date regarding the British movements off the coast, and the German Admiralty soon learned all about this extension of the Blockade off West Fjord. It was so serious a threat to Germany's communications, such an important menace to her essential supplies, that something must be done about it.

But the story is so long and tragic that it must be considered separately in a later chapter. In the meanwhile, at Admiral de Chair's request, a British submarine was sent to patrol off the coast. It was hoped that her invisibility might make her particularly suitable for this special work. E-13 was eventually sent from Great Yarmouth to cruise south of Trondhjem, but the time was badly chosen, as the weather was bad; she developed engine trouble and had to return to her base. No other submarine succeeded her, and the ore problem was never solved after all. German steamers continued to be sighted, but they were careful to remain within Norwegian territory.

Those students who may wonder at the price the Big Blockade of 24 ships was costing the British nation will find it not too abstruse a task, and for their information it may be added that the 10th Cruiser Squadron was burning in coal about 600,000 tons a year. Under one heading alone the expense of controlling the northern seas was thus very considerable, yet it was extraordinarily well spent even at a period when money seemed to be of no consideration. Seventy or eighty vessels a week were being examined, and that all such work could be done month after month in all weathers without an accident was a remarkable proof of sound seamanship. Big liners cannot be handled with the facility which belongs to a destroyer, or even a light cruiser. The average passenger steamer has less fine lines and a wider turning circle, so a great deal of manoeuvring had to be done by the patrol before she was in a suitable position for lowering the boarding party. The conditions of wind and sea at a particular moment had to be considered in relation to the other vessel, and of

L

course the oared boat must be given both a lee and the shortest distance to cover.

Neutral steamers were not always too helpful, and the Captain of a patrol liner had to think of the lurking submarine, the drift of his own ship, and much besides. Sooner or later, and quite likely during the middle watch, when human nature is always at its weakest, one of these seventy or eighty intercepted vessels would be in collision with the examining ship, and no amount of good fortune could prevent one or two accidents of this nature. "I have been closer than I had meant to be on one or two occasions when boarding vessels," writes one of the most experienced of Admiral de Chair's commanding officers in a private letter, "and, as a rule, they would not do anything in the way of working their engines to keep clear."

It was at 2 a.m. on July 1 that H.M.S. *Patuca* (the 6,103-tons Elders & Fyffes steamer) was on Patrol "C" away to the north-west of the Hebrides looking out for the Swedish[1] S.S. *Oscar II*, which was about due from Buenos Aires on her way to Christiania, with a cargo of coffee, hides, etc. The Swede was under suspicion, and at the time mentioned had been sighted and stopped. Unfortunately she struck the *Patuca*, crushing in her own bows, and then, steel to steel, the hulls crunched against each other in the swell, rubbing alongside with a terrible crashing until *Patuca's* propeller bored a hole in the *Oscar's* engine-room. The latter began leaking badly, the engine-room filled, the fires were put out, and altogether this single-screw 3,403-tons ship was in such a bad way that she had to be abandoned, the crew being taken aboard the *Patuca*, who was damaged to the extent of her plates being bulged in one side and flange of her propeller being badly bent. However, by means of the collision-mat, shoring up her side, and filling up the spaces between plates with cement, the armed merchant cruiser was able to become fairly seaworthy and to steam at 14 knots for the Clyde, whither she was ordered by the Admiral to proceed.

To the scene of the accident were now sent the 10th Cruiser Squadron ship *Digby*, and the boarding steamer *Royal Scot*. (These armed boarding steamers were a kind of

---

[1] Not to be confused with the Danish steamer of that name.

link between the Blockading Fleet and the trawlers and yachts of the Auxiliary Patrol; their office being especially to look out for suspicious craft which might be minelayers or submarine depot craft. Such vessels as were used in peace-time by the British railways were especially convenient for this purpose, being practically "little liners".) At 10.30 a.m. the *Royal Scot* took the *Oscar* in tow, whilst *Digby* acted as escort; the tug *Plover* was ordered from Stornoway, and the two destroyers *Fury* and *Staunch* from Scapa Flow. Two steam yachts and six trawlers were likewise sent out from Stornoway.

But matters were not looking too rosy. At 1 p.m. the *Oscar's* upper deck was awash and her tow-rope had parted. Three hours later the *Royal Scot* once more had the Swede and began making for Stornoway, but the speed was only four knots. Anyone who has ever tried to tow a vessel of such a size after she has been mined or torpedoed well knows what a laborious and anxious task it is. The stricken vessel takes an awkward sheer and suddenly goes off to starboard on a wild rush like a sailing ship demented; then she will go about on the other tack, out of control, refusing to obey the helm, and every moment the tow-rope threatens to snap under the strain.

So it was with the *Oscar*, and after a trying night she snapped another tow-rope at 5 a.m. of July 2. Unfortunately the grey wet morning turned into wind, which was rising quickly, together with a nasty Atlantic sea. A tug would have been more suitable than the boarding steamer for this kind of work, but somehow the *Plover* failed to locate the *Oscar*; and in vain the *Digby*, together with the armed yacht *Iolaire*, searched the horizon for the missing unit. Matters were getting worse, speed now dropped to three and a half knots, and at 11.30 a.m. the condition of *Oscar* looked so perilous that it was not safe to let the few hands which had been put aboard her remain; so they were removed. Two hours later the rope parted again, though *Royal Scot* managed to get hold once more. At 5 p.m. progress was checked, and an hour later the tow repeated its annoying antics.

By this time the situation approached the desperate, for presently all the wires had gone excepting that attached to the derelict's cable. There was neither steam nor hand gear on her capstan, and the night, with its misty fog, increased the general anxiety. By 2 a.m. of the 3rd there was every evidence that *Oscar* could not last much longer, and during the ensuing hours she yawed about most tantalizingly, parting her tow for the final time. All wires were now gone, she had pulled out the bollards from her deck, further towing seemed impossible, and the *Royal Scot* was so short of water that she had to leave the job and run into Stornoway. Late that afternoon *Digby* and *Fury* tried to pick up the broken wire, but failed; and the derelict developed a list of 40°, the seas now sweeping over her as across a half-tide rock. At 7 p.m. the tragedy ended when *Oscar* disappeared for all time beneath the Atlantic waves.

It had been a trying time for all, but the sequel did not come till after the War, when the case came before the Prize Court, and Lord Sumner, on May 4, 1920, in delivering judgment of the Privy Council, stated that the collision had been caused by the negligent navigation of *Patuca*, who was alone to blame.

CHAPTER XIII

CAUSE AND EFFECT

FROM the date when the *Lusitania* was sunk, that memorable occasion in May, Germany seemed to become curiously and almost continuously entangled with international trouble. And this narrow-sighted tactlessness conspired to assist the British Blockaders, whose duties all the time tended to cause friction among neutrals.

> Fortunately for England [wrote Commodore G. von Schoultz,[1] who, as a Russian naval officer aboard H.M.S. *Benbow*, was able to view sea affairs from a somewhat independent angle], the distant blockade of Germany, the chief weapon of British naval strategy, was so effective that it already, in itself, guaranteed victory to a very large extent. It was also fortunate that international politics and strategy were working in various ways against the main enemy, so as to increase further the already very difficult task of the submarines.

During the summer of 1915 one incident after another mounted up to make Germany's cause internationally unpopular where it might have been precisely the opposite. Before the United States' indignation over *Lusitania's* torpedoing had died down, another sensation arose when the British Leyland liner *Armenian* (8,825 tons) was torpedoed by U-38 and sunk on June 28 some 54 miles N.W. of the Scillies. She was on her way across the Atlantic to Liverpool, and 20 American citizens of her crew were killed. There had been neither search nor visit, and such an attack was plain piracy. But this was only one unfortunate item in a growing list. For months past the Germans in the United States, by means of an elaborate and comprehensive code, had been

---

[1] *With the British Fleet.* By Commodore G. von Schoultz. P. 214.

sending messages from the States to Berlin through the Sayville wireless station. The Ambassador, Count Bernstorff, and Captain Boy-Ed, the Naval Attaché, in particular had found this medium most useful.

The difficulty was that Sayville should be German-owned, but somehow it must be stopped from being of non-neutral service ; so on July 8 the United States Government took over this station for themselves, and thus vanished the only direct means of communication which the Blockade had left to our enemy. From now onwards the Norwegian, Swedish, and Danish American liners would possess an increasing temptation for German agents, and consequently the need of neutral ships being sent into Kirkwall for examination became even more important. Nor was that all. Sweden, nationally, was so pro-German in sympathy that to offend her would seem mere idiocy. Nevertheless, the Germans did not hesitate to capture the Swedish mail steamer *Bjorn*, open her sealed mailbags from Sweden and Russia destined to England, censor their contents, and only after a long delay return these communications.

Naturally great annoyance was aroused, for the Germans had committed an offence against international conduct and the Hague Convention of October 18, 1907, which laid down the principle that the postal correspondence of neutrals or belligerents found at sea in a neutral ship was to be inviolable. And the result of the *Bjorn* affair was a protest by the Swedish Minister at Berlin against such a wrongful interference. On the other hand, Germany's merchants this same summer were busy using the neutral parcels post to America as an ingenious means of carrying on an export trade for manufactured goods of small bulk and high value, such as the finer grades of textiles.

This went on for a time, but in September Britain announced the intention of examining neutral *parcel* (not letter) mails, and warned neutral mail-steamers against carrying the enemy's parcels. This warning for a time had a desired effect. The German Post Office was obliged to suspend accepting parcels for overseas destinations. A new phase began when the merchants commenced posting their parcels in one of the neutral countries, but the Blockading Fleet and the

British Postal Censorship between them made this practice so dangerous that trade could never expand to serious dimensions.

Such tricks as these were typical of the isolation which the 10th Cruiser Squadron was making ever and ever more acute. The shortage of everything in Germany during July could be disguised by no manner of subterfuge when hungry stomachs cried out for food. Austria was feeling the Blockade severely, so that at the end of June she made an appeal to America, though fruitlessly. Germany had made a terrible blunder when she sank the *Armenian*, but her Note to the United States Government a few days later added fuel to the fires of anger. Washington regretted that the German Note was not satisfactory, and was "keenly disappointed" to find Germany regarded itself as exempt from observing the principle that the character and cargo of a merchantman must first be ascertained before the vessel could lawfully be seized or destroyed ; and that the lives of non-combatants may in no case be jeopardized unless the ship should resist after being summoned to submit for examination.

During this period German agents in the United States were stirring up the cotton people against Britain ; and there were not wanting Southern planters who were willing to listen sympathetically. But Mr. Simms, the Representative for Tennessee, pertinently pointed out that after all it was far better for the planters that the Allies, rather than Germany, should have control of the seas, since normally Britain and France were by far the greater cotton consumers.

It was noticeable from June onwards that many Dutch trawlers from Ymuiden were fishing off Iceland, and that large quantities of both fresh and salted fish were being carried in Norwegian vessels from Iceland to Aalesund in Norway. It was, moreover, an open secret among the Scottish experts that the Dutch catches ultimately went into Germany, whilst other information proved that the Aalesund cargoes were carried to our enemies likewise. Now fish was conditional contraband ; that is to say, vessels carrying this commodity could be arrested if the latter were destined for Germany's armed forces or one of her official[1] departments. The British

---

[1] From February 1, 1915, the German Government took over control of all foodstuffs.

Blockade had caused such a shortage of meat in Germany that fish now occupied a position of the primest importance, not merely for civilians, but for the fighting forces. So here was fresh need for the 10th Cruiser Squadron's vigilance, whose efforts were still being hampered by the Foreign Office's release of neutral ships carrying such invaluable cargoes as cotton and oil.

Thus, for all the monotony of the grey patrol life, there was always some new phase dawning, some new question arising. Certainly never had there been a blockade so full of complexities and varieties. But now arrived the strangest demand of all. Looking back on the past with our present knowledge, it may seem that we attributed to our enemy powers of imagination and originality of initiative which he never actually demonstrated ; yet he had sprung several surprises upon us, and none was more lasting in its effect than the long arm of his submarines. All sorts of theories and rumours got about, and I recollect when employed on special patrol off the S.W. Irish coast in 1915, after the *Lusitania* disaster, the persistent legend (still to-day not wholly dead) that U-boats were using certain of those lonely bays as secret depots. Further embellishments stated that the Irish peasants were supplying tins of petrol, that German submarine officers had more than once landed, and the programme of a local cinema had been found in the pocket of a captured U-boat Captain !

Apart from the fact that these ocean-going submarines did not use petrol, and that any craft doing so long a trip as from Heligoland to the Fastnet and back would scarcely gain much benefit from even a dozen gallons of fuel, there was no truth in the other suggestions. The U-boats' radius of action (Hersing's round-the-British-Isles non-fuelling voyage from Germany to the Mediterranean, for example) was such that there was no necessity for a secret base : they carried vast quantities of oil in their tanks.

But the air of mystery in 1915 still existed, and there was upheld a report that a submarine base was being established at Jan Mayen Island under the disguise of a mercantile company. Whether this alleged corporation had justly been suspected, or whether the whole thing was a myth, no one could say : the matter must be investigated carefully, and no sort of doubt allowed to survive. Jan Mayen Island ? Where was it situate ? How many well-informed people had ever heard of it ?

It lies at the "back of the beyond", on the way to the North Pole, in lat. 71° N., between Iceland and Spitzbergen. Nature dropped this volcanic island into the cold Greenland Sea, but endowed it with few qualities of any value ; yet suddenly, in the middle of a great European War, it had won a keen interest. Admiral de Chair selected the *Alcantara* to go and search if there was any truth in the report, and on July 3 she paid her visit. At this date the suggestion was being also put forward that a German wireless station would there be found.

Captain Wardle was destined to have some unusual experiences during those eventful years. He had twice nearly gone to the bottom of the sea in the *Crescent* and the *Calyx*, respectively, and in a later chapter we shall see him fighting a glorious duel ; but here came an interlude of exploration and wondrous contrast, something quite different from waylaying neutrals. The account which he has kindly given me is that of a most interesting adventure, such as could happen to few naval officers in wartime or peace.

After examining the coast through the glasses, it was evident that only a few places were available for landing, the southerly swell, together with the precipitous cliffs against which the surf dashed itself, making the approach inhospitable. There was only one cove in any way suitable for a submarine base, but large quantities of driftwood and wreckage lined the shores on both sides of the island. The outline of the land was found to have been charted incorrectly, but the *Alcantara* used several anchorages, and at one of them some objects resembling huts were seen, but surf prevented further investigation. At another, however, it was possible to go ashore, and here four wooden huts were discovered that had been used by the Austrian Expedition in the year 1882. Still in fair condition, these dwellings contained several bunks, two stoves, two casks of provisions, and six unopened tin-lined cases.

Outside were about a ton of briquettes, whilst an old-fashioned electric cable led from one hut to beach (a distance of 200 yards), where a flat-bottomed surf-boat in good condition was lying. A signal mast some 20 feet high was noticed near the huts. In one of these at last breathed life. A startled movement ! Gleaming eyes ! On the walls there was proof of

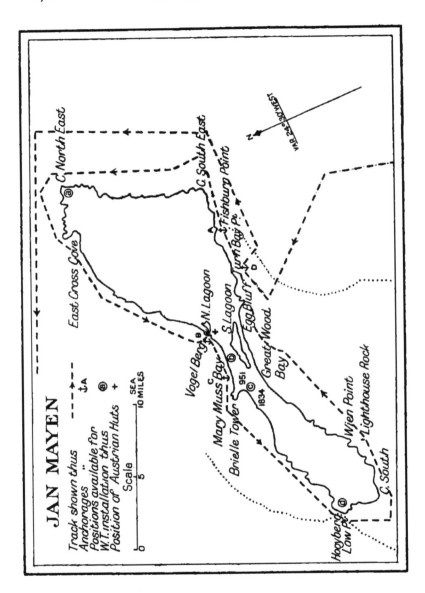

JAN MAYEN

Track shown thus   - - - -
Anchorages   "   ↕A
Positions available for
W.T.installation thus   ⊛
Position of Austrian Huts   +

Scale

|0   5   SEA
                  10 MILES

C.North East
East Cross Cove
C.South East
Fishburg Point
Turn Bay Pt.
N.Lagoon
Vogel Berg
S.Lagoon
Egg Bluff
Great Wood Bay
Mary Muss Bay
951
1834
Brielle Tower
Wfen Point
Lighthouse Rock
C.South
Hooybergs
Low Pt.

VAR.24°.30′WEST
N

a visit by human people ; but the last date written was "27 May, 1914"—two months before the war. The *Alcantara's* parties of exploration ascended four low hills, on two of which poles still remained which had probably once been used for survey.

Having come ashore at a third anchorage, where the beach was shelving, still another hut revealed itself a hundred yards from the sea and in good repair, containing bunk, stove, and several pots. Little else was found on the island except two large iron tanks, red with rust, apparently washed inland with other wreckage. Of wireless, or any indication of a submarine depot, there was not a trace, and the only living creatures comprised a litter of fox-cubs in one of the huts. These wooden buildings, and the other items, were used by trappers on their rare visits, and traps were actually discovered. But it was clear that no one had been to Jan Mayen this present year and, owing to the nature of the ground, signs of a landing would have been plainly visible.

Thus another war myth became wiped out, and definitely no enemy station was being made in these high latitudes, so the *Alcantara* now pushed off westward in the direction of Greenland's icy mountains in order to search for a passage ; but after steaming for 18 hours the ice-pack was encountered stretching E.N.E. Further westward progress being checked, the *Alcantara* steamed to the south, skirting the ice barrier, until the weather became so thick that further investigation was out of the question. It was heavier ice than had been met with off Iceland, and there were observed real detached bergs. Neutrals would not be able for the present to come right north of that island, and here was a second fact established for the Blockaders. So, with a present for the Admiral of a fox-cub, the ship came home.

Nevertheless, unsubstantiated rumours of mysterious depots along the coast of Norway still persisted, and many a keen young British officer not quite free from the influence of juvenile literature evolved daring schemes for revealing these supposed nests. Almost every Commander-in-Chief, no matter in what part of the globe the campaign happened to be, used to receive offers of this sort, but very few were accepted. And it must be confessed that a spirit of adventure had been largely the source of inspiration. Of course, among the

Blockaders one of these novel efforts was planned and put forward for combing out the Norwegian fjords—perhaps a far more formidable task than the inventor had realized— and a motor-schooner with a heavy-oil engine was to be employed. The party were to pretend the expedition was for the purposes of fishing, shooting, and painting, and to consist of a young naval officer, a young subaltern from the Army, and a British civilian who had spent many years in Norway.

The scheme was delightfully boyish, the object being to cruise through all the bays and fjords likely to be available to a U-boat for replenishment of fuel or stores ; discreet information was to be made of the natives, the bases were certain to be located, and the party hoped to destroy at least one submarine. It sounded an ideal adventure trip, and doubtless would have been excellent fun. Luckily, the idea was turned down, and for the best of reasons. There never were U-boat bases in Norway.

By the end of the first week in July 1915 it was possible to look back and take stock of the work which had been done by the Blockading Fleet since its reorganization of last Christmas ; and the figures are remarkable. No fewer than 1,610 ships of various nationalities had been intercepted, regardless of weather, of which the Norwegian (460), Danish (404), Swedish (191), and American (59) formed the most numerous among the neutrals. A total of 396 vessels had been sent into port for examination. That which is still more remarkable can be found in the light of post-war knowledge. Often enough a commanding officer in the 10th Cruiser Squadron would wonder whether, after all, one of the enemy's vessels might not have got through from Germany during the past winter's fogs and dark nights. The chances of climate and the vast expanse of sea were so heavily in favour of a really brave and determined blockade-runner.

It is therefore interesting to state that to-day we know that only one of Germany's ships rushed the patrols, and that was some months previously. She was the ex-British S.S. *Rubens*, 3,600 tons, which the enemy was particularly anxious should reach East Africa with supplies for the German naval and military forces. Changing the name of this merchantman into *Kronberg*, and pretending she was a Dane, the enemy sent her forth in February. She left the Skaw on February 19, and had the pluck to steam between the Orkneys and Shetlands during the darkness. Fortune favoured her daring Captain, and she duly reached East Africa. As in another place[1] I have already narrated her fate, no further reference need be made ; but the proportion of one to 1,610 is so noteworthy that in any future naval wars it will be difficult for any blockading force to attain such an efficient standard.

We have seen at what cost of fuel this barrier was maintained, and the following list is valuable as showing that the Blockading Fleet consisted of 24 ships, 884 officers, and 6,275 men : a personnel of merely 7,159 was causing economic paralysis to the enemy and signing his death warrant. When one considers how insignificant seven thousand lives were regarded by the Armies on the Western Front, and that a single squadron of eight battleships among the Grand Fleet comprised such a number, one realizes that never during the whole European War was such effective work done at so comparatively small an expense.

NUMBERS OF OFFICERS AND MEN SERVING IN THE 10TH CRUISER SQUADRON IN JULY 1915

SHIP	OFFICERS (ROYAL NAVY)	OFFICERS (ROYAL NAVAL RESERVE)	OFFICERS (R.N.V.R.)	MEN
Alsatian	17	48	2	480
Cedric	6	42	—	330
Otway	4	41	—	320
Columbella	3	24	1	270
Patia	4	23	1	200
Mantua	3	40	1	320
Hildebrand	3	26	1	270
Arlanza	4	34	1	220
Teutonic	5	51	1	380
Motagua	3	25	1	200
Alcantara	3	34	1	300
Carried Forward	55	388	10	3,290

[1] *The Königsberg Adventure*, London, 1932, pp. 141-146. It should be added that at the end of November 1914, whilst the old "Edgars" were being paid off after the heavy gale and there was no efficient Blockade till the new year, the S.S. *Rio Negro*, with some of the *Karlsruhe's* survivors from the South Atlantic, got unmolested round the north of Scotland and interned herself at the Norwegian port of Aalesund. (See Chapter VIII of my *The Sea-Raiders*.)

Ship	Officers (Royal Navy)	Officers (Royal Naval Reserve)	Officers (R.N.V.R.)	Men
Brought forward	55	388	10	3,290
Orcoma . .	4	34	1	280
Virginian .	4	36	—	220
Victorian .	3	36	2	200
Oropesa .	3	30	1	200
Orotava . .	4	24	1	200
Andes . .	3	36	1	300
Changuinola .	3	23	1	190
Hilary . .	3	28	1	220
Digby . .	3	19	1	210
Patuca . .	3	24	1	205
Ebro . .	3	29	1	230
Ambrose .	3	29	1	260
India . . .	3	28	1	270
Totals . .	97	764	23	6,275

It will be observed that, whilst nominally a *naval* squadron, the personnel by a considerable majority consisted of mercantile officers in the proportion of seven to one. The numbers of men given are only approximate, but here the ratio in favour of the Mercantile Marine was not less great. Thus, in short, whilst the commanding officers came from the Royal Navy, every one of the ships, and most of the other people, were not professional warriors, but temporarily lent from vessels of commerce. The lesson to be learned is obvious : the strength of a maritime nation is to be found as much in its sea-carriers as in its sea-fighters.

Nor did the King forget to reward such devotion to duty, for early in August came a number of decorations to this Squadron, including a D.S.O. for Captain Trewby, the *Alsatian's* commanding officer ; Commander E. Outram, R.N.R. (her peace-time Master) ; and Engineer-Commander R. Wilson, R.N.R. (her peace-time Chief Engineer). Several petty officers and leading seamen in the flagship were awarded either the D.S.C. or D.S.M., whilst a number of honours went to various other vessels in this hard-worked Squadron.

Nevertheless, the general public still remained ignorant of what all these ships and men represented in the great European drama now ending its first year.

CHAPTER XIV

DURING this summer a Black List of neutral ships had been compiled, though it was not until the end of the following February that it was complete. The principle, however, was useful, and saved much trouble: if the intercepted vessel's name was in this category, she was sent into port without further question. At this date there was still considerable traffic passing through the Blockade to and from Archangel, and many were the stories which shipmasters brought concerning those "mystery men" and secret agents of Germany at work in that port. There was reason, also, for believing that German financiers were sending by neutral steamers to New York large numbers of American bonds, and this placed the west-bound passenger ships under a new suspicion.

During July U-boats had been working both to the east and west of the Shetlands, increasing the risk to vessels that were being sent in under armed guards. This was a source of no little anxiety, for now the interceptions had risen to 115 a week. It was quite clear that the submarines had been instructed at home to find out the positions of our Blockade Patrols, for on July 25 a U-boat armed with two guns stopped a Norwegian steamer, ordered the Master aboard, and asked whether he had seen any British cruisers. Another Norwegian was similarly stopped and interrogated by the submarine as to whether there were other steamers in Liverpool loading for Archangel.

And now there came over the Blockade a condition that was something quite new and equally alarming. It was a phase both complicating and curious. The *Motagua* had

intercepted the Norwegian S.S. *Fimreite*, and an armed guard
was taking the latter into Kirkwall, when, at 4 a.m. on July 23, a
submarine was sighted on the port bow making for the *Fimreite* at high speed. The position was lat. 60°17′ N., long.
8°43′ W., that is to say, in the locality a long distance north-
west of the Hebrides, and a region where U-boats had been
seen on previous occasions.

This morning the German fired a gun, ordered the Master
to stop and send a boat, which was done. The situation for
the armed guard was not pleasant. It was under the care of
a young officer, Mr. P. B. Clarke, Midshipman, R.N.R. If
the U-boat Captain should entertain even the slightest notion
of the Englishmen's presence, what would happen ? The
Midshipman made a pretty shrewd guess, and reckoned that
his first duty to his King and Service was to preserve his four
men ; so, whilst the Norwegian Master was aboard the submarine, Clarke ordered his guard to take off their uniforms,
disguise themselves as much as possible, put their revolvers
in their pockets, and assist the Norwegian crew in lowering
the boats. The Master returned aboard and stated that he
had been questioned as to his destination.

"Where are you bound ?" the German had asked.

"Hull," came the answer.

"Going there direct ?"

"No : via Kirkwall."

(Ah ! The German knew what that meant.)

"Then you have a Prize Crew on board ?"

"Yes : one British officer and four soldiers."

"I shall sink you for trading with the English. Get into
your boats, but you shall not let the Englishmen get in. They
are to be sunk with the ship."

Clarke, however, thought differently, and got his party into
the boats. As soon as the latter were clear, the U-boat opened
fire on the *Fimreite* with a gun. About fifteen projectiles
came whizzing across, one striking the boilers, and down sank
the Norwegian steamer bow first, whilst 29 German officers
and men (most of them in duffle suits) watched the incident
from the submarine's deck. The latter, now fully satisfied,
dived and made off to the westward. For most of that day
the Norwegian's boats flicked about the lonely Atlantic,

but by the mercy of God at 3.30 in the afternoon they were marvellously saved from dying of exposure and starvation. There came along not a steamer, but another Norwegian, and a sailing ship at that. She was the barque *Springbank*, who picked them up, and eventually transferred Clarke with his four men to the *Caliban*, who brought them safely into Stornoway.

Now not long after this incident occurred one of the strangest sequences of the whole War. On June 23 there set sail from New York the barque *Pass of Balmaha*, once a proud possession of the British Mercantile Marine before the conquest by steam, but by this date she had passed into United States ownership, and now she was coming across with a crew of 20 and a cargo of cotton bound for Archangel. A month passed, and she approached the Blockade zone, when the *Victorian* stopped her, put aboard an armed guard, consisting of an officer, petty-officer, with four men, to take her into Kirkwall or Lerwick, according to the wind's decision. During the next couple of days the voyage continued, when the disconcerting sight of U-36 appeared. This evening the 26 people in the sailing ship watched the submarine torpedo and sink a steamer.

Next morning (July 24), at 6 a.m., U-36 again appeared, when she was seen to sink a British trawler and a small coasting steamer. It is not necessary to stress the suspense, during all these hours, of those in the American sailing ship. For the armed guard, at least, the hand of fate could be perceived approaching with the sureness of destiny. "Our turn next!" An hour later U-36 was able to switch her attention to the vessel flying the Stars and Stripes, and came alongside. But the armed guard? What to do in this predicament?

The *Victorian's* officer acted quickly, burnt his secret orders, told his men to borrow clothing from the American crew, and sent his five to stow themselves in the forepeak till the submarine had finished and departed. But the submarine's Captain (Lieut.-Commander Graeff) decided to capture the *Pass of Balmaha*, and put on board Petty-Officer Lamm with orders to take her into Cuxhaven. Germany would be glad to receive the cotton. During these days quite a number of sinkings were being made off north Scotland by other

M

submarines, and Graeff wirelessed through to another U-boat near the Shetlands that the sailing ship was to be found and escorted.

The armed guard was in a quandary, for U-36 continued visible a while; but the Englishmen were expecting every hour to sight one of our patrols, when all would be well. The ship would be again captured and Lamm taken prisoner. Now the extraordinary and sad fact must be mentioned that the *Pass of Balmaha* somehow sailed through a "dead" zone, and, to the chagrin of *Victorian's* party, not one of the familiar Blockading Fleet crossed their path. Why? Because, Patrol "C" having been passed already, there was no other blockade-line south of the Faroes, and in any case the submarine menace just now required that these armed merchant cruisers should not operate too far south. The result was that, with marvellous good fortune, the *Pass of Balmaha* got untouched into the North Sea, past the local patrols of the Shetlands and Orkneys, thence to the southward, and eventually all the way into Cuxhaven, where she arrived early in August, having been picked up and escorted as far as Heligoland by the submarine who had been called up. The *Victorian's* armed guard were taken ashore as prisoners, and Petty-Officer Lamm (undoubtedly a brave and enterprising fellow) was sent for to receive the congratulations of Admiral von Pohl, Commander-in-Chief of the German Navy. And here we must leave the *Pass of Balmaha* for the next eighteen months, until one Christmas morning she reappeared in another rush through the Blockade.[1] If ever a ship had an adventurous career, it was this barque which made our enemies a free gift of the longed-for cotton.

But we have not yet finished with U-36 and Lieut.-Commander Graeff. There had steamed out of Scapa Flow in the glow of a July evening an undistinguished little collier of only 373 tons, similar in type to so many of those steamers which used to bring fuel and other supplies north to the Grand Fleet. The name of this vessel was the *Prince Charles*, and she was scarcely worth a second glance. Away she slowly ambled to the westward, but she saw very few vessels. At

---

[1] See Chapter XXII.

6.20 p.m. on July 24—that is to say, about twelve hours after Graeff had captured the *Pass of Balmaha*—the collier *Prince Charles* happened to be about 10 miles W.N.W. of North Rona Island, that isolated rock which lies between the Hebrides and Shetlands. She now witnessed a sight such as the *Pass of Balmaha* had seen too often.

Little more than two miles away, and apparently stopped, was the *Louise*, a three-masted Danish steamer with one funnel, and fifteen minutes later a submarine alongside was also descried. The *Prince Charles* continued on her course at the slow, steady jog-trot-thump-go, jog-thump-trot-go, after the manner of her breed, when the U-boat (like the fable of the dog with a piece of meat) suddenly left the *Louise*, started up her oil-engines, and hurried at full speed towards the wretched collier, who hoisted her Red Ensign. A German shell came tearing its way towards *Prince Charles*, but fell 1,000 yards beyond; whereupon the collier stopped engines, blew three blasts to indicate her engines were going astern, checked way, and began lowering boats. Meanwhile there came a second shell, which passed between funnel and foremast but fell 50 yards over. Getting pretty well on to the target now!

When the submarine was only 600 yards away, she turned her broadside to the collier and resumed fire. But just then something happened, dramatic and wonderful, surprising beyond all thought; for the smoke-grimed collier hit back, opened fire with her guns, causing the German gunners to desert their post and hop down into the conning-tower quick-quickly. More shells from the *Prince Charles* rained down; frequent hits were registered; the submarine was holed and began to sink by the stern; two men were already killed in the conning-tower; the bows stood up into the air; the sea became black with Germans swimming for their lives; and in one final plunge the submarine disappeared to the bottom for ever. The collier rescued as many as possible, four commissioned officers, two warrant officers, and nine men out of a total of 33 being thus saved and taken prisoners.

So perished U-36.

Who and what was the *Prince Charles* ?

She had just been fitted out as a submarine decoy, and this was the very first of the so-called "Q-ship" actions which

opened up a new chapter in modern naval warfare. Besides
her peace-time Master, Mr. F. N. Maxwell, and crew of nine,
she was now carrying under the command of Lieut. Mark
Wardlaw, R.N., an R.N.R. officer together with nine active-
service ratings. Armed with only a 3-pdr. and a 6-pdr. on
either side, her guns were cleverly concealed by tarpaulins,
but their accurate and rapid fire impressed the survivors
immensely. Rapidity and accuracy were essential ; otherwise
U-36 with her 14-pdr. gun and torpedoes would have sent
the *Prince Charles* to join other steamers down below.

It was well that, with all these submarines now pressing
north, the boom defence at Swarbacks Minn coaling-base
was approaching completion, where already five colliers with
15,000 tons of fuel had arrived. But another awkward
predicament of an armed guard indicated that the new peril
was more than a mere gesture. It was July 28 ; the *Hildebrand*
on the previous day had stopped that familiar *Trondhjemfjord*
(New York to Bergen with general cargo) and ordered her into
Kirkwall with an armed guard, when at 12.25 p.m. a submarine
appeared and began shelling the Norwegian. The Master
altered course to bring the U-boat astern and steamed off
at full speed with the enemy following ; but after half an hour
the German was fast overhauling and again shelling *Trondhjemfjord*, so the latter had no other alternative except to stop.

As usual, the Master (Captain Bang) was ordered aboard
the U-boat with his ship's papers, but he was a very fine,
considerate seafarer. Equally unselfish and thoughtful was
his wife, who happened to be travelling with him. Their
conduct throughout was of a brave independence worthy to
be remembered, and not every neutral would have behaved
as they. Before going off in the lowered boat, Captain Bang
arranged for the disguise of Lieutenant Crawford, R.N.R.,
and the latter's armed guard. The good wife provided Crawford with some of her husband's clothes, and, by that practised
art of dissimulation so natural to her sex, packed the officer's
uniform among her own effects preparatory for removal in
one of the boats. The guard's rifles and other gear were
concealed in the steamer's forepeak.

Scarcely had Captain Bang stepped aboard the submarine
than the latter signalled the *Trondhjemfjord* to abandon ship

immediately. By 1.25 p.m., only an hour after the first encounter, everyone had got into the boats, and at 130 yards the U-boat fired a torpedo which struck the steamer amidships. Over she listed heavily to port, but, owing to a large quantity of sulphuric acid in the cargo, there followed a loud explosion, scattering debris to the height of the mastheads. At 2.51 p.m. the steamship foundered. Once again did that rare thing, a ship under sail, come to the rescue ; for after the submarine had taken in tow for four miles to the southward the boats containing crew and guard, the Norwegian barque *Glance* was met with, who received them on board.

There presently was sighted by *Glance* the Swedish S.S. *Orlando* bound for Sweden, and to this vessel all were transferred, Captain Bang and his party thus continuing their voyage ; but the armed guard were again transferred, this time to the trawler *Princess Juliana,* and thereby reached Thurso after their many adventures. They owed their freedom from capture or injury entirely to Captain Bang, who turned out to be the most loyal friend. When the U-boat commanding officer inquired if the *Trondhjemfjord* had been boarded by a British patrol, or whether an armed guard had been put aboard, Captain Bang lied manfully : he would probably have been shot had the truth been discovered by the Germans.

Captain K. S. Irgens, of the troublesome *Bergensfjord,* which had been stopped west-bound for New York on July 9, was reserved and courteous in manner, and used to have a typewritten letter of protest in good English all in readiness to send through the Boarding Officer for the latter's Captain.

I readily admit your full right to visit and search my ship on the high seas [it would begin], *and to bring it into port for the necessary detention, when there is sufficient evidence to believe that contraband articles are in my cargo ; but if such evidence is not present, I regret not to be able to admit your right to take my ship into port. . . . In such case it will therefore be necessary that you take complete charge of my ship, and the whole responsibility for my ship, passengers, mails and cargo, until my ship is again outside of the "war zone". I shall also ask you in your instructions to your officers in charge of my ship to be aware of the extremely dangerous position, in which my ship will be put, if she is stopped, or signalled to stop, with a British "Prize Crew" on board.*

That was his firm standpoint, and doubtless any one of us in the same situation as Captain Irgens, anxious for the charge committed to him, would have taken up the same attitude ; yet the fact remains that his ship was a perpetual embarrassment to the Blockade, and no steamer gave so much trouble to the Cruiser Squadron Captains. Captain Irgens was proud of his 17 knots speed, and seemed to imagine that he could always get away from our patrols. He was wrong : even after a long chase, interception followed, though she did her utmost to elude them. "I stopped the *Bergensfjord* one night", writes one of these commanding officers to me, "when she was westward-bound north of the Faroes, showing no lights except her sidelights." Sometimes even these were out, and the risk to traffic of a liner tearing about the sea at such a speed on a dark night was one of the conditions which had to be faced.

The *Bergensfjord* must have been highly profitable to her owners during those months, for she wasted little time in port, and on the first of August was again stopped and sent into Kirkwall, this time by the *Alsatian*, for a thorough inspection. Among her cargo were such items as loaded shells and cartridges, but besides her passengers and crew were 24 men working their passage. Once again, too, the Danish S.S. *Oscar II*, New York to Copenhagen, was sent into Kirkwall.

By the end of July the ice was leaving Iceland and a passage quite close to the north shore was being used by sealers and fishermen. It was definitely established that the *Bergensfjord's* favourite route, both outward and homeward, was to pass through lat. 63° N., long. 7° W. (i.e. well north of the Faroes), and she kept to schedule so regularly that she usually was at that spot about 2 p.m. on the Sunday after departure from New York. There is no doubt that Captain Irgens was a very able officer. When the officers of the British armed guards remained on board, they were treated by him with great courtesy and took their meals with the saloon passengers. On requesting to be allowed to pay for their hospitality, the British officers were informed that they were guests of the Norske-Amerika Line.

There now comes into our story one more of those tragedies which are inseparable from grim war. The reader will recollect the institution of that new Patrol "G" off the Norwegian coast for the purpose of interrupting the Narvik ore-steamers, and as recently as August 8 the *Virginian* captured the Swedish S.S. *Vollrath Than*, with 8,000 tons of this contraband bound for the Germans via Rotterdam. Other units normally patrolling this important area were the *Ebro*, *Teutonic*, and *India*. The approaches to West Fjord had gained an increased importance ever since the trawler *Tenby Castle* had demonstrated the rewards of vigilance.

But it could not be long before this tighter control of the Blockade section would be contended. German agents in such ports as Narvik and Bergen would learn all about it from shipmasters and pilots. Exact news of the patrol ships, their names, their cruising stations, would quickly reach Berlin. The latter's reply would consist in sending out either a division of light but fast cruisers to wipe out the patrol and then scurry back home before the Grand Fleet learned too much; or better still and more economical would be the very plan which Admiral de Chair had so much desired for the opposite operation of striking terror by means of the submarine. Since the War we know on the authority of the German naval historian, Captain Gayer, that information did reach Berlin through an agent that "an English cruiser was permanently stationed" off West Fjord, and it was now decided that the best antidote to the interference with the ore-ships was to send forth submarines.

Even on July 11, the *Ebro* sighted a U-boat off this Fjord in lat. 69°22′ N., long. 15°15′ E., but on August 3 there left Borkum for this special service U-22, which during the very first week of War had (with three others) been scouting at the southern end of the North Sea. It was a little time— a whole day and a half—before the vague fear could be established that something terrible had happened. The *Virginian*, on the afternoon of Sunday, August 8, was trying to pass an important signal through to the *India* that the German auxiliary cruiser *Meteor* had started out from the Heligoland Bight that morning and was expected to pass up the Norwegian coast, probably on her way to lay mines in the White Sea. Such information was more than enough to keep the *India* very much on the alert. Actually, however, the *Meteor* was not bound for the White Sea this time, though she had rushed past the coast last June, reached the White Sea, laid a series of minefields[1] (which had disastrous results), and got safely back to Germany. Her mission on August 8 was to lay a minefield in the Moray Firth, so she never got so far north as the *India*. How the *Meteor* succeeded, and the extraordinary adventures which happened to her immediately afterwards, I have narrated in another volume,[2] and they need not here be repeated.

On Sunday, at 8 a.m., the *India* had reported her position, but during the early hours of Tuesday *Virginian* (senior ship in Patrol "G"), after calling her up by wireless for nearly three hours, could get no answer. It was quite certain now that the *India* had met trouble some time between Sunday afternoon and 2.15 a.m. of Tuesday. The full story may now be presented as follows :

It was a mere coincidence that two sad losses—one an armed merchant cruiser, the other an armed boarding steamer —should both occur within twelve hours of each other yet at different parts of the North Sea. It was even still more strange that the *Meteor*, herself an improvised warship, was to suffer such a dramatic fate, and to become so curiously concerned with another submarine, U-28. These, again, were just the chances of war. The commanding officer of *India* was Commander W. G. A. Kennedy, R.N., and he was very busy during Sunday patrolling off the West Fjord through a line which may be described with accuracy as along the parallel of 67°30′ N., from as far west as 11°30′ E. to as far east as 13°30′ E., which brought him very close to the Norwegian coast. The armed trawlers *Saxon* and *Newland* were also hereabouts.

The first incident occurred about 8.30 a.m., when these two trawlers were sighted to the north with the Swedish S.S. *Gloria*. The *India* stopped and sent an officer aboard

---

[1] See map of these positions at p. 111 of my *The Auxiliary Patrol*.
[2] See my *The Sea-Raiders*, Chapter XIII.

to examine *Gloria*, but after a most thorough search, lasting an hour and a half, she was allowed to proceed. At 11 a.m., whilst steaming at 14 knots and zigzagging for fear of submarines, *India* closed the Swedish S.S. *Atland* in order to identify her. The latter was keeping carefully inside the 3-mile limit. At noon came an urgent wireless message from *Virginian* to send the *Gloria* into Kirkwall, so speed was raised to 16½ knots and search was made to the north, but the steamer had vanished, and *India* now eased to 14 knots, but resumed her zigzagging. At 3 p.m. a British steamer in ballast bound for Archangel was spoken, and presently the trawler *Saxon*.

The summer afternoon began to wane, a steamer of sorts was reported coming up from the south-east, and Commander Kennedy altered course to try and intercept. He had just left the bridge temporarily to give the wireless operator an order, leaving Sub-Lieut. E. W. Alltree, R.N.R., in charge, the time being 5.40 p.m. Suddenly the look-out man on the fo'c'sle reported : "Submarine on starboard bow !" Looking in the direction indicated, Alltree saw the white feathery track of a torpedo approaching from only 300 yards away. Commander Kennedy had barely left the wireless-house and reached the next (hurricane) deck, when he heard the alarm gongs sounding.

Running back to the bridge, he was in time to witness the torpedo track foaming at an angle of about 30 degrees from the bow.

"Full speed ahead ! Hard aport !"

The order was obeyed promptly, and at first it looked as if danger had just been averted, for the track seemed to have reached the ship and nothing to have happened. Evidently the missile had gone under the hull !

Then came that ominous thud, with the explosion. A hit !

The torpedo struck its target below No. 3 starboard gun, and immediately the ex-P. & O. liner began to sink by the stern, heeling 10 degrees to port. The Commander ordered messages requesting assistance to be sent out, and then came "Abandon Ship !"

Seven boats had been kept in a state of readiness for such

an emergency, and swung out. In spite of the appalling swiftness of the catastrophe, the most perfect discipline and behaviour continued till the end. Boats were being lowered, life-rafts being prepared, extra lifebelts being served out, whilst down below water was rapidly rising in the engine-room, where a like stoic calmness prevailed till the sea swept the staff away. Unfortunately, as many readers well know, there are few occasions more difficult than that of trying to lower boats from a sinking merchant steamer with the old-fashioned davits. Over and over again it happens that one of the falls (the ropes by which a boat is lowered) runs out with a rush and shoots its people into the water. But especially awkward is the lowering when the ship has a heavy list.

Thus the starboard boats never reached the water, being hopelessly thrown into confusion because the first lifeboat's foremost fall freed itself, ran out, and so made the boat to swing round, fouling two others, whilst the fourth (and last) got stove in against the steep-heeling ship's side. On the port side, however, three out of the four boats were safely lowered and got clear ; but—again an accident which had so often occurred in peace-time to big steamers—the fourth boat capsized as she touched water, just because the stricken vessel had still got so much way. The result was that, notwithstanding all the efforts to save life, there perished nine officers and 107 men, only 189 officers and men surviving, but 157 of these had either dived off the ship or, having gone down with her, came up again.

There is no sadder sight for a sailor than a sinking ship— many of us can never forget the pain during those war years of seeing some noble vessel lurching and wallowing helplessly before the final plunge—yet for the Captain who has nursed his ship through gales and danger zones, only to find her suddenly slipping from under his feet, there is a particularly poignant grief, which is no more capable of being described than the distress of a mother weeping for her firstborn can be expressed in words. Commander Kennedy had neither the time nor the chance to readapt and react to the quickly changing conditions. Five minutes ago he was on the bridge ; then he was trying to save his men ; another swift spasm and he found himself going down with the *India*, clinging to the foremost port davit, till he eventually floated up alive among the wreckage and was hauled into a boat.

Sub-Lieut. Alltree was able to leave in one of the boats that was already about full, and only with difficulty on touching the water could she get away from *India*, which was going ahead at 10 knots in spite of the change in trim. A horrible spectacle then presented itself to him who, a few minutes ago, had been officer-of-the-watch. He saw the vessel's stern go deep down, her bows lift right out of the water, the guns on the fo'c'sle carry away, the hull break in two—and then nothing remained of the 8,000-ton liner that had made so many safe voyages during the last nineteen years, only a confused, meaningless mass of spars, rafts, and broken wreckage floating this way and that. Already 35 men were in the boat, whilst another was dangerously deep, having shipped so much water in the act of being lowered.

Some men were still struggling in the swell to anything that floated, but now a Swedish steamer from a couple of miles away had observed their plight and was coming to their assistance, though the present danger existed in the overcrowded boat being likely to capsize. Sub-Lieut. Alltree, after heading for the steamer, finally decided to make the land, which was some seven miles E.S.E. at Helligvar. He saw the *Saxon* going to rescue those still in the water, but he saw also (after going a couple of miles) the periscope of the submarine. It came towards the boat and dived only when some thirty yards away. At 8.30 that evening Alltree's party reached Helligvar, where the Norwegians received them with kindness, giving them food and rooms for the night. Early in the following morning three bodies were brought ashore by local motor-boats. A Norwegian gunboat took the survivors and bodies to Bodo. Other survivors were picked up by the *Saxon* and the Swedish steamer, thus reaching Narvik together with eleven more bodies. With full honours, and attended by Norwegian naval, military, and civil authorities, the sad funeral ceremonies took place, flowers, evergreens, and wreaths from the kindly Norwegians being placed with the White Ensign, Union Jack, and Red Ensign picked up from the *India*.

But now began a dismal period for eager warriors snatched out of war and death into inactivity. No more chance of toiling for victory against the enemy ; no more days and nights on patrol. They were transferred to an internment camp near Lillehammer, and three long years in a strange land must pass before the War should finish.

Thus did U-22 make matters temporarily easier for the ore-ships, though the Patrol "G" still continued, and on August 13 one of the units intercepted the S.S. *Gotaland* bound for Middlesbrough. This was the Swedish vessel which had picked up 88 of *India's* crew, and she brought news that the *Saxon* had rescued 46. The trawler patrols (including *Tenby Castle*) were now moved some distance south, but still continued their risky and lonely vigil in lat. 64°18′ N., long. 10° E., to intercept shipping in the neighbourhood of Kya Island, whilst submarines continued to operate, and one even stopped a Norwegian steamer and seized mails addressed to the Allies.

Commander Ernst Hashagen, who happened to be serving in U-22, has recently published in his experiences the German version of how the *India* was sunk. "For months past", he writes, "reports had been coming in repeatedly that a British auxiliary cruiser was operating off the Lofotens and disturbing the German ore traffic from Narvik. We were to put a stop to this business by attacking and sinking the ship." The torpedo was fired at 1,200 yards, and, after hitting *India*, the submarine dived to 10 fathoms. When again she was sighted it was because she returned "to the scene of the wreck after about two hours to fish up buoys or other flotsam which may reveal the ship's name, which we do not yet know". But U-22 was frightened by the British trawler and Norwegian, "so we abandon our intent and retire again submerged". Not till the submarine got back to Germany was it learned that the victim had been the *India*.

CHAPTER XV

THE War had been going on for a year, the Blockade had gradually become a fine mesh, so that whilst the Foreign Office still caused some extraordinary releases—to the utter amazement of Admiral Jellicoe and Admiral de Chair—there was in general the denial of most commodities to our enemies. And the effects were manifest now in more than one category. It mattered little that one outward-bound steamer and one inward-bound sailing ship had slipped through the patrol lines, though the facility with which iron ore and cotton arrived in Germany must always seem to posterity a remarkable weakness of the Blockade net. Had the submarine problem and other considerations only permitted a more determined thwarting of the Narvik trade, then the results would have been to Germany so vital that before long the High Sea Fleet might have come out on a raid. The Grand Fleet was based so near to hand that an historic engagement should have followed. And the Germans would have been compelled either to risk a big battle on behalf of their iron supplies, or else gradually to let the War be lost through lack of shells.

By the month of August 1915 the whole of the new oat crop in Germany was confiscated by the military authorities, and meat became both rare and dear, costing 60 per cent more than in England. In Bremen a cotton-importation company was founded with a capital of £200,000 to centralize the importation into Germany and make firm offers to American cotton exporters. Financed by the German banks, this new move was a keen effort to make sure of the second most essential commodity, now that iron seemed so reliable in large quantities.

It was on August 22 that the enemy received an ugly shock. At long last—but only in response to public opinion, our Press, and Parliament—the Foreign Office agreed to declare cotton to be Absolute Contraband, which meant that bales could be seized in neutral ships if the cotton were destined for the Central Powers. And we had waited more than twelve months for such a decision! The official announcement which accompanied this declaration clearly showed a certain sense of shame for delay, and a continued fear of America, rather than a rigid will to starve our enemies of food and munitions. In justification for not having made cotton to be Absolute Contraband long ago, Whitehall defended its dilatoriness thus:

> While circumstances might have justified such action at an earlier period, His Majesty's Government are glad to think that local conditions of American interests likely to be affected are more favourable for such a step than they were a year ago; and, moreover, His Majesty's Government contemplate the initiation of measures to relieve, as far as possible, any abnormal depression which might temporarily disturb market conditions.

Now it is curious to note that during these months, whilst Britain was even nervously anxious to keep friendly with the United States, Germany, in the clumsiest manner of her submarine policy, was again causing Washington great irritation. The *Lusitania* and *Armenian* affairs still rankled, when on August 19, without any visit, search, or warning, a U-boat sank the White Star liner *Arabic* not so very far from the spot where *Lusitania* had perished. Diplomatic relations became strained; Count Bernstorff a week later informed Mr. Lansing that submarine commanders had now been warned not to attack any more merchantmen without warning; and Germany had to promise that full satisfaction would be made for the *Arabic's* sinking. The effect of this climb-down should be carefully noted. From September 24 to the following March 1 (when Germany began her extended submarine campaign), practically no more ships of commerce were sunk by U-boats. So the Blockade operations were not independent proceedings, but subject to the interplay of trans-Atlantic influences.

The German retired naval officer and writer, Captain L. Persius, before he died was able to reveal just after the War that by September 1915 everything was not well with the German Navy, that a spirit of pessimism had set in and the seeds of mutiny, though not yet fructified, were growing. To-day we know from other German writers that Captain Persius was not exaggerating. What was the cause of the discontent ? In part it was the haughty overbearing Prussianism of the officers, the utter disregard of any consideration for the warrant officers, petty officers, and ratings ; but it was partly the inferior food, and the monotonous inactivity, for which the pressure of the Grand Fleet and 10th Cruiser Squadron was largely responsible. The crowding of men together in confined spaces; the ever'asting, never-ceasing drill to keep the men occupied; the repression of all individuality; the severe punishments for trivial faults; the bad commissariat in the lower deck; the desperation of German naval officers, expressed in carousals, their secret smuggling ashore to their own families of parcels of food (sometimes hidden in laundry baskets) which had been rightly intended for the crews ; the friction with America; the failure of submarines as blockaders: all this created a feeling of dejection, promulgated a sense of distrust. "It is so useless to contend against England. Why continue the struggle ?"

So surely and steadily was the British Blockading Fleet doing its duty, whilst unable to see the results. Nevertheless, those British authorities who sat in their office chairs on shore went on blundering. With some difficulty and trouble the American S.S. *Llama*, carrying a large cargo of oil, had been chased by vessels of the 10th Cruiser Squadron and finally captured. An armed guard had run the prevailing risks of submarines and taken her into Kirkwall, yet by a mysterious mentality someone in authority had ordered her release and allowed her to proceed on her way to Germany. She duly arrived at Swinemunde, where her most welcome cargo fetched a high price. "It seemed incredible", Admiral de Chair complained, "that after a year's war experience we should deliberately allow such supplies to reach the enemy after the carrying ships had been intercepted."

If the Blockading Fleet had done nothing else, it would

have been yet worth while for its work in preventing German patriots from getting home to serve in the fighting forces. Still they came aboard neutral ships of all sorts, and still they were arrested. At the beginning of September, six German men were found aboard the Danish S.S. *United States* by the *Oropesa's* Boarding Officer. Before the month's end a German chemist was taken from the Norwegian sailing vessel *Bonanza*. She was bound for Bergen, and doubtless, when he joined her in New York, it was imagined that such a ship might get through without excessive trouble. A week later the *Ebro* found a "wanted" German (working as a trimmer) aboard the Danish S.S. *Jelling* (Baltimore for Copenhagen), whilst another was found in the Swedish S.S. *Avesta* bound for Christiania.

The problem of the Narvik ore-ships had now settled down to the unsatisfactory condition that a large amount of traffic was passing by the inshore channel and kept its course rigidly within territorial waters, thereby reducing the efforts of armed merchant cruisers and trawlers to impotence. But some day there would be a further effort and more raids. In the meantime the Squadron was preparing to face another autumn and winter with the gales of wind and long nights. In every ship of Admiral de Chair's force there had been added on the foremast, well above the height of funnels, the second look-out crow's-nest which had been found so useful in some units. An excellently improved range of vision now ensured that neutrals could be sighted before the merchant cruisers themselves were descried. The wisdom of the Busta Voe base was being proved. The harbour was ideal for the purpose, all ships when inside being totally hidden from any vessels passing outside. However hard it might be blowing, units could lie securely anchored in smooth water and carry on their coaling, watering, or temporary repairs, and then put to sea with 1,000 tons in their bunkers.

The final weeks of the season's submarine activity did not pass without a thrill for the *Patia*. On Saturday night, September 11, about 10 o'clock, she chanced to be on patrol west of the Hebrides, when she collided with the *Oropesa*. The latter was thought to have sustained comparatively small damage, but the *Patia's* fore compartment was flooded, and

Ebro was sent to escort her south to the Clyde. When daylight came, the *Oropesa* revealed injuries which included plates and frames bent from waterline to upper deck, and boat-deck cut into, and she was also leaking. So she was ordered to the Clyde.

But the sequel was amusing. The *Patia's* stem was seriously injured, and the water was up to her collision bulk-head, which was shored up, and ballast was shifted aft so as to bring her stem well up. In this trim she proceeded to steam stern first, but made such slow progress that she headed for the Hebrides for preliminary repairs. In the early hours of Monday morning, whilst it was yet dark, both she and *Ebro* sighted the lights of what seemed to be a steamer, which *Ebro* proceeded to investigate. When the latter came up to the lights, it was no steamer, but a submarine, and so close that the merchant cruiser could not fire at her. The U-boat dived, but presently rose again and showed a light, where-upon the *Ebro* tried to ram, but the enemy (who was evidently on the surface for the charging of her batteries, and was somewhat short of electricity) now disappeared once more.

For *Patia*, steaming stern first at no better than three knots, this sudden submarine zone was very awkward ; in her present condition she seemed destined to share the fate of *India*. This most certainly would have happened immediately had it been daylight. Luckily the time was only three a.m., yet in another two and a half hours the sun would rise, and with it would come the torpedo. The *Patia's* Captain therefore decided to risk a collapse of the bulkhead, went ahead with his engines, whacked her up to 13 knots, with collision mats in place and 200 tons of ballast brought aft, and thus cleared out of the danger area. So well did everything hold that she now carried on direct to the Clyde, where she arrived safely at eleven o'clock on Tuesday evening.

Now that the short northern summer had passed, and the autumn gales had recommenced, the boarding parties and armed guards were in for another strenuous time. The following experience, which happened to a young officer fresh from his initiation in the Merchant Service, but already one of the *Orcoma's* Royal Naval Reserve Midshipmen, shows

N

the unexpected opportunities for making the best of most hard circumstances.

It was September 16; the scene was that cold and lonely area to the north-east of Iceland. The *Orcoma*, at the northern end of Patrol "A", had intercepted the Swedish topsail schooner *Valand*, and decided to send her into Lerwick, making Muckle Flugga if at all possible during the dark hours. The armed guard consisted of Mr. Cyril A. Bamford, Midshipman, R.N.R., together with a couple of seamen and one stoker. For the next three days all went well, except that the fair wind was light and progress slow. The Faroes were not sighted till 9.30 a.m. on the 19th, to the south-east, for the wind had come easterly during the previous afternoon. It now backed and blew a S.E. gale, which was so strong on the 20th that the *Valand* had to heave-to. Presently it increased so violently that Bamford decided to run before it northward, and sighted the Faroes a second time.

Unfortunately, during the night of the 21st, the *Valand's* steering gear broke down, but the gale moderated slightly, and in a few hours repairs were effected, so she was not blown towards Greenland. On the 22nd came a calm, in which the schooner rolled and wallowed painfully to the ugly swell, but on the next day the breeze came S.S.E., which of course was a head wind, and was accompanied by dense banks of fog until the 25th, when an E.N.E. wind cleared away the fog, but the wind backed to the N.E. and by 6 p.m. was blowing a strong gale. To make matters worse, the schooner's provisions were now practically exhausted after ten days' boxing about, but she was carrying a cargo of salted herrings, and on such monotonous fare crew, as well as guards, must now subsist. At 8 p.m. Muckle Flugga was seen to the south-west, but owing to the virulence of the gale, the absence of shore lights on the Shetlands, and the improbability of sighting any of the patrols off Lerwick, Bamford decided to keep further seawards rather than attempt making that port on a lee shore.

On the 26th, at 1 a.m., the battered ship began to show her weakness, and at this dark hour the fore rigging carried away, so that the foremast nearly went overboard into the furious seas ; but by knocking away the port bulwarks, passing wire strops round the schooner's ribs, and rigging up temporary stays, the damage was made good in a few hours. On the evening of the 27th the Midshipman went about on the port tack in an attempt to make Lerwick, but at four a.m. next day the starboard anchor was carried overboard, though happily it was recovered before it had done more than make a dent in the ship's side, and an hour later land was sighted.

It was realized that the ship was now between Fair Island and Sunburgh Head, the N.E. gale having set her to the westward ; so Lerwick was out of the question, and Kirkwall in the Orkneys (being another lee shore) had likewise to be ignored. The schooner's gear was all rotten, ropes and canvas kept carrying away, until the lower topsail was the only sound sail in the ship. Bamford therefore decided to go all the way down Scotland's east coast, running before the N.E. gale, and try entering the Firth of Forth. This, being a wide entrance, would be the wisest if a lengthy course. Already thirteen days had passed.

Now on the 29th land was observed, and then a town (which the schooner's Master believed to be Aberdeen, though it must have been Montrose), and sail was reduced so as to make the Bell Rock during daylight. At 6 p.m. two flashing lights were picked up—a four-flash light on the starboard bow, and a red-and-white flash light on the port beam. They disappeared, so the supposition was made that they came from fishing craft signalling each other. Bamford was not quite satisfied, and at 10 p.m. picked up the four-flash light again. As May Island (off the Firth of Forth) was the only lighthouse with four flashes, Bamford told the Master to heave-to for the night. This was done, and in the morning there was May Island showing up abaft the port beam ; the other light had been Bell Rock.

Another disappointment followed. The *Valand* next steered a course to sail up the Forth through the southern channel, i.e. leaving May Island to starboard, but destroyer patrols instructed her to enter by the northern channel, leaving May Island to port. Terribly hard lines thus to spend from daylight to dusk on the 30th beating back against the gale, but at length the Island was weathered and they anchored in Largo Roads, whence Leith was reached the following day. Thus ended a thrilling voyage of more than a fortnight in which Swedes and Britons worked together harmoniously, contended with death, and brought an ill-found schooner through great peril. There was an absence of proper navigational instruments or charts, and the sun was never visible from the time they left the Shetlands. In an age when seamanship is said to have been ruined by steam, one rejoices to put on record this fine achievement. Mr. Bamford well deserved the Distinguished Service Cross which he was awarded.

Strangely enough, on the very day that this party had first boarded the *Valand*, the *Orcoma* had sent another armed guard (consisting of Sub-Lieut. D. L. Edwards, R.N.R., with two marines and a stoker) from much the same Iceland locality to take the intercepted Norwegian brigantine *Haugar* likewise into Lerwick. She was another of the herring-carriers, and her cargo doubtless was intended ultimately for Germany. After sighting the Faroes at daybreak of the 18th, Sub-Lieut. Edwards agreed with the Master that it was better to heave-to during the S.E. gale. The *Haugar* was fifty years old, labouring heavily, and leaking badly, so that the pump had to be kept going continually; yet still she made water.

These months of hostilities brought about some curious developments, and who could have imagined that a steamship's junior officer, a sergeant and private, R.M.L.I., and a retired naval stoker should be trimming a brigantine's sails whilst the Norwegian crew toiled at the pumps? On the 19th heavy seas poured on to the decks, and the topmast backstay burst, though a preventer was rigged. On the 21st the Faroes were seen for a second time, and were not yet weathered. Sub-Lieut. Edwards and the Master agreed to go through Dimon Fjord and thus save considerable time, but when only half a mile from the high land the wind suddenly dropped, and the tide began sweeping the ship shorewards. Here was an alarming predicament, for darkness had settled down, no lights were visible, and as the *Haugar* drove westward she came so close to the rocks as almost to scrape them. Picture, too, a fatal rocky ledge just to leeward and running out in such a manner that to evade it were impossible.

What to be done ?

Abandon ship ! So the lifeboat was hoisted out by the topsail-halyards, and the remains of the provisions which an armed guard always brought with them were dropped in with all hands. They pulled off, yet could find no place to land, watched sorrowfully their vessel drifting inevitably on and on to her doom. Just then a miracle happened : to the surprise of Britons and Norwegians the tide hurled her between the jagged rocks without touching them. Incredible, but true ! The *Haugar* was still a living creature ! What double luck ! For the lifeboat was leaking so badly that one of the guards had to keep bailing with a bucket as fast as he could work. They were between the unapproachable shore and the deep dark sea. Back they rowed to the brigantine, scrambled aboard, only to notice that the ship's compass had been smashed to pieces by the main boom. Another was unearthed from below, and rigged, though it was very small.

The S.S.E. breeze then sprang up, and they tacked to the south of Sydero, but on the 22nd the only provisions available were hard bread and salt fish. Next day ensued a calm, followed by a N.N.E. gale, and on the 25th they were hove-to. The seas stove in part of the bulwarks, the fiendish wind carrying away a jib and staysail, whilst the ancient hull crashed her opening sides till the leaks could scarce be kept under control. Next afternoon land was sighted north of the Orkneys, but it could not be weathered, so out into the Atlantic they had to stand. On the 27th, in spite of the strong N.N.E. wind, they carried on, hoping to catch a glimpse of the Orkneys shore before dark.

In this expectation they were disappointed, and heavy squalls kept straining the ship in every part, whilst the atrocious seas which leapt aboard made pumping barely possible. At next daybreak Noup Head was recognized, and that evening, with four feet of water in the hold, the brigantine came to anchor in Kirkwall after 13 days of hellish delight, during which every man was constantly wet through and had to snatch sleep whilst lying in his saturated clothing. The neutral had been brought to port for examination as ordered, but would the authorities in London ever realize the price that had been paid ?

Two days after this episode had ended, H.M.S. *Mantua*, another unit of the Blockading Fleet, but in Patrol "A" between Iceland and the Hebrides, sent an armed guard under Sub-Lieut. A. M. Eastty, R.N.R., to take the Swedish S.S. *Avesta* into Kirkwall, and he suffered a thrilling suspense, though differing in kind from the two sailing-ship experiences. On October 1, at 6.45 in the morning, an enemy submarine was sighted on the port bow, and the *Avesta* hoisted Swedish colours. The armed guard, in accordance with the now established custom, was ordered by their Sub-Lieutenant to keep out of sight and hide their uniforms, Eastty himself removing his naval cap and jacket. He also instructed the Master that, if compelled to stop, he was to hide the guard and make no mention of their presence.

To this the Swede answered that he would probably have to give some reason for being on his present course, as the Germans were aware that this steamship line made a northerly track on their homeward voyage ; so Eastty told him to say the *Avesta* was proceeding into Kirkwall voluntarily. Perhaps, ordinarily, this yarn might have been accepted, but only perhaps. It so happened, unluckily, that among the crew was a German trying to get home, and if the U-boat commanding officer insisted on an examination, would the German hold his tongue ?

Not likely !

Matters now began to look lively, and the submarine to approach. Up went the latter's signal to "stop immediately", but the *Avesta* kept her course and speed. Less than a mile separated them ; at any moment the Master would be compelled to lower boat, go off and be catechized.

Just at this stage smoke appeared to the eastward, and the shape of a steamer. Ah! One of the 10th Cruiser Squadron! The U-boat had seen her too, and forthwith changed her plans, steering off to the N.W. and hiding herself in a friendly rain squall.

Tension was released ; there would soon be the protection of guns. Now the sequel is that, when the steamer arrived, she turned out to be, not British, but the American oil-tanker

Polarine bound west across the Atlantic. She had given the U-boat quite a scare, and unconsciously had saved Eastty's companions, who all arrived safely eighteen hours later in Kirkwall as ordered, where the German member of the crew was duly handed over.

CHAPTER XVI

On earlier pages mention was made of the *Caribbean*, which formerly served in Admiral de Chair's squadron and during March was one of the vessels watching the Norwegian coast. It was well that this 5,824-tons Royal Mail Line steamer had since been paid off, but an interesting commentary and comparison between sail and steam cannot be omitted. We have seen that, in spite of all wind and sea could threaten, those two ill-found sailing vessels *Valand* and *Haugar* by good handling won through to harbour.

During that same gale of September 26 the *Caribbean* got into serious difficulties. She had been fitted out as a receiving ship for dockyard workmen, and whilst on passage to Scapa Flow took in a great deal of water. During the afternoon she was heard sending out "S O S" supplications on her wireless whilst off Cape Wrath. The *Arlanza* would have been despatched to her assistance, but was too far away, so Admiral Jellicoe ordered the light cruiser *Birkenhead*, together with tugs and others, to make for the spot. Pathetic signals, "Ship drifting to westward", "Water gaining on fires", flashed across the ether, but in the early hours of the 27th most of the crew were taken off. At 7.30 a.m. down went the *Caribbean*, beaten by the weather, and in her perished fifteen lives.

Changes of commanding officers, as well as of ships, brought their own contrasts. It was all such an unusual life into which everyone had been plunged. One Captain, for example, after his new appointment, brought his armed merchant cruiser into Scapa, handed her over, rushed across to a certain crack battleship, took command, and an hour later put to sea. A great and sudden change he found from the bridge of a liner to that of a heavy-armoured man-of-war which was to distinguish herself at Jutland. Every Admiral and Captain in the Grand Fleet continued to extol the wonderful work which the Blockading Fleet was patiently performing, yet how little did the British public south of Scapa realize all the risks and perils which were involved!

In October Admiral de Chair's Fleet was strengthened by the addition of the Royal Mail Line *Almanzora*, 16,034 tons, her commanding officer, Captain W. D. Church, R.N., having formerly commanded the light cruiser *Weymouth*. Another change, but from a man-of-war one-third of the liner's tonnage. *Almanzora* was still being built at Belfast when the Admiralty took her over early in 1915. No efforts of the builders were wasted on superfluities, and she must be got ready as an armed merchant cruiser without delay. Her second-in-command, Commander W. C. Tarrant, R.N.R., tells me that she was a mere shell of hull with engines, only absolute essentials—such as magazines, store-rooms, accommodation for personnel—being installed, and these items occupied such a comparatively small portion that when you walked through the great wide spaces you had the impression of visiting a series of enormous steel tanks. As a fighting unit, and the most modern of her class, she was very efficient with her eight 6-inch guns, two 6-pdr. anti-aircraft, a Maxim, as well as depth charges at the stern for use against submarines.

A great portion of her time was spent off Iceland, patrolling between there and the Greenland ice-barrier, where blizzards and gales, fog and ice, became the normal conditions. Navigation was extremely difficult, the position of ice changing almost hourly, and temperatures of below zero were quite common. For those on deck life was a great trial, for the look-out men an agony; yet blockade-runners and raiders might at any hour come along with the blizzard. Even below, where heating arrangements existed, the temperature frequently fell so low that officers and men rarely removed thick overcoats and mufflers.

It was only with the greatest difficulty that ships were boarded by any of the patrols during the latter half of October, and on the night of October 15–16 there was some pretty boatmanship when the *Hildebrand* (Captain Hugh Edwards,

R.N.) put a party aboard the Norwegian S.S. *Corona*, bound from Baltimore for Bergen with a cargo of grain. Duty must come first, and orders are orders. There were men known to be among the crew who were "wanted", and they must be fetched in spite of the weather. But the *Corona* was found to have sprung a leak, and was sinking, so all hands (numbering nineteen) were taken off to the *Hildebrand*, which stood by. They were carefully examined, and six who had joined at Baltimore were placed under arrest.

In the meanwhile Admiral de Chair despatched the *Otway* at full speed to take charge of what would probably be salvage operations, but on the way met with the Danish S.S. *United States* bound east. She had to be boarded, and an armed guard brought her into Kirkwall, where an Austrian aviator was discovered among the passengers. The *Hildebrand* stuck to the leaky *Corona* during the night, and at 8.30 next morning the water was eighteen inches over the latter's stokehold plates. It was wild weather, with wicked seas, but Captain Edwards soon after midday managed to get her in tow by shackling on wire hawsers to the steamer's own cable, in accordance with the recognized principles of towage ; for by this means the heavy cable makes a sag and takes off something from the sudden jerking which happens when the sea is all valleys and crests.

Such was the strain, however, that four hours later this cable parted. Hours of anxious work followed, yet, notwithstanding the considerable sea running and the condition of darkness, the *Corona* was again connected up. It was an act of exceptionally fine seamanship, and somehow the tow continued till 6.45 a.m. on the 17th, when Captain Edwards received orders to cast off. The Norwegian steamer was now in a hopeless state, and the *Hildebrand* sank her as a dangerous derelict. Lucky it was that *Corona* had met with the life-saving patrol.

The persistence with which people of German nationality still endeavoured to reach home was as surprising as it was expressive of the subtle assistance at work in America by the enemy's sympathizers. Only a few days after the *Corona's* foundering there came the Danish S.S. *Hellig Olav*, carrying 242 passengers from New York for Copenhagen. She was stopped by the *Victorian*, and no fewer than 86 turned out to be Germans, of whom a dozen were men.   What a mighty power is optimism that all these should have expected to reach home via the Blockade !   Nevertheless, only a week later that old acquaintance, *Oscar II*, was heard by *Columbella* calling up Bergen, so that the patrol later in the day was able to intercept her before the *Oscar* reached a European port.   The *Oscar* had come from New York with general cargo and 183 passengers, of whom 11 women and children, besides five men, turned out to be Germans.

What did our Blockade look like through the eyes of a neutral ?   It is always interesting to get another's impressions, and less than three months previously a special correspondent of the New York *Evening Post* had travelled in this very ship eastward.

Two days before we sighted land [he recorded], it was rumoured among the first-class passengers that a rendezvous had been made with an English warship for the morning of August 7 at nine o'clock.   Anyway, promptly at that hour a converted cruiser was seen far ahead, shoving determinedly toward our starboard bow.   It had no name, carried no flag, and was painted a dirty-leaden black.   A few minutes later a British Naval Lieutenant and six British seamen were on board, with a case of provisions and some wine—a prize crew being forbidden to touch the ship's food.   Our wireless was at once dismantled, the wireless house locked, and the key deposited in the Lieutenant's pocket.   A British sailor with loaded rifle stood guard at the steering wheel ; another patrolled the bridge, where the Lieutenant had now taken command ; a third was in the look-out.   But our Danish flag still hung from the stern.

The writer then goes on to say that the *Oscar* was detained at Kirkwall only a couple of days, and, after being released, arrived at Christiania, where

we met the Norwegian American liner *Bergensfjord*.   Her last trip across had been even more exciting than our own.   For, after slipping through the English web unobserved, and arriving within Norwegian waters, she had carelessly strayed out beyond the 3-mile limit, been pounced upon by a British cruiser and taken ignominiously back to Kirkwall.   The British Admiralty had reported the matter to the owners of the Norwegian American Line, asking them to dismiss the Captain.   They had refused.   Captain Hiortdahl, they declared, by passing through the dangerous waters as quickly as possible, was not only saving them money in coal and provisions, but was safeguarding the ship and the lives of the passengers. Besides, he was a good Captain—otherwise he could never have given the British cruisers the slip, as he had done three times out of every four since the war began.

Captain Hiortdahl, continued the correspondent, declared he "would keep on trying to run the British Blockade just as before", that is to say, by putting out the ship's lights as he approached Scotland, and would "continue to make a secret of the ship's daily run and her whereabouts", his wireless operators having been ordered by him not to send any messages when near England, but to try to pick up all news passing between ships.

The reader will recognize more than one error in this narration, yet it indicates the kind of elusive spirit with which the unceasingly vigilant Blockade lines had to contend. One marvels that such protracted watchfulness could be kept up in long stretches of 60 days without any leave, except perhaps a walk of an hour or two at Busta Voe, which was not too entertaining for men accustomed to taste the delights of towns. Unquestionably those who were sent as armed guards in the crazy sailing ships had the worst to bear. We have considered two particular instances, but they were by no means unique. It was the *Hildebrand* who on October 30 met with the Danish sailing ship *Maracaibo* and found she had on board an armed guard from *Orotava*. During the last 13 days the *Maracaibo* had been trying to reach Lerwick, but the south-easterly gales had prevented her from making any headway, so that the supplies for guard and Danish crew had run distressingly short. Luckily, Captain Hugh Edwards was able to send aboard provisions for another eight days.

Occasionally some special service would summon an armed merchant cruiser from her patrol and temporarily weaken the line. Early in October, when Russian affairs were causing the Allies so much anxiety, the *Arlanza* was sent to Archangel to convey a certain person, but, alas, she hit one of those mines with which the Germans had fouled the White Sea tracks, though she was towed safely into Yukanskie Roads, whither the Russians sent repairing materials and diving

H.M.S. "ALMANZORA" ON PATROL

H.M.S. "ALMANZORA'S" 6-INCH GUN AND CREW IN THE ARCTIC

ARCTIC DRESS

plant. The enemy were as ceaseless in their varied efforts as the Blockaders were continuous in their control, and the shortage of cotton was now worrying Germany most seriously. How could the bales be imported notwithstanding Admiral de Chair's Fleet ?

The Norwegian S.S. *Eir* during the middle of October showed what could be done. She had 5,600 tons of cotton in her holds, nominally for Gothenburg, and, after being boarded and examined at Kirkwall, was permitted to carry on to that Swedish port. It is true that she did actually touch at Gothenburg, and there landed 1,500 tons, amounting to 1,600 bales. Five days later she left Sweden with the remaining 7,000 bales, ostensibly to land them at Copenhagen, the matter having been arranged by a shipping agent from Denmark, who was said to be an "American", though he spoke with a strong German accent.

The latter had also arranged that, in addition to the local Swedish pilot required by regulations to take her through the Gothenburg waters, there was another pilot whom the "American" had put aboard privately, and was to take charge after the Swede finished his sectional duties. The private pilot then took over from him and guided *Eir* down the Cattegat, but he did not bring the ship into Copenhagen, where an alleged consignee was awaiting delivery. Novelists have certainly prejudiced us in favour of blockade-runners and those brave seamen who are willing to take big risks, and we find ourselves unable to resist some admiration when the odds against them were great. Certainly about this mysterious second pilot there was a halo of romantic adventure. A kind of "Captain Kettle" with an adventurous past, he was in reality a disguised German. Taking every advantage of a fog, he kept away from territorial waters of Denmark or Sweden into the open sea, where by arrangement there waited a German torpedo-boat, who promptly "captured" the *Eir*, conducted her down the Cattegat, and so into the German port of Lübeck, where the 7,000 bales were landed to our enemy's great joy.

It was a smart trick, and shows how needfully critical should be the Blockade details of examination, how extra cautious should be the attitude towards neutral shipments.

For the American agent by now had disappeared, the alleged consignee in Copenhagen was found never to have existed, and the *Eir* herself had a rather strange career. She had formerly belonged to an owner in Christiania, who sold her to a resident in Bergen, but the latter sold her to somebody in America whilst *Eir* was on her way across the Atlantic !

Immediately after this incident came the Order-in-Council dated October 20, 1915, by which an important change was made in Blockade procedure : the neutral or enemy character of a vessel was no longer to be determined by the flag she was entitled to fly. This was an alteration of that Order of October 29, 1914, by which Britain—in reply to American pressure—had resigned certain of her rights claimed in the Order of August 20, 1914. Under the new policy Britain sought to prevent goods aboard neutral ships nominally intended for Denmark or Scandinavia (but really *en route* for Germany) from reaching the enemy at all. We thus come face to face with the well-known phrase, "The Doctrine of Continuous Voyage". Since August 1915 there had been in force a rationing policy of contiguous neutrals, on the basis of pre-War imports. Thus, if Germany's neighbours had exceeded these figures, there was a *prima facie* case for seizing the goods. But was it legal ? Was it in accord with the Law of Nations ?

The point had been settled in the affirmative only a month previously by the now historic decision of the *Kim* case. The *Kim* was a Norwegian steamer which, in the autumn of 1914, was carrying foodstuffs from New York ostensibly consigned to neutrals in Copenhagen. She was, however, intercepted by a British patrol, taken into port, and her cargo claimed by the Crown as contraband. The matter came before the Prize Court a year later, and was remarkable as being the first occasion in which this tribunal had an opportunity of dealing with the Continuous Voyage doctrine. It is fitting, therefore, that we should quote the judgment which the President, Sir Samuel Evans, delivered on September 16, 1915 :

> The doctrine of "continuous voyage" was first applied by the English Prize Courts to unlawful trading. There is no reported case in our Courts where the doctrine is applied in terms to the carriage of

contraband. But it was so applied and extended by the United States Courts against this country in the time of the American Civil War ; and its application was acceded to by the British Government of the day. . . . A compromise was attempted by the London Conference in the unratified Declaration of London. . . . I have no hesitation in pronouncing that, in my view, the doctrine of continuous voyage . . . had become part of the law of nations at the commencement of the present war. . . . The result is that the Court is not restricted in its vision to the primary consignment of the goods in these cases to the neutral port of Copenhagen ; but is entitled and bound to take a more extended outlook in order to ascertain whether this neutral destination was merely ostensible, and, if so, what the real ultimate destination was.

This decision, then, which related to large quantities of lard and fats ultimately intended for Germany, legalized Britain's pressure, which could be expressed by such means as rationing, or giving the Customs officials power to withhold bunker coal at their discretion from neutral steamers, whose owners were informed that only could such fuel be obtained by an undertaking to carry no cargo of enemy origin or destination.

On October 21, 1915, however, there followed further friction with the United States, who presented a Note to Great Britain contesting the legality of interference with neutral ships or cargoes.

Many vessels [America objected] have been detained while search was being made for evidence of the contraband character of their cargoes or of an intention to evade the non-intercourse measures of Great Britain. The question, consequently, has been one of evidence to support a belief of—in many cases a bare suspicion of—enemy destination, or occasionally of enemy origin of the goods involved.

The Note added an historical comment that

an examination of the instructions issued to naval commanders of the United States, Great Britain, Russia, Japan, Spain, Germany, and France from 1888 to the beginning of the present War shows that search in port was not contemplated by the Government of any of these countries. On the contrary . . . search at sea was the procedure.

One may interrupt this argument by saying that whilst Britain had not established the old technical blockade, whereby we could have confiscated ships and goods more readily than at present, we also claimed that modern conditions justified bringing vessels into port for purposes of search. And to anyone who has read the preceding chapters in this volume it must be obvious that the weather between Iceland and Scotland or Norway, or even the prevailing risk from submarines, made it essential to modify the ancient principle to the extent of the nearest convenient port.

But America would have none of that. She objected to the seizure of vessels at sea "upon conjectural suspicion and the practice of bringing them into port", and hoped that Britain would instruct our officers "to refrain from these vexatious and illegal practices". Furthermore, the United States called attention to the "so-called Blockade" measures as imposed by the Order-in-Council dated March 11, 1915, and protested that Britain had been unsuccessful in her efforts to distinguish between enemy and neutral trade these last six months, so that American commercial interests were hampered. She argued that the British Blockade was not effective, and therefore not binding. "It is common knowledge", continued the Note, "that the German coasts are open to trade with the Scandinavian countries, and that German naval vessels cruise both in the North Sea and the Baltic and seize and bring into German ports neutral vessels bound for Scandinavian and Danish ports."

Thus arose another of those crises at an awkward moment, just when we were tightening up the Blockade to make it more efficient. Whilst at the back of this American diplomatic pressure were the wealthy Chicago meat-packers, yet it needed some ingenuity to overcome the plea that in stopping American cargoes Britain was discriminatory, inasmuch as Scandinavia and Denmark could still carry goods into Germany. Once more, then, did the rope of friendship binding Britain to America come under a heavy strain, yet even now it failed to snap. Only a spirit of self-restraint and common sense between the two English-speaking nations could avert disaster; but Germany had committed so many submarine follies that at least she could win no transatlantic sympathy. Had she possessed clean hands, no doubt the situation would have been for us far more complicated.

GOING OFF TO BOARD
Leaving an armed Merchant Cruiser to examine a
neutral Steamer.

H.M.S. "TEUTONIC"
The old White Star Liner which performed excellent service in the
Blockading Fleet.

The problem for Britain remained that about 10 million men out of 70 million men, women, and children in Germany were now under the latter's military control, and the 10 million must still be separated from the sinews of war. In London the new War Trade Advisory Committee, and the General Black List Committee, both of which were at work this autumn, were the symbols of a more detailed control to be expressed through the Blockading Fleet. The *Kim* judgment had given a strong legal backing, a greater confidence, yet for practical purposes it had not gone quite far enough : it did not appear adequately to justify seizure of cargoes "upon grounds purely quantitative". Large consignments of coffee, cocoa, dried fruits, American canned meat, were still being allowed to get through. It was also learned by Boarding Officers in the course of their inquiries that German trawlers had been making a practice of coming out ostensibly into the Baltic to fish, but had actually proceeded to Danish and Scandinavian harbours, where they loaded with provisions and thence returned home. This went on until the three neutral Governments stopped such transactions, and in a similar manner exportation of fish into Germany was no longer so easy.

Some of the neutral shipmasters were not too discreet in chattering on their wireless, and there was plenty of evidence that they took a huge delight when occasionally they did manage to slip through. One day, for example, the *Cedric* intercepted a signal from *Kristianiafjord* to *Bergensfjord* in Norwegian. It was translated and found to boast that the former had slipped through the patrol line during a rain squall. Undoubtedly a certain number of vessels occasionally had such luck, but in this case, as in others, it happened usually when west-bound, so the result was not always serious. But the fact to be emphasized is that when Whitehall required any particular vessel to be stopped—whether bound east or west— hardly ever did the patrols fail to intercept.

By October Lerwick had begun to be used largely as an examination port additional to Kirkwall, yet it was into the latter that the *Polarine* had to be sent next month. We mentioned this vessel's name recently in connection with Sub-Lieut. Eastty's experience when a U-boat was just about

o

to attack the Swedish S.S. *Avesta* on October 1. All un-conscious of having saved *Avesta* and the British armed guard, the *Polarine* had sped out into the Atlantic. The sequel came on November 4, when another patrol—this time the *Teutonic*—chanced to meet *Polarine*, now returning from Pennsylvania with a cargo of oil for Copenhagen, and was sent into port. It was found that, though she now belonged to the Standard Oil Company of New York, she was the ex-German S.S. *Ems,* and her present second engineer was German too. The Master refused all responsibility for navigation of the ship when the armed guard took over. One wonders if the second engineer to-day has ever learned that the smoke from his funnel was the cause of robbing a brother officer in a U-boat from doing a profitable day's work ?

Neutral skippers were being encouraged with handsome rewards by their owners if only the ship got through the Blockade safely. Little wonder, then, that, spurred on in this manner, all shipmasters used every advantage of weather, wind, and darkness. Even the smaller craft were earning unusual profits. The Master of a Danish sailing ship bound from the Faroes to Norway with 400 barrels of whale oil admitted he was to receive, personally, £100 if he ran the blockade, and £50 if he failed. He was stopped by the *Andes* and sent into Lerwick.

But a most illuminating case was that of the Danish S.S. *Hillerod*, 2,942 tons, owned by Messrs. Brix-Hansen & Co. of Copenhagen. It was one of the most flagrant instances of a neutral vessel carrying contraband for a German destination. This steamer was 23 years old, had been built at West Hartle-pool, but recently had been Greek-owned until she was sold to Denmark. Very ingeniously were efforts made by the shore people to keep everything quietly but efficiently organized, yet by a curious coincidence it was the same *Teutonic* who brought matters to a head on the very day that the *Polarine* was seized.

All sorts of dummy men and subterfuges in those times were employed to cover the real firms who were putting up the money and buying on Germany's behalf. In this story there enters quite early a Joseph Westerberg, by birth a Swede, by age 54, who, when a young man of 27, had become a citizen of the United States and till the end of 1913 was living in Chicago, where he practised as a lawyer. He came back to Sweden and became American Consular Agent at Malmo. His salary was only about £200 a year, yet suddenly, on June 22, 1915, never previously having had any such vast transaction, or any purchasing of oil, he entered into an important charter-party with Brix-Hansen & Co. to carry a full cargo of oil from America to Scandinavia at a lump sum of Kr. 300,000 (about £16,500).

In that month Westerberg sent a man named Hansen to America, who bought the required oil for 117,784 dollars (about £23,556). The cost of insurance increased this figure to more than £25,000. Obviously the Consular Agent himself did not find all these sums. Then whence did they come? The bankers were Kuhn, Loeb & Co., of the United States, and in close touch with Germany; the oil was purchased in America from the Pure Oil Company, and 730,000 gallons of this lubricant were put aboard the *Hillerod* at Philadelphia, whither she had arrived safely. At this date Germany needed fats and lubricants almost more than she required cotton and iron ore. She was willing to pay any price, and Captain J. Ankersen, the steamer's Master, was promised a good reward if only he could bring this valuable cargo through the Blockade. It was manifested to Trondhjem and Gothenburg, yet it was not needed in either of those ports, for the supply both in Norway and Sweden was far greater than the normal.

Unfortunately the plotters gave themselves away by their wireless messages before the ship started from America. Even in August the New York insurance brokers were inquiring by radiogram to Mannheim asking the Mannheimer Versicherungs-Gesellschaft (of Mannheim) for authority to cover lubricating oil per *Hillerod* to Gothenburg. This message, plucked from the air by the British Postal Censorship, conveyed its own meaning. Then, on October 21, Kuhn, Loeb & Co. sent a wireless addressed to Warburg of Hamburg notifying them:

> . . . *Steamer ready to sail.*

That simple statement was adequate to warn the patrols that the *Hillerod* was coming and might be expected in the

Blockade area about a certain date. Actually the steamer did leave Philadelphia on the day mentioned, but not before the Master had received the following interesting letter from his owners sent c/o a Philadelphia firm of shipping agents :

Brix-Hansen & Co.,
Copenhagen,
16th September, 1915.

Captain J. Ankersen,
S.S. "Hillerod",
C/o Messrs. Flint, Goering & Co.
Philadelphia.

Dear Sir,

Hoping that on the receipt of this you will have arrived safely. We send you enclosed copy of the Charter-party, by which you will observe that the S.S. "Hillerod" is fixed homeward from America with a cargo of oil from Philadelphia to Trondhjem and Gothenburg, and beyond this we request you to acquaint yourself with the contents of the Charter-party.

As experience with regard to oil ships has thus far shown that these are very frequently arrested and detained for a considerable period in England, we request you to do your utmost to bring your ship back without arrest, and contingent bringing into port by the British, which is now either done by following a northern course—for, of course, you are to discharge in Trondhjem—or in some other manner.

As you will see from the enclosed certificate, we have secured ourselves in every way in connection with any possible arrest, and providing therefore you should succeed (if the ship should, notwithstanding, be brought into Kirkwall) in limiting the inspection to at most two days, we hereby promise you an extra gratuity of Kr. 1,000, which, of course, will also be due if the ship is not taken into port.

We now request you to do your utmost to get rapid despatch at Philadelphia, and wishing you a good voyage home.

Yours etc.
(Signed) Brix-Hansen & Co.

But the *Hillerod* had a "good voyage" only until lat. 58°28′ N., i.e. west of the Hebrides, when the *Teutonic's* armed guard went aboard on November 4, and three days later the oil-ship was handed over to the Customs authorities in Kirkwall. From that hour her fate was sealed. On November 16, by order of the Contraband Committee, the *Hillerod* was seized as a prize, and placed in the Prize Court for adjudication. The case came before Sir Samuel Evans, who called attention to the co-operation of Danes and an American Consular Agent "being caught in the actual carrying of Absolute Contraband to the enemy". When the case later came before the Judicial Committee of the Privy Council it was Lord Sumner who bluntly remarked that Kuhn, Loeb & Co. "were a firm much concerned in financing, and facilitating, trade with Germany, and have two partners who are associated with a House in Hamburg". "Their Lordships", continued the learned judge, "have no doubt that this cargo of contraband had an ulterior destination in Germany, and that, when they carried it, Messrs. Brix-Hansen & Co. were fully alive to the fact." The Court also entertained no doubt that Westerberg never was the owner of the cargo, but that he was Mr. H. C. Hansen's agent, and not his principal, and lent his respectable name and office to cover this questionable traffic.

So the *Hillerod* and her much-needed lubricating oil never reached our enemies. Condemned on the ground that it was Absolute Contraband with a German destination, the President had found that the shipowners were directly con-cerned in an attempt to carry the oil to the enemy. Sir Samuel Evans therefore condemned both ship and cargo, and, this judgment having been afterwards confirmed by the Privy Council, the matter ended.

CHAPTER XVII

WE have noted the friction caused by the Blockade. Now, in order to convince neutrals that this control of contraband was the concern of the Allies as a whole, France was asked if she would care to join us in the Northern Patrol. She agreed to send two ships, but these proved small and unsuitable for the strenuous work, so Britain decided to lend her a couple from Admiral de Chair's command. During the first half of November 1915 the *Digby* was accordingly assigned for temporary transfer to the French Navy, who renamed her the *Artois*, and presently too the *Oropesa* was handed over to become the *Champagne*.

The latter did not rejoin Admiral de Chair's flag as a blockade unit, but worked between France and Archangel on White Sea duties. The *Artois*, however, by the beginning of February was back on Patrol "C". At first this rough-and-tumble life in the chilly north was too strange an experience for the Latin sailors to relish such labours, and they did not appreciate British naval drinks of rum or beer. This necessitated occasional visits to Brest for the replenishment of wine stores. But after a while the *Artois* settled down to the job, and in doing good work demonstrated to the world that France with Britain was united in the determination to restrict enemy trade supplies. The ceaseless gales, the blinding snow, the frequent fogs, the almost continuous darkness of the Blockade region, were in violent contrast with conditions that many of the French crew had previously experienced. Here was an area of 220,000 square miles which formed the key-position of the maritime war, and it was a gesture of sea brotherhood that some share in its patrol should now be undertaken.

But on those well-tried British officers and men who were now in their second winter of hard vigilance and boarding, physical effects were being manifested. Accidents could not be avoided, pneumonia was not preventable, and no fewer than three operations for appendicitis were performed in the Squadron at sea within the first year. Apart from the Blockade Fleet's strictly belligerent duties, there were frequently incidents where charity, rather than animosity, was extended. Some poor old sailing ship battered by the storm would be met with, such as the Norwegian *Songelv*, which the *Victorian* found with all rigging crippled. A tug was requisitioned to assist the unfortunate into port. It was a welcome relief after much contending.

In this same November the *Patuca* found the Norwegian S.S. *Kong Haakon* on voyage from Baltimore for Christiania with rye and wheat. The cargo had shifted, the *Kong Haakon* was listing 12 degrees to port, and she had only 12 hours' coal left in her bunkers even steaming at four knots. She had been burning red and green flares of distress, which had been observed by another Norwegian steamer, *Quernstad*, who, on being boarded in the evening by *Patuca*, reported a sister's predicament. One of *Kong Haakon's* crew had been injured by the heavy seas, but now he could be attended by *Patuca's* medical officers.

The *Patuca* was compelled to take *Kong Haakon* in tow next day, as the last eleven days of north-easterly gales had finally exhausted the coal. The wind now once more increased to gale force, but the tow continued all that day and night till the following afternoon, when the armed trawler *Alberta* came out and took the Norwegian at three knots into Stornoway, where she arrived another day later. It had been a narrow escape, for the plight of a plucky steamer with her Captain and crew drifting back into the Atlantic beam on to a north-easterly gale, bereft of fuel, is a picture too painful for contemplation.

It is unpleasant, none the less, to remember the trouble which the Norske-Amerika liners were still creating. To-day we have evidence that these steamers deliberately laid themselves out to attract German passengers, and that luggage conveyed by this line could still contain contraband without much risk of interference by the officials. The general opinion in the Blockading Fleet was that such ships were definitely engaged in non-neutral service, and thus were liable to seizure. Nor can the reader who has followed their evasions fail to reach any other verdict.

Another instance soon occurred. The *Kristianiafjord* was expected from New York about mid-November, so all patrols were warned to look out, and signalling by wireless was reduced to a minimum. Early in the morning of the 15th it was learnt that "a large steamer proceeding N.E. at high speed" had been sighted north-west of the Hebrides. The Admiral therefore wirelessed *Teutonic* (on Patrol "A") to cut her off before reaching Muckle Flugga, and it is yet another proof of the marvellous efficiency in the 10th Cruiser Squadron that this evening, an hour before midnight, the Admiral in his cabin aboard the *Alsatian* received from *Teutonic* a message which read something like this :

Have intercepted "Kristianiafjord" in lat. 61°10′ N., long. 0°50′ W., steaming at high speed without navigation lights.

On glancing at the chart, the position was found to be off Muckle Flugga pretty near to where *Bergensfjord* had also been caught at an earlier date. But the *Kristianiafjord's* Master was, in the opinion of all seafarers, open to grave censure. Here was a passenger steamer acting in such a manner that she might have been taken for a German raider or mine-layer and sunk by gunfire after the briefest interval. Had the conditions been reversed, and this Northern Blockade been in German hands, we know perfectly well that the Norwegian would have been shelled at sight. In any case, the loss of innocent passengers' lives would have been on the Master's responsibility for such reckless conduct.

Negotiations were reopened between the British Foreign Office in November, and it was agreed with the Norske-Amerika Line that its steamers need not call for inspection at British ports when outward bound and proceeding in ballast from Bergen to the U.S.A., *provided* the British Consul at Bergen was satisfied such ships carried no goods ; that the vessel followed a predetermined course, of which due notice was to be given; and that the average speed of the Company's cargo-boats and liners was to be communicated to the Admiralty.

The Andrew Johnsen Line also agreed with this undertaking, stating that their cargo ships "make a maximum speed of about ten miles and downwards according to the conditions of the weather", whilst the speed of their passenger steamers averaged fifteen. This line further agreed to the Foreign Office's suggestion that the Company's officials should search the luggage of any passenger travelling with more than two trunks, and examine all passengers' luggage where contraband was suspected.

Throughout the War the attitude of the Norwegian Naval authorities towards Britain was entirely correct, and even considerate, especially with regard to patrols and the interpreting of internment regulations in the kindliest manner. But, obviously, Norway had to stand aloof. It is quite conceivable, too, that Germany had made representations concerning those of our armed trawlers on the look-out for the ore-ships. At any rate, during November a Norwegian naval vessel closed one of the trawlers and protested strongly against their operating in West Fjord, interfering with shipping and using wireless. The Norwegian officer claimed that northward of the line Skomvaer-Light-Gunna-Sound-Island comprised territorial waters. So the trawlers were now shifted south of that demarcation. As an example of Norwegian naval sympathy, let the following be related.

The armed trawler *Tenby Castle*, during a heavy gale of November 23, received considerable damage off that coast, her decks being swept by the terrific seas. She therefore put into Bessiker (near Kya Island) to effect repairs, which took three days. Along came the Norwegian gunboat *Hidalgo*, from whom assistance was received, so that in due course the trawler got back to Lerwick. There was no internment, but rather an acceptable and welcome sea courtesy. A week later the armed trawler *Newland*, also employed off the Norwegian coast, suffered such damage by the gale that her boats were smashed and she developed serious leaks, but she managed to reach Lerwick.

Terrible weather occurred this month, and once again

an armed guard had an unforgettable experience. It was on Tuesday, November 2, that this party had been rowed off from the *Columbella* to the United States sailing vessel *Andrew Welch*, bound from San Francisco to Helmstad with a cargo of beans. Excitements came quickly, for, whilst trying to make Lerwick, several submarines were sighted before rounding Muckle Flugga four days later. On that Saturday wind and sea were so bad in the Blockade area that boarding operations were out of the question, and off Noss Head the *Andrew Welch* had to heave-to.

That was awkward enough, but the gale got worse, and so did the tempers of the neutral crew, who insisted that the ship should make for Helmstad. To this, of course, the British officer would not consent, whereupon the Americans struck work. As the armed guard were unable to trim sails and keep the ship going without help, this led to an impasse. A compromise was eventually made, and it was decided to run for Aberdeen. This was done, the *Andrew Welch* actually arriving off there on Thursday, the 11th, and a small steamer was spoken who promised to send out a tug.

The sailing ship backed and filled, but no tug came forth, and then such a heavy gale blew up from the N.N.W. that the *Andrew Welch* had to heave-to until Sunday. In the end, the crew again refusing work, the pumps having gone wrong, and the ship's drinking supply becoming exhausted, the officer of the guard agreed to run into the Norwegian port of Christiansand, where she duly arrived.

It was noticeable that fewer Germans were now attempting to reach home as passengers or stowaways, the news having got round the world that such efforts were hardly likely to succeed. Thus when *Changuinola* boarded the Swedish S.S. *Signe* (Rio de Janeiro for Christiania) it was learnt that her seven German stowaways had been landed at Corcubion by advice of the Swedish Consul. Nevertheless, a number of alien women still travelled, who were suspected of smuggling packages of rubber, which the enemy so much needed. At the beginning of December, one Saturday night, whilst the *Alsatian's* wardroom officers were in the midst of a highly successful concert on the high seas, the proceedings were rudely interrupted by meeting with the Scandinavian-American liner *Hellig Olav* from New York. The ships stopped, and off went the boarding party, who discovered among the passengers seven German and two Austrian women, and a one-armed Austrian man.

Greater respect for the Blockade was likewise being manifested by American exporters, for when the Norske-Amerika *Kristianiafjord* was about to sail from New York in the first week of November for Christiania with products destined "for resident buyers in Sweden" the packers suddenly ordered the loading to be stopped, fearing the Blockade would confiscate the goods on the principle which had been established in the *Kim* case. Such fears were not without justification, since the United States exports to Norway and Sweden during the first three quarters of 1915 had increased seven times over the amounts during the corresponding period of 1914; such swollen buying by Scandinavia being obviously on Germany's behalf. But cotton by November was so well kept out of Germany that the Kaiser's Government permitted its use solely for Army purposes.

But another important milestone in the War was just being passed. When the Boarding Officer came off from *Alsatian's* cheery Saturday night entertainment, during which the Admiral had contributed a song, there was an interesting item in the *Hellig Olav's* daily paper, whose wireless news included the following :

The State trial in New York against Hamburg-American Line and members of German Embassy closed yesterday. Verdict "Guilty" against four out of five defendants. Sentence later. . . . Evidence of Buenz showed complicity of Boy Ed, the German Naval Attaché, besides constant monetary subventions and instructions from German Government.

This was good news for the Blockaders. It meant that at last the United States Government were putting a stop to those improper activities, the trickeries and deceits ; the assisting of Germans to engage in anti-Allies plotting and propaganda, to smuggle contraband in small parcels, to send couriers backwards and forwards ; to supply colliers for over-seas raiders. The Sayville wireless station, as we have seen, had been taken out of German hands, and now the enemy's spy system in America was to receive a heavy blow. Mr.

Lansing, the United States Secretary of State, informed Count Bernstorff that Captain Boy Ed, the Naval Attaché, and Captain von Papen, the Military Attaché, were "no longer *personæ gratæ* to my Government", and requested their immediate recall.

But neither showed any signs of departing. On December 10 Mr. Lansing again wrote to the Ambassador lest the Government "be compelled to take action without awaiting the recall of the Attachés". At length, after this undignified display of bad German manners, Bernstorff replied that the Kaiser had agreed to their recall. The final act of the unseemly affair ended with the departure of von Papen on December 21 for Holland, and of Boy Ed on January 1. It was a highly significant crisis, for it showed the trend of future events. Notwithstanding all that might have resulted from Anglo-American unpleasantness over the Blockade, yet it was German diplomatists who were turned out of the country, and a year later Count Bernstorff went too.

Whatever difficulties might arise in the future with President Wilson's people because of the 10th Cruiser Squadron's activities, no problem now could be incapable of solution. Germany had ruined her own interests, created an unfavourable impression, lost any sympathy which the harshness of the Blockade might have won for herself. She was disgraced, discredited, dismissed from that respect which she had formerly owned. Between Washington and Whitehall there would assuredly be more than one repetition of trouble, but it would be capable of adjustment without any severance of diplomacy.

Of course, like the bad weather, the *Bergensfjord* continued as a steady nuisance to the Blockaders, and two days after the *Hellig Olav* visitation the *Bergensfjord* was stopped, when two German subjects were discovered, though one was over military age. One of the firemen in the Swedish S.S. *Kronprinz Gustaf* (on her way from Rio de Janeiro) also was found to be a German subject. Similarly, the *Frederik VIII* came along from New York with several passengers of enemy nationality and of military age. Although they claimed to belong to the Red Cross, this did not prevent the liner being sent in for examination.

Next came several incidents similar in character and fruitful of trouble with the American Government. There was no doubt that these Scandinavian and Danish steamers were carrying by the medium of postal packages a considerable trade between Germany and the United States, thus to some extent cheating the Blockade. By mid-December the time arrived for drastic action. First approached our old acquaintance the *Oscar II*, who heralded her advent twenty-four hours previously by her wireless chatter. When she was taken into Kirkwall 734 bags of parcels en route from the U.S.A. for Norway, Sweden, and Denmark were removed. The *Alcantara* stopped the Danish S.S. *United States* bound west with a parcel mail. The weather was too bad for boarding, so she was escorted to the lee of the Shetlands, whence an armed guard took her all the way down to Greenock. Some thousands of postal packages from Germany, containing merchandise for America, were then removed. At this time 58 sacks of parcel post were seized aboard the S.S. *Stockholm*, also bound west, together with 597 parcel bags in the above-mentioned *Frederik VIII*.

All this caused a great outcry in the U.S.A., where public sentiment was so injured that a protest was lodged with the British Government, who, before replying, consulted the French Government, because (wrote Sir Edward Grey to the American Ambassador) this raised "important questions of principle". A final answer was made in the following February, Britain taking up the standpoint that she had censored, not the neutral-borne letter mails, but only the parcels. This was the rigid discrimination. When, a few days later, the *Bergensfjord* came on her next west-bound voyage and was intercepted, she carried 30 bags of parcel mails duly certified as not being "of enemy origin", so she was allowed to proceed after one male German had been taken off.

But this December weather was trying severely even the stoutest and most recently built vessels of the Blockading Fleet ; and those of us who were patrolling other areas off the British Isles will not easily forget those heartbreaking gales or menacing seas which rolled in from the Atlantic mercilessly. In Admiral de Chair's armed merchant cruisers, which at this date numbered 21, the following serious defects now developed owing to stress of weather. The *Hildebrand's* foremost deck-house during one gale had become so damaged that the water got below and rendered the stokers' quarters uninhabitable. A few days later a leak developed in her hull, letting in about two tons of water an hour. But still she stuck to her patrol. The *Almanzora's* fresh-water pipes froze and burst, icicles forming a series of festoons. The *Mantua* developed such leaks that she had to be dry-docked and repaired. The *Hildebrand* became so much worse that she, too, was sent off for the Clyde shipbuilders to deal with. During the height of that horrible gale on December 30 the *Orotava's*[1] steam steering-gear became disabled through breaking of her rudder chain. With immense difficulty repairs were effected and damage made good by midnight. The *Hilary* developed defects in her tail shaft owing to her engines racing in heavy seas.

And so the strain on ships as well as personnel had to be borne. It was now decided to withdraw those lonely patrol trawlers from Norwegian waters, since they could be of little use during the winter. But for the plucky officers and men of the boarding parties and armed guards, who were the very instruments of the Blockade, there could be no relief. If they should fail, then the whole idea must collapse, and the pressure on Germany would vanish. So into their open boats the party would go, risking life and limb to climb aboard the stranger. It had almost to be hurricane weather before such visits were delayed. The inspiration was not merely a matter of personal honour, the reputation of the ship, the esteem of the Squadron, but the fact that for days some "wanted" ship had been awaited with eagerness.

The British intelligence during the War is known to have been wonderful, and its help in regard to the Blockade developed into a system which combed all the world's ports and shipping. A signal would reach the *Alsatian* something like this:

Four-masted sailing ship "Cabilla" left Valparaiso two months ago, boatswain said to be German. Brown hair, blue eyes, scar across right cheek. Pretends he is Dane. Ship to be sent in if met with. Captain suspected of enemy sympathies.

---

[1] During bad weather on December 7 the *Orotava's* seaboat was washed right overboard.

Or it might be :

Intercepted letter from Master of German S.S. "Mirami" interned at Bahia states following three engineers and second mate have left in Swedish S.S. "Katrina" to fight for Germany. Expected to pass through Blockade area between Thursday and Saturday next.

Then would follow the names and descriptions of the five men, who would become wonder-struck when approaching the Shetlands to find themselves picked out from among the other passengers and removed in a boat. But their coming had been known for weeks.

So it was with the Norwegian barque *Skomvaer*, which had left Buenos Aires last October 15, and was ordered to be taken into port when met with. It was now December 21 when the *Otway* stopped her and sent an armed guard on board consisting of Sub-Lieut. S. F. Carter; R.N.R., a Midshipman, R.N.R., and four seamen with eight days' provisions. Although bound for Lerwick, it was an impossible task. Nothing but strong easterly winds blew for the next eleven days, so no headway was made. Frequently ships of the patrol would be spoken, but it was a dull, miserable Christmas for six Britons and the twenty-one Norwegians.

On the day after this came the *Orotava*, who supplied another eight days' provisions, and on January 1 *Cedric* gave them some more. That afternoon the wind veered to S.W. and W., so that at last *Skomvaer* passed Muckle Flugga and arrived off Lerwick two days later. Such a dull sailer was the barque that, owing to the contrary and baffling winds, she was boxing about off that harbour from January 3 to 8, unable to get in. There now breezed up a northerly gale, so Carter tried to make Kirkwall, but on the 9th the wind backed to S.W., inducing him to make once more for Lerwick. On the 10th the wind veered to W.N.W. and Lerwick was out of the question.

By this time there remained only five days' drinking water, and it was blowing very hard, with a high sea. The crew complained to the Master respecting the ship's safety, and he insisted that she must run for it. To this Carter consented with reluctance, and the *Skomvaer* ran to the south-east. This brought them to the Norwegian coast, where a pilot was picked up, yet even now there ensued two weary days of calms with heavy snow squalls. They tried to reach Stavanger, but were eventually taken by a couple of small tugs into Flekkefjord, where they arrived on January 14. Thus nearly a month had been spent on short rations and with no little anxiety, yet to no purpose, so far as the Blockade was concerned. Flekkefjord happened to be the destination for which the *Skomvaer* had sailed with her cargo of Quebrachi wood three months ago, and now the question was the matter of internment. By a reversal of circumstances, surely the armed guard themselves would be detained ? Along came a Norwegian destroyer, who obtained particulars, went away for orders, and came back with permission from the authorities that the armed guard might leave the country as soon as possible. The result was that all six took passage in a Norwegian steamer to Newcastle and thence travelled to Liverpool, where they rejoined the *Otway*, which had come up the Mersey. It should be added that the *Skomvaer's* Master for days had been supplying the guard with bread, milk, and tea, but he refused to accept payment ; and the *Skomvaer's* owners would not make any claim for the barque's delay.

Nor was she the only vessel that suffered at the merciless hands of these gales. I remember a few days before that Christmas seeing in Queenstown a most unusual and interesting ship lying at anchor. As I steamed past I recollect trying to puzzle out what part she could possibly be playing in the Great War. This was the historic *Morning*, which, until the year 1902, was the Norwegian whaler *Morgen*, when she was purchased by the Royal Geographical Society and sent out to the Antarctic, where she discovered a new island, reached Captain Scott's famous *Discovery*, then came home again in 1904 and returned to her career as a whaler.

Now in December 1915 she was loaded at Brest with ammunition for Archangel, left Queenstown late in December, bunkered at the Faroes, then got caught in the S.E. gale and began leaking so badly that she foundered on the morning of Christmas Eve. Most of the boats were stove in, the whole crew were drowned, with the exception of the Second Mate and the Master (Andrew Smith), who were found and rescued from an open boat by the *Cedric* on December 28. The sufferings of these two men, after being four days exposed to such cold and violent weather, needs no stressing ; but the anguish and nervous suspense, the hopeless outlook, the one-in-a-million chance of ever being seen amid lonely crested waves, reduced them to a state of exhaustion. A few hours later they would have succumbed.

So the year ended dramatically on sea. Only one armed guard so far had been taken prisoners, though two had their prizes sunk under them by submarines. The cheerful willingness of these young officers and men, who undertook such constant risk without the satisfaction of being allowed to strike a blow in defence of their own safety, was, as Admiral de Chair so well appreciated, remarkable. During 1915 that huge area of 220,000 square miles had been intermittently patrolled in all weathers and conditions. Not even the ever pressing U-boats had stopped the patrols, though the latter's lines had to be shifted according to the submarines' presence.

No fewer than 3,108 ships had been intercepted, of whom 696 had been sent into port under armed guards. That is to say, about 700 vessels could have carried their contraband for enemy destination except for this vigilance. But the cost in lives had been high : 63 British officers and 800 men had gone down with their ships. The result of this first year's experience showed that, whilst far more neutral steamers and sailors were trying to get through, far fewer actually succeeded. Another striking feature was that, though the Admiral was in close touch with units by wireless and pre-serving a continuous control, seldom did one sight another.

The *Alsatian* was a kind of huge telegraph sorting office always on the move—a great intelligence exchange, through which about 70 messages in or out passed every day not-withstanding the restriction of signalling to a minimum. The flagship herself between January 1 and December 31 had steamed 71,500 miles, an equivalent to having gone more than twice round the world ; and she had consumed 40,287 tons of coal. The wear and tear of machinery, alone ; the labour in coaling ; the navigation and constant checking of positions ; the lowering and hoisting of boats : all these

P

items when multiplied by a score of units represented only a fraction of the big efforts being made to defeat Germany by sea. The pity was that the bureaucrats had not allowed the Blockaders a freer hand, nor imposed a sterner policy on neutrals. But with regard to the personal work of those serving under Admiral de Chair, everyone in the Grand Fleet shared in Admiral Jellicoe's remark that officers and men of the 10th Cruiser Squadron "deserve all that their country can do for them".

By the year's conclusion Britain's arrangement with the leading traders of Denmark, Holland, and Switzerland, under which the trusts were made sole consignees of goods that must not be re-exported into Germany, had been rendered possible only because the Squadron was a controlling force. It was so real a threat, so powerful a lever in bargaining, that without this patrol force such agreements could never have been enforced. When the managers or directors of the principal Dutch shipping lines, trading companies, or banks had given their promise to Britain, there was a moral obligation imposed against our enemies, who were not insensitive to such isolation. Nevertheless, smuggling from Holland into Germany was as rampant as it was difficult to check. Large quantities of rubber found their way from the Netherlands to Germany and Austria by registered letter post. The fat which Germany so badly needed was sent by the Dutch inside chocolate, or in wooden piles specially hollowed out. Large quantities of soap, containing fat, mysteriously travelled, and quantities of "honey" consisted of rubber solution.

One vessel left Amsterdam loaded with 110 tons of margarine, passed through the locks, crossed the Zuyder Zee, thence by inland waterway through Zwolle towards the German frontier; but it was stopped by detectives just before reaching the latter. As to the Narvik trade, it was proved by records that between August 1914 and December 1915 there had reached Germany via Rotterdam several million tons of iron ore. Whether this was turned into shells, guns, mines, or submarines, it is regrettable that the supply could not have been stopped. Admiral M. W. W. P. Consett, who was British Naval Attaché in Scandinavia during 1912–1919, supports the seriousness of this view. "Nothing would have hastened the end of the War more effectively than the sinking of ships trading in ore between Sweden and Germany."[1]

In regard to the other commodities, the Netherlands Overseas Trust, whilst fully conscious of the smuggling, were unable to prevent this leakage. They could not keep goods always under their eyes after arrival and delivery to the first consignee, in spite of some 600 officials working for the Trust. German buyers came over and offered prices three or even four times those obtainable in Holland. Smuggling attained such magnitude that on a certain venture, where woods ran across the German-Dutch frontier, some 200 men, women, and children might be engaged at a particular date. Indeed it was admitted in the Netherlands Parliament that 37,000 people by February 1916 had been caught in the act of smuggling.

By land and water did such supplies find their way into Germany and thereby partially negative the Blockaders' efforts afloat. Just as in the eighteenth century those who smuggled brandy, tobacco, wines, and silks from the Continent to the English coast had to invent all sorts of tricks and concealments, so it was during the Great War from the Low Countries to Germany. Ships, for example, would have anchors made of copper but disguised. An engine was found with its water-tank filled with fat. "Onions" were really rubber balls. And so the game went on. There was only one remedy, and that was to make the rationing more severe, but it must be applied to Norway and Sweden as well.

---

[1] *The Triumph of Unarmed Forces*, London, 1923, p. 80.

CHAPTER XVIII

THE ART OF BOARDING

THE reader will have not failed to observe in the preceding chapters that the essential and indispensable features of the Blockade were the interception, stoppage, and boarding of ships. This was so much more than a mere routine affair, yet it occurred with such regular daily frequency during three long years that it is well to set down for all time exactly the procedure which took place in order that we may perceive the toil and hazard of boatmanship, whilst leaving for posterity a complete record that may be of value. I have in the following pages endeavoured to present a composite picture of exactly what went on, the details having been supplied to me by a number of officers, each an expert in his own department.

We shall view the subject as seen respectively by the Admiral, the Captain, the Second-in-Command, the Examining Officers, the boatmen, the sullen neutral shipmaster.

Let us imagine ourselves aboard the armed merchant cruiser. From the crow's-nest high up the mast the smoke of a ship has been sighted by one of the look-outs, who kept two-hour watches only, since that was quite long enough when ultra-vigilance was so important. Course would be altered and speed quickened to intercept her before the stranger could sight the patrol; but then the neutral would usually turn away and try evasion. By this time the cruiser would be working up to full speed, and presently the two converging courses would nearly reach the point of contact; but before coming within gun range the merchant cruiser's buglers would sound off "Action Stations", men would come rushing forth, and the ship be cleared for an engagement, with guns trained on the neutral, magazines opened, stretcher-parties and first-aid parties at their posts, fire-hose connected up, and everything ready for a fight. Who could say offhand that this was not a raider in disguise?

Flag-signals have been hoisted ordering the vessel to stop immediately; if this was not complied with there would be first a blank charge fired, and then a live shell across her bows. The next duty was to manœuvre towards the ship, zigzagging and keeping outside of torpedo range, lower the boarding boat, then turn away and signal the stranger to approach the boat, whose examining officers would then climb aboard. Sometimes during a gale, says Admiral de Chair, "I have witnessed the boarding boats capsized and sunk alongside the craft they were boarding. The way we generally managed to get alongside was to order the ship to steer a certain course at right angles (if the weather was not too bad) to the wind and sea. Then we would go round ahead of her and, with our ship pointing in the same direction, lower our boat under our lee, then steam ahead, ordering the other craft to steam ahead too. The latter would come up to the boat, so there was less need for rowing, the stranger giving the boat her lee. The intercepting patrol would then steam round and come up astern ready for the boarding boat to return."

That was the general principle in the *Alsatian* and others, but some commanding officers modified the method according to their own ideas and the different handling which each ship required. Whilst the general practice was to steam very slowly ahead, bringing the seas just on one bow, lowering the boat to leeward, the *Alcantara* acted as follows. This somewhat flat-bottomed vessel had been built for the River Plate trade, so that her draught was light in proportion to her top-hamper: in a wind she drifted fast to leeward. Admiral Wardle (her late Captain) tells me that he therefore lowered his boat to *windward*, left her, and then went astern, to clear the boat. Even when it was blowing hard, this unusual seamanship exactly suited *Alcantara*.

Vessels of the 10th Cruiser Squadron had orders to stop the stranger at about 5,000 yards. In very bad weather the *Alcantara* would keep the wind about four points on the bow before going astern. "In *Almanzora*", says Commander

W. C. Tarrant, R.N.R., "we had single wires through the davits to the boat. This meant no awkward fall blocks to hook on or unhook. These wires met inboard at a buffer spring attached to a single threefold purchase. The travelling block of the purchase ran on wheels on deck."

"I much preferred my way in *Alcantara*," says Admiral Wardle, "of having a double-ended boat on No. 2 hatch, so that I could hoist out on either side."

Such a boat carried only six men, whereas the thirteen or fifteen would be in the normal service cutter. The latter, whilst bigger, was less handy when arriving alongside a tall steel side, and disaster came when the cutter, having drifted under a ship's counter, was crushed by the steamer's heavy roll. Captain John Kiddle, who was in the *Alsatian*, informs me that "all our boats were of the ordinary Merchant Service pattern, stowing *inboard* on the boat-deck. The foremost boat each side was kept permanently turned out and secured in (Naval) Service fashion, with gripes and griping spar. The reason for this was that they were rather larger than the others and blocked the gangway badly if kept turned in. We had not a seaboat proper, as understood in the Service, but a small double-ender was stowed on the fore-deck, being hoisted out and in by two derricks and winches. One of these derricks was topped to plumb the boat in the inboard-position, and one to swing out for lowering into the water."

In the accompanying photograph will be seen the *Alsatian's* boat swung out ready for lowering. This particular one was sometimes fitted with an outboard motor, and is just taking the Boarding Officers Lieut.-Commander J. W. Williams, R.N.R., and Paymaster Sub.-Lieut. J. Barton, with a crew of seven, to examine a steamer. No patent dropping gear was fitted. "An eye with a lizard[1] was used to steady the boat as far as possible", says the latter, "when lowering in a seaway, but, considering the height above water of the *Alsatian's* foredeck, the boat was apt to bump badly if the ship had any movement. Fenders were used, of course, to obviate this. When the boat was nearing the water, the winch had to be let run, and I can assure you it had to be smart

---

[1] A lizard is a wire or rope having a thimble fitted at one end. This will be recognized in the photograph.

"AWAY SEA-BOAT'S CREW!"
Boarding officers and crew of the Flagship about to be lowered
into the water.

work unhooking. The way in which the boarding boat's crew —officers and men—carried out this evolution in all sorts of weather was beyond praise. As you can imagine, the slightest fault would have meant the boat capsizing; but during the time I served in the ship we were lucky. It was the only method that could be used, as the boat deck was some 25 to 30 feet further up."

Sometimes the boat would hoist sail for the run down to the stranger's lee side; at other times she would be rowed. It was ticklish business coming alongside a hull whose rivets stood out like domes and had a nasty habit of catching against the boat's gunwale. When a capsize followed, or the boat became swamped by the backwash, not rarely were the crew rescued by the ship to be boarded. The admiration by the Royal Navy for the way the Royal Naval Reserve handled these open boats remains one of the abiding results of the Blockade. Captain Kiddle describes it as "absolutely superb". "The handling of these boarding boats", says Admiral de Chair, "became a fine art, and it was inspiring to see how they were hoisted out and sent away in the heaviest sea, with the ship rolling heavily; yet the appliances were of the simplest— just an ordinary span and heavy hook—the boat being lifted out of its crutches and dropped over the side on to the crest of a wave, disappearing the next moment as the ship rolled away and the boat sank far down in the trough of a sea below the bilge of the ship."

Admiral de Chair was experiencing conditions that belonged to the old days of oak and canvas. On several occasions he had to visit his ships in heavy weather, and the method was thus. Having brought the strange ship 200 yards astern, the boat would be hoisted out, the Admiral stepping in from the lee gangway as the boat rose level with the upper deck. Then both ships steamed ahead, the stranger giving the boat a lee; and the process would be repeated on the return trip. "The boats' crews in my flagship were mostly composed of Newfoundland fishermen, who were marvellous boatmen, accustomed as they were to handle their little dories on the Banks of Newfoundland."

"We had about 25 of these Newfoundlanders," adds Captain Kiddle, "and they were sterling seamen." Those who remember Kipling's *Captains Courageous* need no reminder of the hard conditions under which these men had been brought up to work line-fishing on the Banks from open boats that often get lost in the fog, leaving the men to die of cold and starvation. Accustomed to boarding their own schooners during terrible weather, which sometimes get driven right across from America to Europe, this hard school of gallant men were the world's greatest experts for the Blockade job. In winter the ice on these schooners' bulwarks, rigging, anchors, and so on at times becomes seriously weighty, and even the seas which leap aboard become solid frozen masses, so that the ship settles down deep in the water beyond her correct water-line and she founders. Even since the War there have been cases where several of these fine schooners, bereft of chart, compass, or sufficient food and water, have fought death during week after week before getting home again.

No sons of Empire did better work during the Great War than these seafarers. Without such specialist boat-handlers, together with the English and Scottish fishermen, it is difficult to imagine the Blockade could have been a practical combing of neutrals. Rehearsals still went on; every time an armed merchant cruiser entered Busta Voe to coal, it was "Abandon Ship!" and away went all boats for an hour's sail or pull round.

Two of the ablest Boarding Officers in the whole Blockading Fleet were Lieutenant-Commander (now Captain) J. W. Williams, R.N.R., and Paymaster Sub-Lieut. J. Barton, R.N.R. (later Lieutenant R.N.V.R.), both of whom served in the flagship, and their co-operation was ideal. They raised ship-visiting and examination to such a standard that it can never be beaten, combining the qualities of physical courage with tact and personal dominance over all the bluffs and reticence of evasive foreigners. Captain Williams brought to his task a strong, independent character that had been moulded by long years of hard service and stern discipline under the Red Ensign. The respect of these two officers one for the other was typical of what was existent in other units of the Fleet. "I had the great fortune to have with me John Barton, an ex-amateur champion boxer of the Midlands," says the former. "John knew not personal fear. Day and night,

LIEUT.-COMMANDER J. W. WILLIAMS, D.S.O., R.N.R.

One of the most experienced Boarding Officers. Now
Marine Superintendent of the White Star Line.

gale or calm, he was always the same—full of go. In spite of
my warning, he would attach to his person a heavy Service
revolver and bandolier full of cartridges : sufficient weight to
sink any ordinary man 'without trace'.   On one occasion this
practice was nearly his undoing.

"We were boarding a very awkward ship in a rather nasty
gale, with high seas running. The ship was rolling badly, and
there were many projections from her side which would have
sunk us had we been unable to keep our boat clear. John made
a spring for the ship's side—caught the ropes and ladder—but
our boat hove up under him and he very quickly found
himself, as it were, turned into the sinker of a deep-sea
lead. He managed, however, to slip his armoury, and
came to the surface, having absorbed quite a quantity of
the North Sea, and swearing that his 'Gieve's' waistcoat was
wonderful.

"Sailing ships were the most difficult to board, and we
were very nearly washed right on board—boat and all—on
several occasions. Experience, self-confidence, and nerve were
required by the Boarding Officer. I had two years' experience,
and it was astonishing how we soon found that we could
board ships in nearly all weathers. At any time, day or
night, we were called away, assisted in the darkness by our
searchlights, running before the wind under a small lugsail
towards our prize, which would be lost to sight in the trough of
each sea, and eventually rounding up to leeward of the ship
for examination. The dark hull of our own ship (with her
searchlight ever watching) was always near with guns trained
on in case our prize turned out to be a raider. It was always
understood that in such a case fire was to be opened and the
boarding boat with crew sacrificed."

"Personally," Lieutenant Barton informs me, "I rather
enjoyed the boarding stunts in *daylight*, but on a dark night
with a really heavy sea running it was really poisonous.   In
putting my boat alongside, it was always necessary to anticipate
the skipper being a hostile neutral, in which case it was not
difficult to run me down 'accidentally'.   I often think of the
many times when I have been waiting, keeping my seaboat
head on to the seas, for the good old *Alsatian* to pick me up.
Then I would see her coming along, showing 50 feet of her

forefoot—as she often did in heavy weather. Those were great days!"

Proud of one's ship! But proud, also, of the boat's crew! In the photograph Lieutenant Williams is sitting, Cox'n Leslie is standing at his left, and Michael Lynch next to them. Lieutenant Barton (in Paymaster's uniform) is standing holding the hook, which had to be disconnected. "Michael Lynch was my stroke oar from August 1914 to the end of the War, and he was plus 10 at his job. A man of great strength and staying power, he never got rattled, and in fending-off with the butt of an oar he repeatedly saved us all when alongside small tramp steamers with flush deck-ports, which, as we came up on a big sea, would have caught our gunwale and capsized us."

This officer's personal narrative of being lowered from the tall deck of *Alsatian* is full of interest as we glance at the photograph and think of the boat hanging as high as a big house. The crux of lowering or being hoisted was the act of connecting or releasing the massive steel hook. "I always took charge of it myself, both when leaving and returning. Although I am pretty strong physically, it was just all I could handle. In leaving the flagship, we would be dropped while she had way on (about two knots), and the instant we touched water the stroke oar would unship the after of the two lizards, and I would unship the hook. The cox'n would put the helm over, and then the bowman would let go for'ard. This would put us clear of the flagship. It was very much more difficult returning, as the flagship would have considerable speed on because of the submarines; and in heavy weather the baring of her forefoot was most impressive.

"I had to place my seaboat so that, as she passed us, the long steadying-line from the deck would just trail over us. I would then sing out: 'All hands on steadying-line!' The fore-and-aft lizards would then be made fast to the fore-and-aft thwarts, and the hook would come down with a run, which I would grab and jamb on to the ring. Then the job would be to keep it engaged while the winches were taking the weight. It was just a gamble whether I hooked on while the seaboat was on the crest of a sea or in a trough: if the latter, we would quickly have a heap of slack—both chain and fall—so I had to see we did not become disengaged.

"On the instant of engaging the hook I would roar out : 'All fast !' The officer on deck in charge of hoisting and lowering would pass the word to the winch controlling the outboard derrick, and the winchman would give it full steam. The instant we were clear of the water (and often before !) the signalman watching from the bridge would sing out : 'Boat clear of water !' The commanding officer would instantly give the order : 'Full ahead all four (propellers) !' and the ship would begin to feel the impetus."

It was an unforgettable sight for this boatload of men to be sitting poised on a great wave watching and waiting for the *Alsatian* some four miles distant with all her guns trained on the suspect. Then the short quick suspense, the strain on connected gear, the rattle of the winches. Never once occurred the slightest hitch, and this was due to the smartness of the seaboat as well as of Lieut.-Commander Alfred Freer, R.N.R., on deck, who was responsible for the whole evolution of "Away seaboat's crew !"

Up the neutral's rope ladder would climb the two officers with their signalman, leaving the boat dancing about below in charge of the cox'n and four oarsmen. The reception aboard the neutral varied. In the case of Holland and Denmark there was little cause for complaint, but the Swedish shipmasters were truculent and difficult, who had to be addressed in unmistakable terms. Immediately would begin the examination, the first duty being to look at the steamer's boats. For what purpose ? Well, to ensure that they were not mere camouflage of guns. Having at last been satisfied that this was no raider, one Boarding Officer would get what information he could out of the Master, whilst the other British officer did the same with the steamer's Chief Officer, the signalman having a yarn with one of the ship's company.

The ship's papers were examined—certificate of registry, bills of lading, manifest, bill of health—from which were extracted such items as her nationality, tonnage, owners, ports bound from and to, passengers, crew, cargo, consignees of the latter, and so on. Next (if everything was all correct) would be semaphored back to the armed merchant cruiser :

"Holds and crew examined. Nothing suspicious to report."

"If you are satisfied, return on board and let her proceed," would come the answer.

"Boat leaving," the Boarding Officer would then flap back.

The stranger would be given the flag of the day, good for the next three days. This, on being hoisted, would allow her to pass the next patrols unmolested.

"Flag of day till noon Thursday N for nuts P for pudding Q for queen."

So with this message from the cruiser the neutral would flutter her bunting, start her engines again, and pass on.

The flagship was in wireless touch with the Admiralty, and if an armed guard had been put aboard, further instructions would soon come out of the ether.

"It was generally with the greatest respect, and some trepidation," says Captain Williams, "that we were received by the Captains, crews, and passengers of the ships examined. All hands were first mustered and their identities checked off on the manifests and crew lists. The description of wanted people (as supplied to us by the Naval Intelligence Department) was carefully checked off also. Next holds and cargo manifests were examined and a report signalled to our Captain, who made the decision as to whether the ship had to be taken in for examination. If this was found necessary, a prize crew, consisting generally of one officer and five or six men—all of course armed—was sent on board."

Nor was this escort into port always devoid of humour when those in charge were lacking in experience. "The R.N.V.R. officers of the prize crews taking our captures into Kirkwall and other ports were at the beginning more full of zeal and the 'will-to-win' spirit than experienced in the ways of the sea. Once, when entering Kirkwall, the naval shore-station was throwing signal after signal—International Code, semaphore, etc.—into the ship, which was a Dutchman. The Captain was entirely baffled, but our R.N.V.R. hero, not to be beaten, put the naval signal station out of action by hoisting every flag he had in the ship, and came to anchor before the astonished yeoman-of-signals had recovered from the shock."

It was impressed on officers that they were to perform their difficult work whilst showing every courtesy to the neutrals. "Soon after commissioning the *Calyx*," recollects Admiral Wardle, "I told the senior R.N.R. Lieutenant to have a yarn with the young R.N.R. Sub-Lieutenant who would be the first to go in charge of a Prize Crew. It was a necessary precaution, for the senior Lieutenant came back later to say he had given him a good twenty minutes on the subject of tact, and had then tested him with the following question : 'Supposing, when you get on board, the neutral Captain does not ask you to use his cabin ?' The answer came pat : 'Then he'll b——y well have to lump it.' However, this young officer did very good work later."

Admiral Wardle also relates the following two incidents, which illustrate the elusiveness of the neutral skippers. "One dark night, blowing a full gale, I intercepted one of the Danish East Asiatic liners, and, as we could not board, because of the weather, Admiral de Chair signalled me to keep her till we could. Later on, while I was below, the officer-of-the-watch reported she had switched off all lights and disappeared. An anxious moment, after the Admiral's signal ! A brain-wave caused me to steer along the course she would have to go to the Cattegat, and I was much relieved about two hours later to see a light in the distance. It was the liner ! She had by now considered herself safe and switched on her navigation lights !"

Through the same over-confidence did another evader fall into Admiral Wardle's hands. "I caught a Swedish ship with ammunition on board in much the same way. I was patrolling near the Norwegian coast, well inside or to the east of the main patrol line. She had got through the main line, and, thinking herself quite safe, had switched on her navigation lights. The Captain was very annoyed. I sent him in with an armed guard under an R.N.R. Midshipman. I think it was on this occasion that the Captain put a revolver on the table and the Midshipman took it up, unloaded it, and pocketed it !"

Whilst the Boarding Officers each carried a revolver, the men of the armed guard had rifles and bayonets. The food they brought on board consisted of bully beef, biscuits, and water. "Anyone acquainted with ships", explains Commander Tarrant, "will at once recognize that to examine and search thoroughly even a small cargo vessel at sea is an impossibility. To discover contraband it is necessary to remove and search the whole of the cargo, and when it is stated that the vessels dealt with carried anything up to 15,000 tons of cargo, this point will be readily appreciated. For this reason, as far as cargo was concerned, the Boarding Officers were only able to carry out a comparatively superficial examination."

How wideawake both Boarding and Customs Officers had to be may be understood from some of the blockade-runners' tricks. I have come across instances of rubber being made up as coffee-beans and enclosed in bags; whilst other bags containing mails to or from Germany would be secreted in private cabins. The Captain's "wife" might be in reality a German courier travelling backwards and forwards from America. "Hollow masts", says Admiral de Chair, "and double bulkheads filled with contraband; forbidden metals (riveted to the ship below the waterline); sections of honeycomb filled with rubber solution; macaroni covering sticks of aluminium"—were all tried and discovered. The Customs Officers obviously could not pull every package of (say) a 10,000-tons steamer to pieces; for there was a standing order that the neutral was not to be detained more than a short time. But X-ray photography was found of immense assistance.

When a neutral was ordered into port, it was the duty of the armed guard's officer to ensure that she steered a proper course. Before starting off, this officer would receive by semaphore from his mother-ship the present exact position, so he could be independent of the neutral skipper's reckoning. The latter was not suffered to interfere with the allotted course into the examination port, for which reason both day and night the British officer was on the bridge protected by a couple of the armed guard. From the time of first boarding to that when she was either allowed to proceed or be sent into port varied according to circumstances, but it might last an hour or less. All sorts of amusing and strange incidents would crop up unexpectedly, as, for example, when the Dutch S.S

Amsterdam, outward-bound for Halifax, even had the temerity to ask the *Alsatian* if the latter would kindly supply the steamer with a chart "from Cape Race to Halifax". Back came the signal : "Very sorry cannot spare chart."

Another stranger would send a message : "Tell Captain that Norwegian S.S. *Augusta*, carrying timber for Iceland, has sprung a leak and requires assistance in lat. 61°33′ N., long. 14°40′ W." It was a fact that two Dutch trawlers from Ymuiden were in these waters spying for Germany, but their names and fishing numbers were known to the Blockaders. On the other hand, when any British trawler was fishing the Iceland grounds, or on passage, and had urgent information to communicate to H.M. ships, she used to hoist a basket over her fishing burgee. Finally, as a measure of further isolating Germany, it was insisted that all vessels trading with Iceland, or fishing in those waters, must have either a declaration (attested by one of the British accredited agents in Iceland) that she was working from an Iceland base and would not take her catch thence to Scandinavia or Holland, or else a declaration, attested by the British consular office in Norway, that the catch would be sold to British Government buyers.

The most difficult examination problem to the end of the war was how to intercept the letters which were being carried aboard neutral ships individually by members of the crew or passengers on behalf of Germany. But the busiest time was during the herring season off northern Iceland, when one armed merchant cruiser might have to send in ten or more fish-carriers to port with a corresponding number of guards, thus seriously depleting that ship's personnel. All these items were different in kind from the navigational dilemmas, which were as real as they were brilliantly overcome. In ordinary peace-time procedure a steamer advances directly from one position to another, keeping a steady course. But for vessels of the 10th Cruiser Squadron the courses were frequently being altered, "dead reckoning" (after much zig-zagging, stopping to board, and so forth) was of little help, the frequent fogs shut out sun and stars ; whilst, between Iceland and Greenland in particular, the navigators had to contend with unknown currents and considerable magnetic attraction. A wireless direction-finder was fitted to the *Alsatian*, but originally to no other units; yet, in spite of every conceivable drawback, the navigational standard continued to the end remarkably high. Perhaps it has never been surpassed in the whole history of seafaring.

CHAPTER XIX

FINE SEAMANSHIP

WE have repeatedly stressed the prevailing fear that sooner or later the Germans would send through the Blockade a raider disguised as any of the numerous neutral steamers or sailing vessels. Until the end of 1915, apart from the *Kaiser Wilhelm der Grosse*, which rushed through during the first week of war, ere the Blockade had been properly instituted, not one raider had slipped past, although the *Rio Negro* and the S.S. *Kronberg* (ex-*Rubens*), carrying supplies to the enemy's forces in East Africa, had succeeded during the winter of 1914–15; so also during the winter of 1915–1916 another supply ship, the S.S. *Marie*, managed to be so evasive that by March 1916 she arrived with guns, arms, and ammunition at the German East African Sudi Bay.[1] But hitherto no raiders had made the attempt.

This condition was altered when, towards the close of December 1915, Count Nikolaus zu Dohna-Schlodien started out from Germany in the S.S. *Moewe*, hugged the Norwegian coast, sighted the Sule Skerry Lighthouse (west of the Orkneys), laid a minefield on New Year's Day, and then, after this night operation, carried on into the Atlantic, where he spent some highly successful weeks capturing and sinking ship after ship, till he returned north, passed through the Blockade zone at the end of February 1916, and steamed safely into Wilhelmshaven on March 4.[2] It was an extraordinarily fine achievement, and, whilst such a double evasion of our patrols could have been possible only by selecting the period of long

---

[1] For further details see my *The Königsberg Adventure*.
[2] Full accounts of the *Moewe's* two voyages will be found in my *The Sea Raiders*.

Q

black nights, yet here was a further embarrassing proof that even the most efficient blockade ever organized could not be made absolutely tight. The sinking of H.M.S. *Edward VII* on January 6, after striking one of *Moewe's* mines, was a visual demonstration of this truth. Still, even the 10th Cruiser Squadron could not do impossibilities, though it had done wonders; and the award of a K.C.B. on New Year's Day to Admiral de Chair, to the joy of all in the Squadron and the Grand Fleet, was a measure of appreciation for unprecedented vigilant toil.

During the year 1915 a total of 3,098 vessels of various nationalities had been intercepted, of which 743 had been sent in for examination. These figures are sufficiently eloquent to us who have perceived something of the efforts requisite for such individual work; yet the sad aspect is that the higher powers in Whitehall had released so many ships to the neutrals containing petroleum, wool, fish, rye, wheat, hides, cotton-seed cake, linseed, maize, lubricating oil, whale oil, meat, flour, lard, and so on.

The British public now became alarmed at this attitude of the Foreign Office, and in January 1916 the Press took up the matter with vehemence. The *Daily Mail* called attention to "the sham blockade", whilst the *Morning Post* criticized it as "the makebelieve blockade". Rumours that Cabinet Ministers would be impeached began to spread, Parliament was uneasy, and finally, on January 26, Sir Edward Grey, Secretary for Foreign Affairs, was compelled in the House of Commons to explain and defend the practice of allowing neutral countries to receive that which the Navy would have denied them.

"If", he argued, referring to the principle of release after seizure and examination, "the ship has goods destined for a neutral port for bona-fide consumption of a neutral country, without which that country would be starved of some essential supplies, then that cargo was released and not put into the Prize Court." As a rule the decision was made by the Contra-band Committee, though in several cases the Cabinet dealt with the ships and did not consult that Committee. If these "reckless" charges were true, added Sir Edward (referring evidently to the Press campaign), "and I was a naval officer,

I should want to shoot the Secretary of State for Foreign Affairs. . . . The thing that matters is the dispiriting effect it has on our seamen. There never was a time in the whole history of this country when we . . . have owed a greater tribute of gratitude and admiration to the Navy."

But the whole vindication of the Foreign Office was summed up in the Minister's apology that this Department "has to do its best to retain the good will of the neutrals", so that the War Office, Admiralty, and Ministry of Munitions might still get what they needed from the United States, Scandinavia, Denmark, and Holland. The Foreign Office was charged with the duty of keeping diplomatic relations so correct that supplies to Britain were not stopped, whilst at the same time the enemy's supplies through neutral channels were restricted.

Such delicate nicety can be appreciated, yet there were not lacking many well-informed men, both inside and out of the House, who still demanded a firmer policy; such, for instance, as that which Turkey was enforcing at this time. She had no regard whatsoever for neutral trade, and allowed no goods to pass through the Dardanelles except those coming to herself. Thus Roumania had to suffer.

Many people in England, further, considered there were far too many Blockade Committees around Whitehall, and that the time had come when all the diffuse contraband machinery might be tightened up. Perhaps this criticism was not so short of the target, for Lord Robert Cecil (then Under-Secretary for Foreign Affairs) admitted that we "were suffering in this Department because we were organized for peace and not for war. . . there have been too many committees. If we had only one committee, I would say we had too many." Nevertheless, this month were added the Foreign Trade Department of the Foreign Office, as well as the Finance Department.

Severe rationing (which Admiral Jellicoe had advocated) was now, however, introduced with surprising success, and the still more surprising acquiescence of neutral traders. Furthermore, it was tested in the Prize Court in the case of the *Baron Sternblad*, and the burden of proof (that excessive imports were coming into a neutral country) was shifted from the Crown to the consignee. Certainly the outlook of neutral countries was now none too pleasant, since Germany would not sell her valuable dyes to Norway unless the latter sent her copper ; and Germany would not allow Holland to have coal except the latter gave her meat.

Gradually, therefore, between the pressure of Britain on the one side and Germany on the other, the position of neutral Europe became an unenviable one ; so that the Norwegians, Danes, and Dutch began to look round and ask themselves a plain question : Which of the belligerents will come out of this war victorious ?   Whom shall I have to reckon with at the conclusion ?   And these three countries, from their vantage point of distance, perceived that, whatever else might happen on land or sea, it was the Blockade which was going to be the deciding factor, that this institution, however inconvenient, was gaining strength, and must be accepted.   Such a realization, coupled with the trade agreements being made with Britain, and the horror aroused by German submarine methods at sea, had the effect of inclining these three nations in Britain's favour.

In Sweden, none the less, the pro-German sympathy was still obstinate, and early this year there was even some loose talk of her joining in the war on Germany's side. Such an attitude was negatived at the beginning of February 1916 by a section of the Swedish Press which prudently demontrated four propositions :

(1) It is almost unthinkable that the British Fleet will be beaten in the present war.

(2) Sweden would risk her existence as a free country if she entered the war voluntarily.

(3) With regard to the Blockade demands, Sweden must give up her right of exporting goods to Germany just now ; otherwise this would be regarded as a breach of neutrality and Sweden would be in conflict with Britain.

(4) As Sweden has had to put up with the German submarine blockade, so she must tolerate the British Blockade.

It has been well said that "Denmark was Germany's larder, and Sweden her workshop",[1] but the embargo now being placed on all neutral goods in excess of certain figures was to make Germany's economic distress still more acute. Under what new regime such control was to be enforced will presently be made manifest. It is to be noted that what with the numbers of vessels employed for Army transport, tenders to the Grand Fleet, patrols, and many other purposes in different theatres of the War, and the sinkings by enemy action, together with the necessity for bringing commodities into the country with regularity, there was already a shortage of tonnage, and the Allies were largely dependent for carriers on neutral owners. If those were driven into the enemy's arms, Britain would have starved, her armies have collapsed, and there would have been no materials for France, Italy, or Belgium in the manufacture of their munitions.

By the beginning of January 1916 the French auxiliary cruiser *Champagne* (late British armed merchant cruiser *Oropesa*), under the command of Capitaine de Frégate C. Berthelot, called at Swarbacks Minn with 200 Russian naval ratings from Serbia for Archangel, and found herself dragging during one of the usual Shetlands gales, but she came to no harm. It was an introduction to the wild weather which our French friends would find so trying. The Swedes were still very troublesome, and on January 11 the *Alsatian* caught the S.S. *Kronprinsessan Victoria* north of the Faroes in a determined attempt at evasion. Her Master, Captain Snobohm, was much annoyed at being sent into Lerwick, and considered it was "hard luck being caught", as he admitted to have made four voyages and been diverted to a British port only twice, whilst he knew of four ships of this line which had evaded capture altogether. She was bound from Buenos Aires for Christiania with so much coffee, cocoa, and wool that the freightage on the cargo (valued at £300,000) amounted to £100,000, paid before sailing and passed through the Bank. When the boarding party climbed up the rope ladder it was discovered that the Master was sending a wireless message to his owners. This was promptly jammed by the *Alsatian*.

---

[1] Admiral Consett, *The Triumph of Unarmed Forces*, vide supra, p. 93.

In like manner a few days later the *Bergensfjord*, shortly before being boarded, was heard wirelessing to the S.S. *New Sweden*, and again the jamming was started.

The *Kronprinsessan Victoria* was quite a bad case. Captain Snobohm handed over a mailbag, and, when pressed for other papers, produced from his cabin several large packets sealed and addressed, remarking that he believed them to contain duplicate manifests, but "did not know for certain". On being opened, the contents were found to be enclosed in a second cover, also addressed. When this cover was opened, there were revealed manifests which disagreed with the manifests originally produced ; part, if not all, of the cargo being consigned to German interests direct.

Captain Snobohm had thus been caught in the act, and showed great nervousness. He admitted that the ship had twice been captured, and that his original intention had been to run as far north as lat. 64° N., but owing to bad weather and the presence of his wife on board, who was ill, he had run east on lat. 62°48′ N. He much regretted he had not gone further north, as thus he might have escaped.

So violently blew the January gales that ships in Busta Voe emulated the *Champagne*, and dragged badly, even with two anchors down. Coaling had to be stopped, steam raised, and the boom gate vessel dragged her anchors too. The shore end of the net (secured to a large rock) carried away owing to the rock splitting under the heavy strain. The other French auxiliary cruiser, *Artois* (late *Digby*), Capitaine de Frêgate J. de Marguêray, had the misfortune to be damaged by a collier who, in coming alongside, made a hole in the cruiser's bow with the crown of the collier's anchor.

Meanwhile ships on patrol were having a thrilling time. The *Patia*, although hove-to, shipped a sea so heavy that it damaged her bridge, injured an officer, and strained her hull, allowing salt water to contaminate her freshwater tanks. This caused the ship's company to be laid out with gastric trouble, and she had to be sent to the Clyde for repairs. The *Orotava* had her wheelhouse and all bridge-fittings smashed, and she was obliged to run before the gale, endeavouring to use hand steering-gear, but without success. The *Orcoma* also came off badly, having buckled her main deck. These

facts are mentioned because they show the utter merciless-
ness even to vessels whose structure was as splendid as the seamanship of her officers. The American S.S. *Ausable*, on her
way towards Kirkwall, when hove-to in the gale received such
punishment that the port side of her bridge was severely
damaged, two boats were stove in, the officer in charge of
the armed guard and one of his marines, together with
the *Ausable's* officer-of-the-watch, being all washed off the
bridge.

But there were some further glorious battles this month
between ships and men against the terrible forces of wind and
wave, the mere recital of which must quicken every reader's
imagination. Frequently encounters like these never reach
print except in some exaggerated and unseamanlike recital,
so that it would be a pity not to record them now. On January
24—the same day as the *Ausable's* mishap—the armed
merchant cruiser *Ebro*, Commander V. F. R. Dugmore, R.N.,
intercepted that fine Norwegian barque *Beechbank*, once a
pride of the British Merchant Service. She was now trying
to make Lerwick, but had lost her fore and main topmasts,
her mizzen t'gallantmast, and nearly all her sails as well as
boats.

The *Ebro* tried taking her in tow, but without success,
so stood by her till morning. An armed guard was on board
under Lieutenant Wynn, R.N.R. The Norwegian crew
became difficult to manage, and would not go aloft, so the
cutting away of the mizzen topsail and other aerial work had
to be done by the Norwegian Master and Lieut. Wynn, who
now took charge of the ship. Next day it was blowing a
whole gale—force 10—and the waves made it utterly impossible
for communication by boat, yet the *Ebro* was again trying to
take the barque in tow. And now occurred another of those
proofs that in the days of steam we still have seamanship of
a standard that was not excelled in the days of the clippers or
of Nelson's wooden walls.

As the *Ebro* was shortly due for coaling, and contained
only 22 per cent of her normal fuel, she was very light and
nearly as unmanageable on the water as a bladder. How to
connect up? Here was the difficulty. However, Commander
Dugmore made a bold and ingenious experiment. He veered

an anchor and six shackles of cable,[1] which had the same effect as a drogue or "sea-anchor" and kept her fairly steady head on to the W.S.W. gale. The *Ebro* then got a line aboard the barque by firing a rocket, and eventually the Norwegians were able to haul a 6-inch wire attached to the line. The wire was secured to the *Beechbank's* chain cable, of which 90 fathoms were slacked out, and with this enormous scope the *Ebro*, soon after midday on the 25th, was able to take the sailing ship in tow. Speed was only two knots, but a second wire (5½-inch) had also been attached, and in spite of the weather everything held throughout next day until 10 a.m. of the 27th, when happily she brought the *Beechbank* safely to anchor in Lerwick and then went off to coal.

Every seaman will recognize that it was the prudence of towing with the weight and sag of a 90-fathom cable which prevented snapping and made the achievement practicable. But the highest praise is due to Commander Dugmore for his cool resource. A few weeks later he received commendation from the Lords of the Admiralty, in March was mentioned in despatches, and in December promoted to Captain.

In the same gale *Almanzora* was being battered about, when Lieut.-Commander Harold Phillips, R.N.R., in the act of assisting to secure the starboard seaboat, fell overboard. The weather made it impossible to attempt saving him by lowering a boat, and he was drowned. A few days later, whilst preparing to board a Norwegian, the after fall of the patrol's boat about to be lowered took charge, the boat was smashed and seven men injured.

And now came the test of *Artois*. She had intercepted the Danish sailing vessel *Vigilant* bound from Gothenburg for Morocco, and there was a special reason why the latter should be examined. At the first attempt to board, the Frenchmen had an accident with their boat and dropped a man overboard, but he was picked up, and the sailing ship visited. She had suffered piteously from the weather; her foremast was gone, her rigging in a shocking state; and her Master requested that his crew should be taken back to the *Artois*. By reason

---

[1] In the Merchant Service a "shackle" represents 15 fathoms; in the Royal Navy it measures 12½ fathoms. A cable's length is 8 shackles, or 100 fathoms. The *Ebro* had thus let out a considerable length, viz. 540 feet.

of the wind and sea this was at last done only with some difficulty, but an attempt to tow the derelict, which was loaded
with wood and leaking badly, failed.

The gale developed its fury, and *Artois* stood by all that
night (February 2) and throughout the next day and night,
but on the 4th got the *Vigilant* in tow. On the 5th there
came another heavy gale from W.S.W., so that the speed of
tow was one knot ! An anti-submarine escort of the armed
steam yacht *Calanthe*, two whalers, and a tug were sent out
from Stornoway, but they could not face it, and had to shelter
under the land. By 9.30 p.m. *Artois* and *Vigilant* were still
crawling ahead, and got under lee of the Butt of Lewis, and
twelve hours later, after protracted efforts and immense
patience, both ships arrived in Stornoway, the wind during
the last half-day having again reached force 10. Our French
brothers of the sea had acquitted themselves with great distinction.

A curious incident befell the *Patuca*. After leaving
Swarbacks Minn, both condensers in her engine-room were
found to be choked with small fish about the size of sardines,
blocking the entrance of the tubes. It was all due to the net
defence at the harbour entrance, for shoals of fish had been
restricted until the boom defence gate should be opened,
and thus they passed in great quantities simultaneously with
the *Patuca* going through. The *Almanzora*, a few days later,
whilst coming into Swarbacks Minn during a gale, fouled
this net defence and wound it round both her propellers.
She anchored under shelter of the land, and managed in time
to clear them, but there was an unpleasant tangle.

The strong February gales, the bitter cold and cheerless
damp, were taking their steady toll. An able seaman was
washed overboad from *Columbella*, an engineer officer in the
Almanzora died of pneumonia, several sailing ships with armed
guards unable to make Lerwick or Kirkwall had been driven
over to the Norwegian coast, and the *Victorian* lost her cutter
in a snow squall, though the boat's crew were all saved. It
was a hard life indeed. But the neutrals' evasiveness showed
little sign yet of dying away. It was learnt that one American
steamer admitted having adopted on a previous voyage the
following ruse. Immediately after leaving New York, she

doused lights to escape interception by British cruisers off the Hudson River, and then shaped a course by the south of Greenland, round the north of Iceland, thence across to the coast of Norway, which she hugged, having the assistance of a Norwegian pilot all the way from New York. She next steamed south and arrived at Gothenburg in Sweden, where much of her cargo was discharged into lighters specially sent across from Germany.

Once more, too, the Danish S.S. *Hellig Olaf* was intercepted and relieved of 10 German passengers travelling from New York for Copenhagen; whilst that experienced *Oscar II*, eastward-bound, must again get herself into trouble. Besides her passengers and cargo (which consisted mostly of flour and oil-cakes), she carried 1,196 bags of letter mails, the greater portion being for Germany and Turkey.

But now a curious catena of events was to follow, which once more demonstrated that the concurrence of happenings in history are far more wonderful than when arbitrarily arranged by the imagination.

CHAPTER XX

On the last day of January 1916 the *Alsatian* learned from a vessel trading with Reykjavik that, in spite of the heavy gales, this winter off Iceland had been exceptional in that even the most northern ports thereof had been free of ice. This strange physical coincidence was much welcomed by Germany's naval staff anxious for the home-coming of Count Dohna-Schlodien after his first voyage in the *Moewe*, for it would enable them to advise him by wireless that he could go right up to the north in avoiding the British patrols.

No one, of course, in the British Navy was aware of the hour, the day, the week, or even the month of his returning; nor even that he intended to come back. But it would be soon too late for the present season of long, dark nights if he delayed much beyond the end of February. Although no other raider than the *Moewe* had passed through the Blockade zone, yet there was always a subconscious feeling that one might suddenly appear at any moment; and this fear was shared by the British trawlers who were fishing off Iceland. So one evening at the beginning of February, when the *Alsatian* sighted a small steamer and switched on her searchlight to investigate, the stranger was so convinced the flagship was an enemy raider that preparations were made to abandon ship, and the boat was being launched. The incident soon died down when each recognized the other as British. The *Alsatian* had lit up a Hull trawler returning home with her catch, who made a present of some fresh fish and confirmed the news that up to date there had been very little ice off Iceland.

The hand of fate now dealt out events amazingly. On February 26, to the surprise of all, the *Alsatian* received orders to hurry south into Liverpool and for Sir Dudley de Chair to repair to the Admiralty. Everyone aboard was fervently hoping this foreshadowed instructions that *Alsatian* was to go out into the Atlantic and seek the *Moewe*. At 18 knots the flagship tore down to the Mersey, arriving in the early hours of the 28th, and that same afternoon, in London, the Admiral was informed of his appointment as Naval Adviser to Lord Robert Cecil, the Minister at the Foreign Office in charge of the Contraband Department.

It was encouraging for the 10th Cruiser Squadron to know at last there were signs that, in response to the agitation in Press and Parliament, the Government were paying more attention to the Blockade procedure, and the Navy could rest assured that Admiral de Chair would see that in future all was well. Certainly no officer, whether in this or any preceding war, possessed such expert practical knowledge of blockading in all its aspects. But that which was a gain to the Foreign Office became a great loss to the Fleet which he had created, organized, trained, and maintained to a unique standard of perfection : its efficiency was the admiration of all other branches of the Service.

The change from rolling about among the northern mists to the solidity of an office chair after eighteen lively months was dramatic. Only three weeks previously, one Sunday morning, the immense bulk of *Alsatian* had been hurled about so indecorously by the south-west gale that during breakfast the ward-room table took command and went crashing through the bulkhead. Luckily no one was hurt, but everything in the cabins got adrift, for she was rolling 30° each way, which exceeded any of her previous efforts.

On March 1 the Admiral was back in Liverpool preparing for his successor, and next day the latter came aboard. It was Vice-Admiral R. G. O. Tupper, who until now had been the Senior Naval Officer in charge of Stornoway, the northern station so closely concerned with the Blockade's operations, so the transition for this officer was both natural and convenient. Actually on Saturday, March 4, Sir Dudley took final leave of his old shipmates before beginning his Foreign Office duties. On Monday Admiral Tupper hoisted his flag in the *Alsatian*, which sailed from the Mersey next day for her patrol.

Now during this brief interim of changing over from one Admiral of the Blockade to another, two startling events had occurred, of which but one was made known immediately, and the other not till some time later. On Thursday, March 2, whilst both Admirals happened to be on board, who should step across the gangway but Captain Wardle of the *Alcantara* ? Whatever could have brought him to Liverpool?

The answer is—a German raider.

This crisis chanced to occur on the very day after Admiral de Chair had first reached London and brought *Alsatian* to Liverpool. In Whitehall he learned the bare outlines, how that the *Alcantara* had met a German raider and that both had gone to the bottom. But now the Admiral's former Flag-Captain of the old *Crescent*, which had once so nearly foundered in the most memorable of gales, was without a ship and relating the most interesting details of his most recent escape from death at sea.

The story,[1] which is as follows, has been given to me by Captain (now Admiral) Wardle himself. It may therefore be regarded as of the highest historical value for future reference. It has also been supplemented by statements made by five other of *Alcantara's* officers, together with information from German sources.

On February 29 the *Alcantara* with *Andes* was on Patrol "G", i.e. to the north-east of the Shetlands, her position at 9 a.m. being lat. 61°45′ N., long. 0°58′ E. That was actually just about the spot which a raider would pass through, whether inward or outward bound, if she were to hug both the Iceland and Norwegian coasts. The *Alcantara* was to have gone into port this afternoon for her routine coaling, but soon after 8 a.m. received a wireless ordering her not to leave, as an armed disguised raider might pass the patrol line to-day. Captain Wardle therefore got ready for action, shifted his men into clean underclothing, and swung out six of his boats.

At 8.55 a.m. smoke was reported bearing W. by N. (true), but almost simultaneously came a signal from *Andes*, who was to the nor'ard, saying, "Enemy in sight

---

[1] This supplements and corrects the account which appears in Chapter XV of my *The Sea Raiders*, certain details having since come to hand.

steering N.E., 15 knots," and describing her. *Alcantara* was steaming N.N.E., so that the smoke seen by the latter was to port, and presently it indicated a one-funnel ship, whereas the *Andes* was in touch with a vessel having two funnels. Captain Wardle's duty seemed to consist of first investigating the one-funnel steamer before proceeding to help *Andes*, who was hull down and chasing the two-funnel supposed enemy. "I did not consider the steamer on my port bow was the enemy," says *Alcantara's* Captain, who at 9.15 a.m., being then about 6,000 yards from the stranger, hoisted "M N" (International Code meaning, "Stop instantly!") and fired two rounds of blank. This one-funnel steamer replied : "I am going to stop. Machinery requires adjusting."

She also hoisted a four-flag signal indicating her number, but on reference to the book, *Signal Letters of All Countries*, she was not to be found therein. That created a sense of suspicion forthwith, so the alarm gongs were rung, the *Alcantara's* company sent to action stations, and the guns trained on the mystery ship. Meanwhile the *Andes* (being then some 14 miles away) signalled : "Enemy has altered course to S.E."

But Captain Wardle replied, using his searchlight Morse shutter : "Am intercepting suspicious vessel. Is enemy still in sight ?"

To this no answer was received. When *Alcantara* and the mystery steamer were now only 4,000 yards apart, the latter was seen to be flying the Norwegian flag at the stern. The Norwegian flag (as was then the custom among neutrals in order to emphasize their nationality to U-boats) was also painted on the hull (1) abaft of midships, (2) on the bows, with her name *Rena* In response to signals, she stated she was bound from Rio de Janeiro for Trondhjem. Now at that time most commanding officers in the Naval Patrols were kept supplied with *Lloyd's Confidential List of Ships*, and after consulting this it seemed as if the particulars, including size and course, bore out *Rena's* statement.

Having heard nothing more from *Andes*, Captain Wardle determined to put an armed guard aboard *Rena* before going to *Andes'* assistance, but the gun's crews were retained at their stations and the guns still trained. *Alcantara* eased to 14 knots, kept clear of the stranger, and the armed guard was getting ready to go off, when *Andes* signalled by search-light : "That is suspicious vessel." The sea was calm, wind light, weather clear, but the sky being overcast made it a good day for searchlight signalling.

Aboard *Alcantara* no preparation for engagement had been omitted, in spite of *Rena's* apparent innocence. Not merely did Captain Wardle manœuvre to anticipate any surprise, but every precaution was taken against fire, even to the ship's stewards filling all baths and buckets with water, closing water-tight doors, turning on hoses and so on. About 10 o'clock, whilst both ships were heading the same way, and the distance between them was 2,500 yards, the boarding boat had just been swung out by the crane on the port side, when a most significant thing happened. Down dropped the Norwegian flag and ensign staff at the *Rena's* stern, and from the dummy steering-box close thereto men were seen clearing away a 5.9-inch gun. Down, too, fell flaps on her side for'ard of the bridge, revealing two more guns. There came a blinding flash, but the *Alcantara's* armed guard had just time to scramble out of their boat (still in mid-air), and the next realization was of a great shock, during which the boat disappeared into fragments and one of the men dropped over the side killed.

So this was the first raider at last, at the end of all the months of waiting ; yet what a coincidence it should happen on the very day Admiral de Chair was in Whitehall ! It may be explained that to-day we know part of the enemy's cleverness consisted in synchronizing the incoming of the *Moewe* through the Blockade with the outgoing of the *Rena*, so that if one should be lost at least the other might escape. The former had gone right up towards Iceland, taken advan-tage of snow squalls by day and the moonless nights before coming south-east towards the Norwegian shores, and then had the good fortune to find a thick fog before she finally picked up Amrum Island off the coast of Schleswig-Holstein and so into Wilhelmshaven.

Fire from *Alcantara* was opened with all speed, though there were a number of misfires. The enemy's first shot evidently aimed to wipe out the boarding party, and the second hit the side right aft, opening up the deck. One shell burst in Captain Wardle's cabin under the bridge ; so, clearly, the German sought to destroy the centre of all control. This succeeded to the extent of cutting all electrical communications, together with the pipes for the telemotor steering-gear. On the enemy's bridge there was a quick-firing pom-pom which rained shells on to *Alcantara's* bridge. How Captain Wardle survived is one of those other mysteries of the sea.

He gave the order to go full speed ahead with the helm hard aport, but, the steering gear on the bridge being disabled, a messenger was sent aft to order the stern steering apparatus to be connected up. This took about ten minutes, during which time *Alcantara* was out of control and closed the enemy, who was turning to starboard. Unfortunately, *Alcantara* could not go full speed, as steam began to fail immediately, owing to damage. But from three 6-inch and one 6-pdr. Captain Wardle's ship was pouring death persistently into the enemy, so that an explosion and conflagration soon blazed under the *Rena's* bridge, and the cordite at her after gun was set on fire.

At about 10.15 the German fired a torpedo, which passed close under *Alcantara's* stern. Whether a second was fired cannot be affirmed definitely, and it will always be a matter of dispute whether *Alcantara* was or was not torpedoed. Admiral Wardle informs me as follows :

"It cannot be said for certain that the *Alcantara* was torpedoed. I am of opinion, and always have been, that she was *not*. I saw one torpedo miss by the stern, and did not see another fired. I do not think that they could have reloaded the tube under the intense fire they were experiencing. . . . I have always considered that the big holes made by high explosive shell would have let sufficient water into the large open spaces, holds, etc., to sink her. . . . The messenger was not killed. I recommended him afterwards for his work. The time—about ten minutes—which elapsed before the ship was under control again was due to the distance the boy had to go, and the delay in getting the message below from the after steering position to connect up. In this connection I should like it recorded that the ship was then conned by the First Lieut.-Commander from aft. (His name was Lieut.- Commander F. M. Main, D.S.O., R.D., R.N.R.). I, on the fore bridge, was powerless to do anything owing to all communications being cut. It would not have looked well for me to be seen leaving the bridge. The *Alcantara* had very few fires on board. This, I think, was due to the enemy's high explosive shells having a quick-acting fuse, and so detonating on the ship's side without penetrating."

This testimony of the enemy's "dud" shells is borne out by Lieutenant John Howell-Price, R.N.R., who noticed that they passed through the decks without bursting well, even going right through four iron bulkheads; but there were many casualties, and the water service pipes were cut, so it was difficult to put out any fires. This officer survived to win not merely the D.S.C. for his excellent work down below in regard to the fires, but also the D.S.O. two years later at the blocking of Zeebrugge. For he was destined to enter the submarine service, and went as second-in-command of H.M. Submarine C-3, which most gallantly wedged herself into the open portion of the Mole.

The *Alcantara* had always been one of the smartest units of the Blockading Fleet, and was a crack gunnery ship, so that the enemy suffered heavily from the first. Whilst the range began at 2,500 yards, it decreased and ended at 800 yards. "One of my gunlayers," adds Admiral Wardle, "at the subsequent court martial, when asked why he knew his shots hit, answered convincingly, 'Couldn't miss, sir!'"

About a quarter of an hour after the helm had been connected up aft the *Alcantara* took a list to starboard, and at 10.32 boats were seen leaving the *Rena*, so Captain Wardle ordered "Cease fire!" The smoke which had obscured the enemy now cleared, and she never fired again except for one solitary shell. "I am now of opinion that this round was caused by a heated gun," suggested the British commanding officer, who found his own vessel thirteen minutes later listing so badly—this time to port—and certainly sinking, that he ordered : "Boat stations. Stop engines. Abandon ship!"

She continued to heel over till the list was 90°, and at 11.8 a.m. sank without explosions. Perfect discipline was maintained throughout, and the greatest gallantry and coolness were manifested during the action. Fifteen boats and rafts floated clear, but one of the former was cut up by the

R

propellers (which were still sending the *Alcantara* ahead at 3 or 4 knots), and its occupants had to swim.

Surgeon J. P. Berry's impressions confirm the wonderful coolness of his shipmates in danger. "The chief thing which struck me was the complete absence of any panic at any time.... Some time after we had begun to list, I noticed the men from the after part of the ship trooping past, quite quietly, chatting to each other: it never struck me they were abandoning ship. When I discovered this, I sent all my wounded (they could all walk—luckily) along with the men from aft to get to the deck where the boats were. The men nearest them helped them, and those in front made way for them. This made a great impression on me, as, at the time, the ship was so far over that one expected her to go at any time. In the boats everyone did their utmost to pick up those still in the water."

The *Andes*, who joined in a later stage of the action, did not close nearer than 6,000 yards; but, after *Alcantara* foundered, both *Andes* and the cruiser *Comus* arrived on the spot and shelled the enemy till she sank at 1 p.m. Captain Wardle's quick transference from the bridge of a lofty liner down her inclined side into the chilly February sea was such as few commanding officers have had to make; yet even at the climax of tragedy there was comedy. "I took a header off the bilge keel just as she was sinking," he told me, "and shortly after coming to the surface I heard a voice say, 'Your cap, sir!' One of the crew was swimming cap-in-hand towards me." Disciplined good behaviour right to the last! And presently this commanding officer, bereft of his ship, found himself seated with a front view of the artillery practice by *Andes* and *Comus*. "I was sitting on a raft in a good position to mark the fall of shot. The *Comus* made very pretty shooting."

There had now arrived on the scene the destroyer *Munster*, who rescued Captain Wardle, whilst the other two vessels picked up the remaining survivors. Unfortunately two British officers and 67 men perished. Of the *Rena*'s complement there were picked up five officers and 115 men—rather less than half of the company which had so recently left Germany. On March 3, whilst Admiral de Chair was still

THE "MOEWE" MEDAL

The bronze medal issued by the Germans in anger against the British Blockade and Admiral de Chair.

aboard the *Alsatian* in Liverpool, the *Andes* steamed up the
Mersey with one German officer and 110 men.

It remains now to be added that *Rena* was only her temporary, assumed name.   The raider was really the *Greif*,
which had left Kiel some 56 hours previously bound for the
Atlantic on a raiding voyage similar to that of *Moewe*.   From
Kiel she had steamed to Hamburg, whence she had departed
on February 27, her intention being to go round the north
of Iceland.   Built in 1914 as the *Guben*, she was just an ordinary trader commissioned as a man-of-war after the manner
of a British Q-ship.   Her naval commanding officer, Fregatten-
Kapitän Rudolf Tietze, was killed whilst in the boat, by
a shell or splinter, the body and boat both being presently
taken aboard the *Comus*.   He had been the last to leave the
sinking, burning ship, and had got about a hundred yards
away, when the upper part of his head was torn off.

After the *Moewe's* safe arrival in Germany there was issued
in that country a bronze medal to direct thought and hate on
Admiral de Chair as the personification of all that was so
fearsome in the Blockade.   It was a curious Teutonic mentality
which sought to will Sir Dudley's death and eternal damnation
in the same fashion that the well-known hymn of hate was
supposed to injure Britain generally.   Not content with the
wish-to-destroy, German wireless messages also announced
that the Admiral had been killed.   This medal, which measures
about 3 inches across, will be found in the accompanying
illustration, and was obtained by one of our spies during the
War (in 1917). It thus reached the Foreign Office and the
Admiral, who has been kind enough to lend it me.

On the obverse side is a seagull with a fish in its mouth
flying defiantly over a chain that is guarded by two somnolent
sea-lions, the symbolism being that of the *Moewe* (seagull)
travelling so high with its possession as to evade the sleepy
Blockade Fleet !   The inscription below reads :

WIE DIE MÖVE DER SEELOWEN SPOTTET

On the other side are the words :

DEM BRITISCHEN VICE-ADMIRAL DUDLEY DE CHAIR
GEWIDMET

Although this historic duel demonstrated to the enemy that the British sea-lions were not half so sleepy as might be inferred, yet the incident indicated also that a new phase had begun : the Blockading ships must contend not merely with elusive neutrals, but with enemy vessels pretending to be Scandinavians and most cunningly disguised as such. The use of torpedoes whilst the examining cruiser was in the act of lowering a boat was to add a fresh anxiety to the already overworked British naval officers. Big liners cannot be handled with the facility of destroyers, so that the evasion of torpedoes, whether from surface or submarine vessel, became no easier as time passed. The *Alcantara* was of 15,831 tons, and built only in 1914. Her loss was not easily to be dismissed in those days when shipping shortage was becoming serious enough ; yet it was worth while. Had the *Greif* got through into the Atlantic, the losses to the Allies' merchant vessels would have been so notable that we could now afford to lose an armed merchant cruiser every time a raider was destroyed.

CHAPTER XXI

THE position now settled down to a final struggle. Whilst the *Alcantara's* loss had reminded us that extreme vulnerability was the weakest feature of a Blockade controlled by armed merchant steamers, yet it was still effective in spite of the fact that on a selected date not more than a dozen ships might be on patrol, whilst the rest were either repairing their gale-battered hulls or filling up with coal.

The institution of a Ministry of Blockade at the end of February, and the appointment of Lord Robert Cecil in charge, gave a new impetus. It also signified a closer relationship between the Foreign Office and the Blockading Fleet. "The first thing I did when I went to the Blockade Ministry", related this Minister, "was to obtain the assistance of a distinguished naval officer, Admiral de Chair. I went to Mr. Balfour (then First Lord of the Admiralty) and asked whether he would mind my entering into correspondence with Sir John Jellicoe, so that the Admiral, without using the ordinary official channels, could write me if he had any criticisms to make. Mr. Balfour gladly acceded to the request."

This was an excellent beginning, and the co-ordinating of all the various Committees under one head was likely to become beneficial. In Parliament there was still dissatisfaction with the Foreign Office, and that gallant old Admiral, Lord Beresford, with his bluff, blunt manner, in February did not hesitate to attack that department. "If we had maintained an efficient blockade, the War would now have been over. Instead of ships going before the Prize Court, they went before the Contraband Committee." As to those Orders-in-Council and Proclamations, he criticized, there had been fourteen between August 4, 1914, and February 22, 1916. They contained a great number of contradictions, and their language "might be understood by clever lawyers, but seamen did not understand it".

On the other hand the financial drain upon Germany was enormous. Before the War she was exporting 500 million pounds' worth of goods annually. The Blockade stopped that almost dead, and to this day Germany has never recovered vitality. Another means of tightening the Blockade was the Navicert system, which began on March 11, 1916, and worked extraordinarily well until April of the following year, when it was no longer required. "Navicert" was really a code name for a letter of assurance permitting shipment through the Blockade, such assurance being granted only when there was no evidence of intended enemy destination being acquired. The object was to placate American shippers by saving them both expense and trouble caused by seizure and scrutiny of cargoes. But, also, it enabled Britain to prevent undesirable shipments.

The Navicert method was applied to cargoes from the U.S.A. to Norway, Sweden, and Denmark, and about 30,000 of these letters were granted out of 40,000 applications. The latter had to be submitted to the British Ambassador at Washington, who then cabled the Foreign Office in London, where each application was considered on its merits, and within forty-eight hours was cabled back to Washington either "Accipe" (which was approval), or "Nolo" (which meant refusal). The Ambassador, in the case of the former, now issued to the shipper a navicert, one copy of which accompanied the shipment, so that when the cargo reached the Blockade the examining officers, by checking navicerts with the manifest, could at once see if the cargo was in order.

The system between the above countries became so satisfactory and, whilst being welcomed by exporters, importers, and shipowners alike, making for accuracy and rapidity, it was also a valuable means of extracting guarantees from neutral merchants. It was only the Swedes who deliberately and intentionally placed every possible obstacle in the way. Further, an Anglo-Danish commercial agreement was made in February, and an Anglo-Dutch agreement was signed, whereby we obtained a large proportion of Holland's surplus agricultural produce. Similarly, the extension of the Black List system was one more valuable weapon. This grew out of the postal and telegraphic censorship ; for by inspecting the mails and cables Britain learned which were the firms in America and Scandinavia who were engaged in trade with Germany, and who were the dummy consignees. Thus any firm known to have an interest in enemy trade was denied British shipping or insurance. Finally, in March, was established a Jute Control which further extracted useful guarantees from neutral produce merchants to whom jute wrappings were essential.

All neutral shipping lines had to undertake that they would not carry goods of blacklisted firms, else the steamers would be refused British bunker coal. This bunker control became a most powerful lever, since neutral ships could not have their fuel unless they visited a British port of examination and guaranteed not to handle prohibited goods. And before the summer was out an Anglo-Norwegian agreement provided that all the fish caught and landed in Norway after August 18, 1916, was to be under British option of purchase, except that the Norwegians could export 15 per cent of the whole. A similar agreement was made with Denmark, though at first the Danish fishermen were reluctant. This was overcome by the reply that, unless they agreed, Britain would stop the oil-fuel which was necessary for the fishermen's motor-boats.

All this artificial purchasing was a most expensive and quite original mode of blockade. Between January 1916 and the end of March 1917 it cost Britain the colossal sum of £37,000,000, of which £22,000,000 was net loss. The chief purchases were £21,000,000 for Norwegian fish, with a net loss to us of £16,000,000. On the other hand, it diverted 456,000 tons of fish from reaching the enemy, which was a most serious matter, seeing that Germany was receiving so little meat. Similarly, the livestock which we were now obtaining from Switzerland, Denmark, and Holland was a complete denuding of Germany's butchers' shops, and for personal domestic evidence of this meat absence we have only to read some of our enemy's post-War literature. Whereas Holland was exporting some 66,000 cattle to Germany a year, this figure came down to nil by 1917.

Another stopping up of leakage was achieved in April 1916, when the Allied Governments made the important announcement that whereas both Letter Post and Parcel Post had been abused by the enemy for transmission of contraband packages —and the Hague Convention of 1907 (relating to the immunity of mails) could not be held to apply to other than bona-fide correspondence—in future goods despatched as postal packages would be searched and seized as if they were in any other form. Goods concealed in wrappers, envelopes, and letters would be similarly dealt with ; yet we would continue to respect genuine correspondence. The reason for this measure will be obvious to the reader, and those mail steamers running between the U.S.A. and Scandinavia would in future be taken into port for thorough search. There had of late been two bad cases where a couple of Dutch steamers had been found carrying contraband for Germany in postal packets. One was the twin-screw Hollandsche-Lloyd liner *Tubantia* of Amsterdam. This 13,911-tons vessel was found to be carrying 174½ lbs. of rubber. The 5,933-tons Rotterdamsche-Lloyd single-screw S.S. *Medan* had seven packets of crude rubber thus discovered.

Thus, in short, the trend now had set in rather to exercise a control over goods at their source than on their voyage ; to employ agreement and subtlety in preference to friction and force ; to turn neutrals into Britain's friends instead of her enemies ; to make them trade with Britain on terms so advantageous that any zest for doing business with Germany was dulled. All this was astute economic strategy, and the heavy price was worth the bargain—at its worst it was cheaper than prolonging the War. As the months sped by, the Blockade became rather a matter of statistics than seafaring ; of card-index, clerks, cables, and conferences, in lieu of gales, guns, patrols, and chases. A pleasant official luncheon at the Savoy to meet the Dutch Agricultural Delegates, with Lord Robert Cecil presiding, the Netherlands Minister on his right, Admiral Sir Dudley de Chair, and other distinguished personages; or a similar entertainment at the Carlton to meet Norwegian oil-and-fat delegates; did more to harm Germany's larder than the sternest threats. In brief, the Blockade was now becoming more of a business affair and less of a naval operation.

We had made such agreements with Holland, Denmark, and Norway that by the dawn of 1917 practically no overseas goods were reaching Germany, and even Sweden had come to some arrangement regarding cotton and lubricating oils. Nevertheless, the stoppage of the iron ore trade (1) down the Norwegian coast, and (2) down the Gulf of Bothnia to the Baltic ports of Germany, was never achieved. That was one definitely weak feature of our Blockade. Moreover, the British Government's policy of (so-to-speak) "buying up the world"—or at least north neutral Europe—and at the sellers' own price, was the surest road to ultimate bankruptcy—it could not be prolonged. Moreover, we were allowing ourselves to suffer a kind of international blackmail, and other countries were profiting by our nervousness. But there was not money enough in the whole British Empire to purchase *complete* neutral exportation, so a certain amount of goods trickled into Germany from Scandinavia to the last. There was a further reason for this in that the latter wanted Germany's dyes and coal.

Additional to the economic pressure-by-agreement on Germany and Austria, there came now another lasting influence which was in process of ripening during 1916. Germany's manner of conducting her submarine campaign was turning American tolerance into anger. The torpedoing of the British passenger S.S. *Sussex* in the English Channel on March 24, 1916, when some American citizens were travelling, was another incident which caused German-American relations to become strained, and during the rest of that year a breach between those two nations seemed bound to occur before many more months elapsed. Side by side with this development was the gradual change of policy at the Foreign Office in the right direction : it had, in the early stages of the War, been influenced by the Declaration of London, but the peak of that ascendancy had been passed. In March 1916 was issued one more Order-in-Council by which Article 19 of the Declaration of London ceased to be adopted.

This Article read :

Whatever may be the ulterior destination of a vessel or of her cargo, she cannot be captured for breach of blockade if, at the moment, she is on her way to a non-blockaded port.

The scrapping of this objectionable clause robbed neutral ships and cargoes of an immunity that interfered with the practical application of sea-control. It had been a condition altogether too favourable for the enemy, of which we have seen many an instance. But even in the following June Austrian goods were found in the letter mails of the notorious Danish *Oscar II*. The case came into the Prize Court, who declared these commodities to be enemy property and to be sold. Finally, in June, Lord Robert Cecil attended a conference in Paris to consider whether even the partial adoption and enforcement of the vicious Declaration of London should be continued any longer, and on July 7 came the now famous "Maritime Rights" Order-in-Council which killed the last bit of allegiance to the Declaration of London.

The Order now asserted it was the intention of Britain and her Allies "to exercise their belligerent rights at sea in strict accordance with the Law of Nations"; and simultaneously the Foreign Office issued a memorandum explaining to neutral Powers the grounds for this new Order. "The rules laid down in the Declaration of London", it announced, "could not stand the strain imposed by the test of rapidly changing conditions and tendencies which could not have been foreseen." Here was a most remarkable change which indicated that the full circle had been completed since August 1914, and that we were back at the stage of sanity. The Order-in-Council of July 7, 1916, meant a return to International Law, but it meant also how unutterably foolish had been the previous piecemeal and ever-changing policy. "That document—perhaps the most pitiable confession ever forced in public from the lips of any civilized Government—announced in formal terms to the world that the whole system under which the Executive had up to that time assumed to control the war at sea, as distinct from its conduct by the Courts of Prize, had been mistaken, and was now to be withdrawn."[1] The principle of continuous voyage had triumphed; the Declaration of London was stone dead, and a new vitality was given to the Law of Nations. *Magna est veritas, et prevalebit!*

---

[1] Bowles, *The Strength of England*, p. 207.

Now when Admiral Tupper took over the 10th Cruiser Squadron he found his predecessor's organization and routine so excellent that very slight alteration could be made. At first he had 22 armed merchant cruisers and four armed trawlers. The *Ebro* and *Motagua* were sent in March to patrol off Iceland, looking out for raiders ; but only one more of such mystery ships was to run the blockade for the present. The days were getting longer and the nights too short for those excursions. The German S.S. *Libau*, disguised as the Norwegian *Aud*, came through, but we knew all about her, and she was intentionally not hindered. On April 16, at 7.15 p.m., she was scrutinized at a distance of 200 yards by one of the armed merchant cruisers, but there was no object in doing more. For this was Karl Spindler's ship on her way to land arms at the western coast of Ireland for the rebellion of Easter. She had been watched by the British Navy during the greater part of her voyage. She now lies at the bottom of the sea outside Queenstown. I saw her German White Ensign the other day hanging up, framed, in the house of one who was responsible for her capture.

It is true that towards the end of July another raider did set out from Germany, and, as usual, hugged the Norwegian coast. Here, curiously enough, she came across the S.S. *Eskimo*, which the reader will remember as forming one of the 10th Cruiser Squadron until found so small and unsuitable that, like *Calyx*, she had to be paid off. This Wilson liner was now back trading between Christiania and Newcastle, when, on July 26, the raider off Risoer, *and in Norwegian territorial waters*, captured her, taking her back to Germany. So the raider got no further towards the Atlantic.

There were still interesting experiences for the Blockaders during this year, and some of the last of the dying race of famous sailing ships were wafted through the zone. On May 17 the *Alsatian* intercepted the Norwegian barque *Kosmos*, 1,227 tons, bound from New York for Christiansand. She was none other than the once well-known British *Glenesk*, built as far back as the year 1869, when sailing ships were not yet dominated by steam. Then ten days later the *Alsatian* stopped the *Fox II*. She was now a Dane of 228 tons, and that rare creature, an auxiliary with steam and sail. She was on her way from the wilds of Greenland, and her Master reported he had been held up 36 hours amid a field of ice in those Davis Straits which used to imperil our Elizabethan ships.

Another famous four-masted barque, now Norwegian and named the *Alonso*, but still remembered as that fine British *Tinto Hall* (1,723 tons), sailed into the gaze of *Alsatian*, from whose deck the accompanying delightful photograph was taken on June 16. Here she is seen on the starboard tack bound for New York. She had passed through some vicissitudes, having been used as a whaling depot by the Norwegians, but such was the demand now for shipping, and so high were prices, that she was back (in water ballast) on the high seas. A few months later (October 8) the *Alsatian* intercepted another relic of the sailing-ship era. This was the 2,648 tons *Cedarbank*, formerly British, but Norwegian-owned during 1916. She was on her way from New York with barley for Leith, having been over a month on her voyage.

The tension on the Masters of British merchant ships during these months has never been properly appreciated by the public. At the mercy of mines, submarines, and raiders, charged with the heavy responsibility of getting ship and cargo safe to port, these officers were keyed up to expect any sudden peril at the most unexpected hour. One morning the *Alsatian*, about breakfast-time, sighted a steamer of 2,820 tons, and the latter's Master was so sure about the flagship being a German raider that he threw overboard his confidential instructions and was trying to escape in a fog-bank. All ended well when both vessels recognized each other as British. The zone could not be made quite inviolable; there might still be more raiders when the nights lengthened again; but during this summer a monthly average of about 240 ships were being intercepted and allowed to proceed, whilst about a dozen were evading our patrols. A Norwegian shipmaster told one of the *Alsatian's* Boarding Officers this June that neutral shipmasters considered the weakest part of our Blockade to be that which was nearest the ice. "They often had rumours of ships passing through that belt." In view of an incident to be mentioned later, this statement should be noted.

By the middle of 1916 the Blockade had become really effective beyond all criticism, but the rationing policy and the

THE NORWEGIAN BARQUE "ALONSO"
She was formerly the British "Tinto Hall", and is here sailing through
the Blockade.

BRITISH BOARDING-BOAT ALONGSIDE A WHALER

Navicert system relied on the 10th Cruiser Squadron's enforcement. Rightly has it been claimed that the Battle of Jutland was largely a sequel to these stringent measures. For the Germans were getting desperate; the big raid intended for the bombardment of Sunderland had for its object the enticing of the Grand Fleet into submarine traps, and therein partly succeeded. If only Britain's main fleet could be crippled, then the Blockade with its vulnerable merchant cruisers would collapse. But, forasmuch as the battle convinced Germany she must never undertake such a trial of strength again, the Blockade thereafter became even more firmly established.

It is, however, not to be disguised that our enemy missed a gorgeous opportunity. If, instead of the occasional and unarmoured but slow converted cargo ships, she had sent out into the Blockade zone one first-class high-speed battle-cruiser (e.g. the *Von der Tann*), determined to do or die, such a unit within forty-eight hours could have sent to the bottom practically every patrol of the 10th Cruiser Squadron and then interned herself in Iceland or Norway. The effect on neutral opinion would have been for Germany magnificent, the release of supplies to her starving people a godsend, whilst the moral effect on the Allies would have been profound. The loss of so many crack liners with their experienced naval personnel, and the wiping out (for even a few weeks) of the barrier against Germany, might have altered the ultimate conclusion of hostilities. But no such enterprising venture was undertaken—the Blockade had sapped the enemy's physical and moral strength; their spirit was flickering out unfed. The most she could now attain was to cut off our supplies by intensifying her submarine warfare on the principle of sinking at sight everything approaching the British Isles. And herein she all but succeeded. She should have used that pressure more violently at an earlier date.

The armed guards were still having strange and varied experiences. Both the *Bergensfjord* and *Kristianiafjord* continued to give trouble and be caught; but by June the fear of losing facilities for coaling caused such ships to call at Kirkwall voluntarily. And now Dutch liners were coming home round the north of Scotland in preference to using the English Channel.

But the postal and cable censorship was assisting the Blockade Fleet in the most efficient manner, of which the following instances are sufficiently convincing evidence. The S.S. *Pythia*, Galveston for Gothenburg, was carrying a cargo of cotton actually intended for Germany, and was therefore arrested and sent into the Prize Court. The information as to the true destination was obtained by intercepted cables and letters. The following example gave the trick away completely. This letter was sent from Messrs. Joseph Kallmann & Co. of Gothenburg, Sweden, to the Texas Export & Import Co. of Galveston, Texas :

For your guidance,
Cotton has been declared forbidden for export from Sweden ; thus nothing can be transhipped to Germany or other countries. . . . We would, besides, recommend you to tell every Captain to go very far north of Shetlands, right in to Norway, sliding down the coast, where there is hardly any risk of being caught. . . . We have directed several boats like this, and they have come clear of interference. . . . Avoid all touch with England and its cruisers is the keynote, of course, to successful arrival here.

The instruction to go right away north of the Shetlands into Norwegian waters and thence "sliding" down the coast had indeed been carried out frequently, as we have seen.

Then there was the subtle manner by which the Foreign Office detected the enemy destination of a cargo. Let us suppose, for the sake of argument, that the Norske-Amerika liner *Bergensfjord*, New York for Christiania, has her usual mixed assortment of perhaps two hundred different commodities for perhaps a dozen Norwegian consignees. How are we going to find out if some or all of these packages are really meant to reach Germany ? The task is first to look up the consignees in a Norwegian directory and examine them one by one. If you find that Mr. Johannsen is really in business as a ship chandler but is receiving large quantities of detonating fuses ; or a leather merchant is accepting a big consignment of wheat ; or a small grocer has addressed to him ten times the amount of cocoa above his normal requirements ; then there is reason for suspicion. If, moreover, the other consignees are known to have intimate relationship with German firms, or do not appear at all in the directory, then they may be regarded as agents for contraband.

All the above, then, are worthy of investigation ; so the files of intercepted wireless messages, letters, and cablegrams are examined. It will be surprising if the shipper has not telegraphed details to Hamburg or Rotterdam of the shipment coming via Christiania ; so when all this information is sifted and collected there will be found quite enough evidence that at least a big part of the *Bergensfjord's* cargo consists of contraband, and may be put into the Prize Court.

We have seen that resort was made by the contraband-runners to every subterfuge, and each seizure caused some new method of trickery. In order to defeat the censorship, use was made of code words (even to a complicated extent) and aliases. Couriers took a chance in these liners and hoped not to be found out. Both they and the dummy consignees were well paid for their services, and large amounts of money changed hands in those months. It was a long time before traders in the U.S.A. woke up to the fact that, when they wirelessed Germany saying goods were being forwarded by a specified steamer, these messages were being plucked out of the ether by Britain. Later on, after the neutrals learned of the tapping, they sent over couriers, who at first brought written communications, until these letters began to be examined, and then only verbal messages were sent.

Before the Blockade reached its height of efficiency there was probably not one trick of the contraband trade unknown to the Foreign Office ; nor was there one neutral trader whose characteristics could not be produced within a few moments. By the end of 1916 there were 250,000 index-cards giving all the essential facts at a glance. Not merely was there preserved a copy of every trade cable and radiogram intercepted since the beginning of War, but all important intercepted letters had been photographed. A Scandinavian, Danish, or Dutch consignee had only once to be found out as an intermediary for the enemy and the man's name went on the Black List, and the next consignment went into the Prize Court. So close was the attention paid in Whitehall by the staff that one particular cargo would be watched for days and days through telegrams, wireless messages, letters, and the interception of the ship by the 10th Cruiser Squadron, until the arrival in Kirkwall.

The Customs Officers, themselves highly experienced, became wondrously skilled. At first it seemed a hopeless task when several ships were brought in daily, each cargo consisting of perhaps 400 separate items. The first duty was to separate the large number of genuine, reliable, and regular consignees who were above suspicion. The next was to lay aside those goods of which Germany and Austria were known not to be in need. Thus perhaps three-quarters of the entire cargo could be accounted for without much worrying. Of the final quarter, however, there would be every need for scrutiny, and by comparing the Scandinavian names with those on the Black List it was remarkably easy now to infer which remained contraband and which could not be questioned. Here would be the hides, the cotton, the fats, the lubricating oils whose history had been watched for weeks; so they must be seized. And those other goods that seemed above suspicion could go forward only on receipt of guarantees against re-exportation to the enemy.

Never was the interception of letters more fruitfully employed than in regard to the firm of K. & E. Neumond, and this episode is one of the most intriguing stories of the Blockade. It is yet another case of historical fact being more surprising than mere invention. Here was a business house at Frankfort-on-Main engaged as grain and feeding-stuff importers. They also carried on their trade at New York, New Orleans, Galveston, and St. Louis. The two partners were Karl and Eugen Neumond, of whom the former had opened the New York branch about the year 1912. Now it chanced that at the outbreak of hostilities Karl was in Germany, though he managed to travel back to America, and this was to have important results.

This firm was specially appointed by the German Government to send grain and flour to Germany via Copenhagen, the arrangement being made in September 1914 with an official of the War Ministry named Ludwig Eyber; and before the end of November large shipments of grain as well as flour were indeed despatched, the office in Copenhagen—be it noted—having been opened only after hostilities began. Meanwhile Karl Neumond was in touch with a Dr. Heinrich F. Albert, Counsellor of the Ministry of the Interior of the German Empire, who had come to America as member of a commission for purchasing supplies and making financial arrangements for Germany, other members of this commission including Dr. Dernburg (whom we mentioned in an earlier chapter) and Prince Hatzfeld.

Dr. Albert was Germany's leading bagman and blockade-runner. A brilliant man of business, a commercial colossus, he was yet somewhat of a mystery. His offices were in the Hamburg-Amerika Building, 45 Broadway, New York, where he continued in close touch with Bernstorff, von Papen, Boy-Ed, spies, propagandists, and all sorts of queer people. But he was spending some 2,000,000 to 3,000,000 dollars weekly. Before his career was checked, he despatched considerable quantities of supplies through the Blockade, and was the medium also for selling £100,000,000 worth of German securities. These figures will indicate the extent of his operations.

Dr. Albert's purchasing was on behalf of the Zentral Einkaufs Gesellschaft (Z.E.G.), which was a company established to centralize the import into Germany of foodstuffs, fats, and other commodities. On this corporation the German Government had conferred very large powers. It was financed with credits opened by the Disconto Gesellschaft of Berlin, the money being found by the German Government. The Neumond firm was assisted in Europe by Christensen & Schrei of Copenhagen, as well as by Beckmann & Joergensen of Rotterdam, besides the Guaranty Trust and others in America.

Telegrams were sent through the European firms, Neumond's name often being disguised as Newman, the goods being referred to as "shares", the shipments as "transfers", the word "Crossley" being used to signify "Christensen & Schrei". But it was an indiscreet radiogram from the Disconto Gesellschaft, late in August 1915, to the Guaranty Trust which connected Neumond with five rubber shipments of the previous year. The postal censorship now had little difficulty in correctly guessing the code, and in January 1916 the first batch of Neumond's mails was intercepted on its way to America, followed by more interceptions in March and April. After two more batches were stopped the Neumond mail was sent by a courier.

By great cleverness the key to the code in the above correspondence was found on the principle that $a = k$, $c = p$, and so forth, but an occasional shifting of the alphabet by one or two places was also necessary. In order to make deciphering more difficult, the Neumond correspondence was full of dummy words, entirely meaningless and intended to deceive. Also the meaning of code words differed at different times, and it was written partly in German but partly in English. Sooner or later, of course, any code can be unravelled. By collating passages in which the same code-words occurred, or in which the same subject was discussed (*a*) with, or (*b*) without, the use of a code, Neumond's messages were at last discovered to be as clear as sunlight.

Now the Neumonds had a foolish habit of sending written confirmations of their code telegrams, and this helped the British censorship considerably. It explained much that was invaluable to the Blockaders, but it was only after some of the correspondence was removed from a courier that the whole code was disclosed, and an elaborate system of sending cables through intermediaries in Holland and Scandinavia was revealed. On January 1, 1916, Neumond of Frankfort sent the following letter to Neumond of New York, which was read by the British censor with interest :

Confirmation of sales by E. Neumond. We omitted this from the last mail despatch from Copenhagen because we feared England might open the letters, but we will send it by the next mail.

Of course the 10th Cruiser Squadron was careful to intercept the steamer carrying "the next mail". But a wonderful chance in April occurred for the censor to verify the accuracy of his deciphering. Neumond of Frankfort sent in code and cipher to Neumond of New York a letter written on April 22 by H.M. Procurator-General to the Swedish Consul-General, which had reference to a claim of one of these ships in the

Prize Court. The censor then obtained from the Procurator-General's office a copy of the latter's letter. The rest was now easy : it was only necessary to compare the code with the original !

That the Blockade by the spring of 1916 had made matters difficult for the Neumond-Albert cargoes to get across into Germany was proved by the interception of another letter. Eugen Neumond had remained all those months in Germany except for business visits into Scandinavia, but now he was called up for military service this year. He had obtained several postponements, his applications being supported by such powerful influences as Bernstorff, the Reichsbank, and other Bankers in Germany, on the grounds of his utility in obtaining goods for his country. In March did Dr. Albert also write on his behalf and incidentally reveal, not merely that blockade-running had been practised, but that it was decreasing :

The number of reliable and absolutely trustworthy persons on whose co-operation in carrying out shipments from here we can unconditionally rely has gradually so dwindled that the calling up of Herr Neumond would mean practically, if not a cessation, at least a substantial diminution of shipments, already in themselves extremely difficult. In my humble opinion there is still a constant clear necessity to replenish one or another raw material or foodstuffs by means of a shipment from here after the so-called blockade-running fashion.

I may refer in this connection to the proposed rubber consignments and the coming shipments of foodstuffs and oil. Even when Herr Eugen has not himself undertaken the shipment, he has proved useful—practically indispensable—in cable correspondence and in the handling of the business in Scandinavia.

But all this illuminating correspondence and these telegrams ruined their cause and facilitated the work of the Blockade patrols. Such ships as the Norwegian S.S. *Alfred Nobel* (4,769 tons), the Norwegian S.S. *Bjornstjerne Bjornson* (5,268 tons), and the Swedish S.S. *Fridland* (4,960 tons) were intercepted carrying wheat, flour, and cattle-feeding stuffs in the names of the Guaranty Trust Company of New York, and of Norris & Co. But in each case the real shippers were K. & E. Neumond, which in turn meant the German Government. So the goods were seized and thrown into the Prize Court, who, a few months after Armistice, condemned them, holding that K. & E. Neumond in America was an enemy business.

As to Karl, whilst his mail service was never quite scotched till the United States entered the War in April 1917, he himself was then interned as a dangerous enemy. It was the Neumond firm, likewise, which was one of those who used to arrange for a ship to be "captured" collusively by German men-of-war after passing the Blockade. In this way the S.S. *Prins Valdemar* did not bring her cargo into Scandinavia, but it was finally delivered, after reaching port, to Neumond of Frankfort. By the end of September 1916 such cargoes were welcomed in German ports almost as miracles, where the shortage had become acute and the high prices intolerable. During the first three weeks of that month 435 vessels were dealt with by the Blockade Fleet, 123 being sent into port for examination. This remarkably fine record indicates how real the control had become. Still more interesting is the fact that 84 ships during September were sent in from the N.E. of Scotland.

CHAPTER XXII

THE TRIUMPH

The bad weather and dark nights of November 1916 showed that already the Blockade was well into its third winter of strenuous hardship. There had been changes in personnel aboard many ships, yet some officers remained till the very end—a great example of persistency.

It was on November 18 that a curious sequence of events culminated. The *Otway*, which has been previously mentioned in the 10th Cruiser Squadron, was patrolling to the north-westward of the Hebrides under Commodore (nowadays Vice-Admiral) E. L. Booty, when she intercepted the Norwegian S.S. *Older*. The following account, which differs from a previously published version, may be taken as authentic —it was given me by Admiral Booty himself.

"The signals she made in reply to me caused me to be suspicious, and I decided to board her, although I really thought there was too much sea. I found she was a German prize in charge of a German prize crew, who were taking her to Kiel. *Older* had sailed from Newport (Mon.) on November 11 with a cargo of coal for Gibraltar. She was captured by a German submarine on the 13th.[1] On the same day the same submarine sank in about the same position an Italian steamship[2] (by gunfire) bound from Glasgow to Genoa and transferred the crew of 25 to the *Older*, the Master of the Italian ship being taken on board the submarine.

"On the 14th the submarine sank a British trawler[3] by

---

[1] In the western approaches of the English Channel, viz. lat. 47°8′ N. long. 9°6′ W.

[2] *Lela.*

[3] *Hatsuse.* This was 86 miles S.W. by W. of the Fastnet.

gunfire and transferred the crew of eight to the *Older*. The German submarine, with the *Older* in company, apparently started for Kiel on the 13th, after sinking the Italian ship, and sank the trawler *en route*. In the afternoon of the 17th the submarine and *Older* parted company, the German prize crew in the latter consisting of one Lieutenant, one warrant officer, and seven men. When boarded next day by the *Otway*'s party, the Germans defied our Boarding Officer, who, although armed, had only a Midshipman and two armed men to support him.

"I lowered a second boat fully armed, and, as the Boarding Officer signalled, 'They have bombs placed ready to blow up the ship', I replied that I would take off all hands, and that one German should be sent in each boatload. At 4 o'clock the Boarding Officer signalled they had about half an hour before the bombs were timed to explode. The men on board then lowered one of *Older*'s boats, which, with one of *Otway*'s, brought off the remainder. By the time all were on board *Otway* it was rapidly getting dark.

"The whole affair had taken a long time on account of the heavy sea. *Otway* steamed round *Older* all night—not an easy thing in the dark on a dirty night. The bombs did not explode. I re-embarked everyone (except the Germans, who were kept in *Otway*) and sent *Older* in charge of a prize crew to Stornoway, where she arrived on 21st November. She was released and left Stornoway on the 23rd. After effecting some minor repairs, she resumed her voyage to Gibraltar, but was sunk in the Irish Sea by a German submarine en route."

Thus did the neutral ship change hands more than once, and her captors become British prisoners; yet mark again the reversal of fortune in time of war. In the following January the *Otway* intercepted another neutral ship north-west of Ireland, who said she was going to Falmouth for examination. "I put an armed guard on board to see that she did so, and proceeded on my way to Liverpool. She was intercepted by a German submarine a few hours after I left her. The German took the officer of the armed guard off and made him prisoner, and he remained in Germany until the end of the War. The ship was allowed to proceed to Falmouth, and the remainder of the armed guard returned to the *Otway* in due course."

Now on the day after the *Older* was taken into Stornoway Count zu Dohna-Schlodien started out from Germany in the *Moewe* for his second raiding voyage, using his old route of the Norwegian coast, passing through the worst part of the Blockade zone by night. This time he did not go right up to the Arctic, but, favoured with fog, bad visibility, and heavy weather, saved five days on his previous effort and by November 26 was well clear into the Atlantic. As I have already detailed the voyage in another volume,[1] it suffices to say that he again had a successful few months, came back through the blockade during the period March 16-19 after hugging the Iceland coast, and on March 22 was home in Kiel. This was the last attempt she made outside the Baltic.

But there comes still another curious relation between cause and effect. The Admiralty decided to send four ships of the Blockading Fleet into the Atlantic to make a sweep of that ocean and search out the *Moewe*. Thus on December 15 *Almanzora*, *Arlanza*, and *Orcoma* left Liverpool, being joined in the Irish Sea by the *Gloucestershire*.

"During the voyage", says Commander Tarrant, "the same procedure was carried out as on patrol, all ships sighted being boarded in the hope of obtaining news of the enemy. Many were the opinions expressed as to the chances of meeting the raider, and every ship sighted aroused the greatest enthusiasm and hope, never a doubt existing in the mind of a soul on board as to the outcome of an encounter."

But the luck of meeting *Moewe* did not come about.

On the other hand, the absence of these ships was a serious weakening of the Blockading Fleet just at a time when it needed strengthening; for note the following. On December 11 the *Moewe* in the Atlantic captured the British S.S. *Yarrowdale* (4,652 tons) and sent her towards Germany in charge of an officer named Badewitz with 440 prisoners. The *Yarrowdale*, by going fairly north and down the Norwegian coast, did elude the Blockade, and on December 31, 1916, after a plucky attempt, was brought safely into Germany. Thus two enemy vessels got through our barrier. Nor was that all.

---

[1] *The Sea-Raiders.*

On December 21 there left Bremen the most interesting and picturesque raider of the whole War. This was the *Seeadler*, otherwise the *Pass of Balmaha*, which the reader will remember being captured by a U-boat in July 1915 and sent to Cuxhaven. The *Seeadler*, under Count Felix von Luckner, pretended to be Norwegian, passed up the North Sea and boldly through the Blockade, until Christmas morning at 9.30, when, about 180 miles S.W. of Iceland, she was boarded by one of the 10th Cruiser Squadron. This was the *Avenger*, 15,000 tons, one of the very finest of all our auxiliaries. When the War broke out she was being built for the Union Steamship Company of New Zealand, but was completed for the Admiralty, and had recently been added to Admiral Tupper's Squadron.

Both Admiral Tupper and Count Luckner have published their reminiscences, and there still remains something to be cleared up; but one thing is very clear. By the cleverness of her disguise, the *Seeadler* (simulating a vessel named the *Irma*), with a crew picked to resemble blond Norsemen, with faked ship's papers and a log-book stolen from a Norwegian ship named *Maleta*, and many other ingenious subtleties, apparently so bluffed the Boarding Officer that she was allowed to continue her voyage. This she did with some determination, sinking ship after ship both in the Atlantic and Pacific, until her own end came tragically.

So this was the third German to get through during the present winter. And next must be mentioned a fourth which had preceded *Seeadler* but followed the *Moewe*. On the last day of November there steamed from Germany the ex-Hansa S.S. *Wachtfels*, 5,809 tons, now called the *Wolf*, and she had such luck that by December 2 she was on the western side of the Blockade area and near Rockall Bank. She had a really marvellous voyage, raiding in almost every sea of the world, steaming 64,000 miles, and after fifteen months got safely back home. She went right into the Arctic Circle in February 1918, till she was turned back by ice, picked up the Norwegian coast and reached Germany on the 19th. The Spanish S.S. *Igotz Mendi*, which she had captured, likewise got through the Blockade about the same time, but on February 24, when almost home, ran ashore in foggy weather near the Skaw, and the Germans had the misery of being interned. I have before me a letter from an English mercantile officer who remained a prisoner in the *Wolf* for one year and three days. He had been captured in the Indian Ocean.

Admiral Tupper relates in his *Reminiscences* that the *Wolf* outward-bound was disguised as the Dutch S.S. *Gamma*; that she was intercepted at midnight by the *Teutonic* and four hours later by the *Avenger*. But the weather was bad, and, furthermore, the Admiralty had ordered that Dutch mail steamers were to be delayed as little as possible. By an unfortunate mistake the *Wolf* thus got through what otherwise would have been a fatal trap. "Many more ships would have gone through", says Admiral Tupper significantly, "had I shown all the consideration to neutrals that I was supposed to, and the Service would have become a farce." Thus, whatever may have been praiseworthy in the offices of Whitehall, there stands out in the history of the greatest blockade the united protest of the four senior naval officers most intimately concerned with its working : Admiral Jellicoe, Commander-in-Chief of the Grand Fleet ; Admiral de Chair and Admiral Tupper, who commanded the Blockading Fleet ; and Admiral Consett, who watched from his place of duty in Scandinavia the pathetic sight of oversea supplies coming to our enemies through neutral territory, enriching the neutrals and enabling Germany to prolong the War. These unhappy facts can never be forgotten.

It is to be recorded also that, whereas a special green pass was issued to those neutral ships which were above suspicion—or thought to be—and that this certainly facilitated the work of interception, yet by a curious oversight such passes were never afterwards collected again. Nor was it impossible to copy and reprint them. This *acquit à caution* was just a card to show the vessel had cleared from an Allied port. It came into force after the Order-in-Council of February 16, 1917.

But such was the power of the Blockade by reason of the letters of assurance, the control of bunker coal, the censorship of post and cables, that during the last six months of 1916 only three neutral ships of any size reached Scandinavia without examination. Practically all ships were calling at a British or Allied port. So this was to be a terrible winter in Germany, without meat for her people or fodder for raising the young kine, the soil not having yielded its normal harvests of grain and fodder owing to the artificial fertilizers having been completely stopped by the Blockade.

The loss of man power, the demands of the harassed military authorities, the sufferings of civilians in the industrial quarters, the inertia of the High Sea Fleet, the hopeless outlook for the future, now combined to break the enemy's heart. Demoralization set in, the will to conquer weakened, and next came that final disappointment when the institution of regular convoys defended Allied shipping from U-boats, and the United States entered the War with its immense weight in favour of the Allies, just at a welcome time when the units of the 10th Cruiser Squadron had become so few that the strength was not adequate. At least another nine merchant cruisers were needed, but could not be provided. They were required for sweeping the Atlantic, but also for convoying across the same ocean, so a number of Admiral Jellicoe's cruisers reinforced the Blockade Fleet in its final strangling of Germany's vitality. The enemy's answer was to increase her Submarine Blockade pressure; for on February 1, 1917, began her unrestricted U-boat campaign, by which the monthly sinkings of merchant ships rose from 35 to 88 forthwith, in March to 103, and in April (which was the peak of the campaign) to 128.

The aim of this intensification was to force us into peace and thus end the unbearable Blockade. Both Kirkwall and Swarbacks Minn were mined by submarines, and in this the threat against our patrols was direct; but in general the unrestricted phase was to make all boarding still more perilous, though the patrol lines were of less importance than previously, now that other measures had become established. The first thing, for neutrals and the 10th Cruiser Squadron alike, was to steam at full speed, keep zigzagging, and not hang about.

The second precaution still further changed the old character of the blockade; for the examination of neutral ships now took place abroad, and they need no longer risk coming into a port of the United Kingdom. Those coming from the United States and the Panama Canal were examined at Halifax or Kingston (Jamaica). The others were scrutinized at Port Said, or Freetown (W. Africa). Particulars of cargo were telegraphed thence to the Contraband Committee in London, and no ship could proceed until they had cabled their decision. On February 16, 1917, was issued the Order-in-Council in answer to the enemy's declaration of unrestricted submarine warfare. Britain now affirmed that any vessel met at sea, on her way to a neutral port which gave access to enemy territory, without having previously called at a British port for examination, would be deemed to be carrying goods of enemy destination or origin. Such goods would be liable to condemnation in prize, instead of being requisitioned or returned. This was a drastic measure, but it still further took away from the Blockading Fleet their old duties, whilst ensuring as good results.

Incidents and risks still continued, as, for example, on February 8, when the armed merchant cruiser *Moldavia*, having intercepted the Italian *Famiglia*, found she had been stopped by a U-boat, whose armed guard were now taken prisoners, though not before the latter had placed explosives which presently destroyed her. Similarly on February 14, at 6 a.m., the *Alsatian*, after half an hour's examination, sent the Norwegian S.S. *Stralsund*, with an armed guard under Lieut. C. E. Elliott, R.N.R., to Troon. This was a vessel of only 298 tons, with a speed of eight knots, bound from Reykjavik to Genoa with fish. Before the day was over she was stopped by a U-boat, who ordered the Master to abandon ship. This was done, but the German armed guard did not discover the British armed guard, who got away in the boats, being eventually picked up by the armed trawler *Rushcoe*, the *Stralsund* being sunk.

But another modifying influence on the Blockade was heralded when, on February 3, the United States severed diplomatic relationship with Germany and Count Bernstorff at length departed. A couple of months later the American Government officially declared herself (on April 6) at war with Germany, and the recent tendencies of the Blockade now culminated in a still more extended control acting at the port of departure rather than in such harbours as Kirkwall, Lerwick, and Stornoway.

"It is plain enough how we were forced into the war,"

stated President Wilson.[1] "The extraordinary insults and
aggressions of the Imperial German Government left us no
self-respecting choice but to take up arms in defence of our
rights as a free people, and of our honour as a sovereign
government. The military masters of Germany denied us the
right to be neutral."

Thus at long last had Germany's reckless policy towards
the most important neutral country done more harm to
herself than Britain's ultra-cautious neutral regard had
damaged the Allies' cause. But it was a great deal more than
the mere addition of a new friend or the creation of a fresh
enemy ; it signified that the neutral supplies coming from the
New World would be more severely rationed than ever.
Britain, France, and the United States could now snap their
fingers at the rest of the globe. "Between us we regulate nearly
all the essential commodities and the munitions of war, and
we dominate the seas by which they are borne. You neutrals
will have only such goods as we permit, and upon our terms,
or none at all." A policy of a general embargo was adopted
in America, the chief source of contraband diverted its stream
against Germany and Scandinavian countries, so that now
there was virtually no need for a Blockade Fleet to intercept
and examine suspected cargoes—the latter never reached the
holds ! It was not the 10th Cruiser Squadron with its boarding
parties who now did the stoppage, but the Customs Officers
in New York, Boston, Norfolk (Virginia), and other Atlantic
ports. More drastically than Britain had endeavoured, the
United States now enforced blacklisting and the censorship
of postal or telegraphic communications.

The future of the British Blockading Fleet could thus be
clearly defined. Seeing that cargoes were controlled from the
shore, the ships of the 10th Cruiser Squadron were destined
to become superfluous before the year was out. This new
condition was extremely convenient, since the demand for
convoy escort became monthly more insistent. Gradually,
then, this wonderful force which had been created, organized,
and trained by Admiral de Chair, and continued by Admiral
Tupper, now was split into unit after unit till it ceased to

---

[1] In his Flag Day address on June 14, 1917.

exist as a whole. The *Almanzora*, for example, in July 1917, was already busily engaged escorting a convoy of eleven ships from the other side of the Atlantic, and so she continued till Armistice.   To-day we know from German submarine commanding officers that nothing so baffled their tactics as these protected sailings.

It must not, however, be supposed that the final days were devoid of excitement ; in some respects the floating Blockade suffered more injuries than at any other period of its existence. On March 16, 1917, another west-bound raider tried to get through. She was named the *Leopard*, but in reality was the ex-British *Yarrowdale*, which we mentioned previously as one of *Moewe's* prizes. She was stopped by the armed boarding steamer *Dundee*, who in conjunction with H.M.S. *Achilles*, a light cruiser, sank her after an engagement. It was virtually a single-ship engagement, as the *Dundee* had given the death blow before the cruiser could assist. On this same day the merchant cruiser *Motagua* struck a mine but succeeded in reaching Swarbacks Minn. She had the amazing experience of being mined on two occasions. On the first she had her bow blown off, and afterwards her stern. On May 25 the *Hilary* was torpedoed off the east side of the Shetlands and sunk. It was sad that this vessel, which had done so much excellent work all these months and ridden out so many gales, perished during the concluding weeks.

But her loss was an exemplification of the new unrestrained campaign. Only five days previously the two Dutch steamers *Bernisse* (951 tons) and the *Elve* (962 tons) were steaming in company. They had come all the way from Senegal, were bound for Rotterdam, but considered the north of Scotland route safer than the English Channel. On May 20 they were stopped by the *Patia* in lat. 62°4' N., long. 15°10' W., who boarded them. As they had no green ticket of clearance, and the cargo could not be examined at sea, they were sent into Kirkwall with an officer and three men in each case. But then up came a German submarine who torpedoed and sank *Elve*, and torpedoed but failed to sink *Bernisse*. Luckily a British cruiser arrived on the scene, picked up the boats, and towed the *Bernisse* into Kirkwall, where she was temporarily repaired.

The next of these affairs occurred on June 14, when the 15,000-tons patrol *Avenger*—pride of the Blockading Fleet— whilst on her way to Scapa for replenishment of her oil fuel, was torpedoed and sunk at the awful hour of 2 a.m. It was a serious loss in herself, but it showed yet again the extreme vulnerability of this unprotected merchant cruiser class. And, as if to confirm this fact, the *Otway* was similarly sent to the bottom late on the night of July 22. Finally the *Champagne* (which had come back from the French and was again a British patrol) was sunk in the same way on the early morning of October 9 whilst returning from Liverpool. Thus, within six months, four of the 10th Cruiser Squadron had been wiped out. How much longer would it be ere the remainder disappeared ?

But by the end of October the Squadron as a Blockading force came to an end : the people in offices ashore, with their typewriters, telegraphs and files, their network of agreements, trading trusts, and treaties, were carrying on the operation as if it were some world-extensive business with branches on both sides of the Atlantic. It was no longer a seaman's job, and by a curious reversion those very liners which had been so long engaged enforcing the British Blockade were now employed escorting the convoys through the German Submarine Blockade.

A happy relief, indeed, from the unforgettable northern waters, where the winds made mourning in the rigging as if singing a dirge for all seafarers who had perished between the sailing of the Vikings to Iceland and the sinking by submarines ! It was a welcome change for eye-puckered officers and men to get away from snow and ice, from eternal fog and gale, into ocean tracks where the sun ever shines. The untamed sea-horses of the chilly North, with their white manes tossing before the tempests, had been awesome for the boarding parties to behold ; but now there was no more boat-work in the open. Those green mountains of wave, threatening to topple over ships and men—fascinating yet terrifying in their grandeur—now seemed less lofty or bullying. No more of the wild, dreary dawns ; the drab, grey days ; the bleak Shetlands ; the gaunt Muckle Flugga ! It had all passed like a delirious dream, and, instead of chasing evasive

Scandinavian mail-ships, the escorts were at pains to keep the convoys steaming fast enough.

From August 1914 to the end of 1917 the 10th Cruiser Squadron intercepted 8,905 ships, sent 1,816 into port under armed guard, and boarded 4,520 fishing craft. Its strength never exceeded 25 armed merchant cruisers, plus 18 armed trawlers, but frequently the force was much less than this. Its losses (besides H.M.S. *Hawke*) were considerable, a dozen units going to the bottom, viz. the *Oceanic, Viknor, Clan MacNaughton, Bayano, India, Alcantara, Hilary, Avenger, Otway, Champagne*, together with the two trawlers *Thomas Stratton* and *Robert Smith*. It was a heavy price to pay, but it was worth while.

For this biggest of all blockades that the world has ever experienced was so devastatingly effective in breaking the enemy's moral that the first request at Armistice to the Allies was that the Blockade might be raised forthwith. To this day neither Germany nor Austria has recovered from its stringency. The surprising dependence of even most central Europe on sea-borne commerce had thus to be demonstrated by shutting it out during four lean years.

THE END

Lightning Source UK Ltd.
Milton Keynes UK
UKHW022341091019
351322UK00006B/46/P

9 781783 314362